Emily Hobhouse

Feminist, Pacifist, Traitor?

Emily Hobhouse

Feminist, Pacifist, Traitor?

Elsabé Brits

ROBINSON

First published in South Africa in 2016 by Tafelberg, an imprint of NB Publishers

First published in Great Britain in 2018 by Robinson

1 3 5 7 9 10 8 6 4 2

A CIP catalogue record for this book
is available from the British Library.

ISBN: 978-1-47214-091-3

Typeset in Adobe Garamond Pro by Hewer Text UK Ltd, Edinburgh
Printed and bound in Great Britain by Clays Ltd, St Ives Plc

Papers used by Robinson are from well-managed forests and other responsible sources.

Robinson
An imprint of
Little, Brown Book Group
Carmelite House
50 Victoria Embankment
London EC4Y 0DZ

An Hachette UK Company
www.hachette.co.uk

www.littlebrown.co.uk

Contents

Introduction

'To the plain man and woman, outside the political and military worlds, it seems as though in war an arbitrary line is drawn, one side of which is counted barbarism, the other civilisation.

May it not be that, in reality, all war is barbarous, varying only in degree?'

– Emily Hobhouse, 1902

Growing up in South Africa I knew a little about Emily Hobhouse, but only in very broad terms – she was an upper-class British woman, who took the plight of the women and children in concentration camps in a far-off land to heart during the Anglo-Boer War (or the second Boer War, as it was known in the UK). Then one day I came across Rykie van Reenen's book from the 1970s, *Heldin uit die Vreemde*, 'Heroine from Afar', in a bric-a-brac shop. It gave the strong impression that there had been much more to Emily than this.

Emily shortly after the end of the Anglo-Boer War, 1902.

I started reading more about her, including books that my wife, Carol, ordered for me from overseas. I read about the ingenious ploughing plan Emily devised to get the defeated farmers of the Transvaal and the Free State back on their feet after the war, and about the spinning and weaving she taught Boer women to enable them to earn a living. After the First World War, too, she campaigned successfully for food for the children of the 'enemy', feeding thousands of starving children in Leipzig, Germany. During that war, she campaigned at the highest level to bring about peace. It fascinated me that so little was known in South Africa about Emily the liberal socialist, the pacifist and the feminist.

This was how it came about that, fourteen months later, I found myself in a car with Will, a Canadian motel owner, on a dirt track on Vancouver Island. The track wound through an avenue of trees past an asparagus farm and a school, ending at a wooden house. In the doorway stood a small, slightly stooped woman with wispy snow-white hair.

Jennifer Hobhouse Balme. 'Ah! You're here,' she said. 'Welcome!' As we greeted each other, I clasped both my hands around hers.

Finally, after an almost year-long email correspondence, some slight subterfuge to gain access to the British Library in London, a near-indecent search at Vancouver International Airport and a journey of a few thousand kilometres from South Africa, I had arrived in a small fishing village on Cowichan Bay between Vancouver Island and the Mainland.

Jennifer's grandfather, Professor Leonard Trelawny (L. T.) Hobhouse, was Emily's younger brother. Jennifer (born in 1928) is probably the last surviving person who can relate anecdotes about Emily that she heard first-hand from relatives of her great-aunt. I had tracked Jennifer down in September 2013, and we started corresponding. She mentioned that her father, Oliver, had bequeathed her a trunk and a few boxes containing some of Emily's effects, but without providing much detail.

After inviting me inside, she started explaining the family tree in her study on the top floor. L. T. Hobhouse, an eminent professor of sociology, was not only Emily's younger brother but also the sibling who had been closest to her. His son, Oliver Hobhouse, had been the apple of Emily's eye, and finally also her heir. And Oliver was Jennifer's father.

As Oliver's only surviving child, Jennifer inherited everything Emily had bequeathed to him. And after Jennifer married John in

1966, Emily's effects had accompanied her to Canada, when they took up farming there. A small sewing table that had belonged to Emily stood in a corner of the study. Two of Emily's books – *The Brunt of the War and Where It Fell* and *War Without Glamour* – were on the shelf.

On the coffee table lay a pile of handwritten pages, wrapped in now old and worn-out brown paper. 'This is her draft autobiography, just as she left it,' said Jennifer, who herself had written two books on Emily – *To Love One's Enemies* and *Agent of Peace*. Dressmaker's pins that were nearly a century old kept the pages together in order. It was one of only two copies that Emily had written by hand.

Chapters of Emily Hobhouse's draft autobiography.
Some parts of it were typed and others written by hand.

Photo: Elsabé Brits

This is how Emily made changes to her draft autobiography. This part dates from the time after the Anglo-Boer War, when she travelled through the interior of South Africa for nearly six months.

Photo: Elsabé Brits

She had started working on it in 1922 but was unable to complete it before her death. She had typed parts of it, sometimes with the typewriter on her lap as she lay in bed in her last years. The manuscript is in the form of a long letter to the woman who was probably her best friend, Rachel Isabella (Tibbie) Steyn, wife of the Free State president Marthinus Steyn.

'That box contains her material on the Anglo-Boer War,' Jennifer said, pointing to boxes on the floor, 'and in that one is everything on Germany and the First World War . . . You know about the children in Leipzig, don't you? And the Russian babies?' There was a trunk, too.

Inside the trunk was a box. As I lifted it up, there lay three scrapbooks Emily had made; two about her experiences in South Africa, and one about her work in Germany after the First World War. Furthermore, an older scrapbook with sketches made by Emily's mother, and some photos.

To crown it all, the trunk contained four A5 hardcover notebooks, all neatly marked. Diaries. Nowhere had I read or heard of the existence of these notebooks.

These records had survived the Second World War in Oliver's solicitor's office in London, amid hundreds of buildings that had been demolished during the air raids. The trunk also held hundreds of letters and other documents. All of these treasures were here, on an island in Canada. What a wondrous find! (Today, they have been donated to Oxford's Bodleian Library.)

I was literally trembling with excitement. Here I hoped to find answers to many of my questions about the enigmatic and indomitable Emily: who was she really, and what had led to her being spurned by her country, many of her friends and even some of her relatives? Would it have been different if she had been a man?

What had possessed her to travel to a remote dark continent and identify with the plight of people to whom she had no ties? How did she manage to break through the stifling confines of the strict Victorian era in which she had been born and become a citizen of the world?

Emily Hobhouse dared to oppose the mightiest men of her time. Mostly alone in her quest to be a whistle-blower about the atrocities of war, she was a human rights activist decades before it became fashionable. And she paid a heavy price – she was forgotten by history, mostly hated in Britain and labelled a traitor, even though she was a patriot with all her heart.

This is her story.

From slave ship to freedom flight

'I envied the boys the special tutors they had, people whose brains they had the right to pick; of whom they might ask questions. I never had anyone to cut my mental teeth upon. School lessons always bored me . . . They never taught me the things I wanted to know.'

– Emily Hobhouse, 1875

A couple from St Ive in Cornwall (pronounced 'eve', and not to be confused with St Ives) were taken to court because of 'cruelty towards their children'. When the authorities arrived at the house, the mother was distraught at her inability to care for the children because she and her husband were destitute.

The policeman who had searched the house could find no food anywhere. The children were dirty, thin and starving. A doctor who had examined the children stated that they were badly starved, but had not been ill-treated.[1]

The next witness was thirty-one-year-old Emily Hobhouse. She visited the family regularly, she said, and had given them food and milk. She testified that they were poor and neglected. The father was unable to work as he was too weak. She had the deepest sympathy with them. 'It would be no use sending them to prison,' she said, 'because they would only come out worse prepared to fight life's battle.'[2]

The magistrate decided against imprisonment. Emily paid the £10 guarantee for the couple.

Her father, Reginald Hobhouse, was the Archdeacon of Bodmin. She regularly visited the poor in his parish, which included the tiny village of St Ive and the neighbouring village of Pensilva, five miles from Liskeard in Cornwall in the south-west of England.

Emily kept a list of destitute families whom she visited and tried to assist.[3] Among other welfare work in the parish, she founded a library and visited the sick because there was no doctor.[4] But these activities were not enough for her; she had a yearning to do more, to make a greater difference.

Emily Hobhouse had been born on 9 April 1860 into a position of privilege as a member of the Victorian English upper class. On both sides of her family distinguished people had left their mark.

Her mother, Caroline (born 1820), was a daughter of Sir William Lewis Salusbury-Trelawny, the eighth baronet, heir to Harewood House in Calstock, Cornwall.

The first Trelawny who held the title had been made a baronet by Charles I. On Sir William's death in 1857 he had left a substantial inheritance to his children and his wife, Patience Christian Carpenter. Caroline, Emily's mother, inherited ten thousand pounds – an enormous sum at the time.[5]

Emily's mother, Caroline.

Photo: Courtesy of Jennifer Hobhouse Balme

Caroline was an attractive woman with brown hair and blue eyes. Emily described her as someone of 'distinguished bearing, combined with quick parts and a natural manner of extreme charm. She applied her unusual abilities to the education of her children, shewing herself an indulgent and devoted mother.'[6]

The Hobhouse family's history can be traced back to 31 August 1686, when John Hobhouse rented a house near the port of Minehead on the Bristol Channel in Somerset. He was married to Anne Maddox, and their children included their three sons Henry, Isaac and Benjamin. The family became established in the area, and in 1708 Henry Hobhouse opened a shipbuilding yard in Minehead while his brother Isaac started doing business with

9

merchants in the colony of Virginia in North America. From Bristol the family became involved in the shipping industry as shipowners and merchants, and the males became full citizens who were entitled to vote.[7]

The firm of Isaac Hobhouse and Company, which accepted Henry Hobhouse I – a son of Benjamin – as an apprentice in 1729, opened the doors of wealth to the family. Isaac traded between Bristol, the west coast of Africa, the West Indies and the 'plantation colonies' in America.[8] He acquired a large fortune from his commercial interests, which included the slave trade. The ship *Greyhound*, which belonged to Isaac's company, transported slaves from West Africa to Virginia, whereafter it would return to England laden with goods.[9] In a letter to Isaac reference is made to a ship that 'arrives well slaved, I hope shall make a pleasing acc of 'em'.[10] This connection with the slave trade was not kept hidden from the family and Emily was well aware of it.

The family estate and mansion, Hadspen House in Somerset near the village of Bruton, had been purchased by Henry Hobhouse II, an Oxford-educated barrister, in September 1785. Emily's paternal grandfather Henry Hobhouse III (1776–1854) and his wife Harriet Turton (1780–1838) had both died before Emily's birth. Henry III had studied law at Oxford like his father, and had been a solicitor to the Treasury and under-secretary at the Home Office in London under Sir Robert Peel. He had also served as a magistrate in the countryside.[11] By this time the Hobhouses were a distinguished family.

Emily's father, Reginald (born 1818), was one of four sons and four daughters. The boys were all educated at Eton and Balliol College, Oxford. Owing to their good education, the boys Henry IV, Edmund and Arthur all had successful careers.

Emily's father, Reginald, the conservative Archdeacon of Bodmin.

Photo: Courtesy of Jennifer Hobhouse Balme

On completing his studies, Reginald – according to Emily a reserved, humourless, conservative man – became the Anglican rector in the parish of St Ive thanks to Sir Robert Peel, the prime minister for whom his father had worked. Before his marriage to Caroline, he had lived alone for seven years in a cottage opposite the fourteenth-century church. The couple had a big rectory built for them about a hundred metres away.

Emily was the fifth of six surviving children, and the youngest daughter. The children were Caroline ('Carrie', born 1854), Alfred (born 1856), Blanche (born 1857), Maud (born 1858), Emily (born 1860) and Leonard (born 1864).

Emily wrote about her earliest memory from those days: 'I do not know if the sense of having an ego of one's own comes to others at a given moment, or grows imperceptibly, but it was when I was three or four years old that I learnt this. I was sent to see the time . . . I suddenly realised the clock was not me and I was not it but outside it and different . . . It was a curious revelation.'[12]

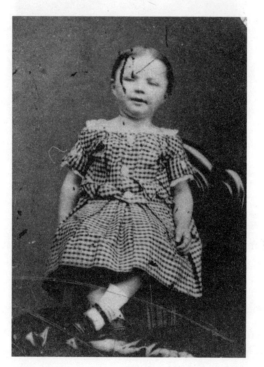

The oldest known photograph of Emily Hobhouse,
at the age of about two (c. 1862).
Photo: Courtesy of Jennifer Hobhouse Balme

The curate at the church in St Ive, St Aubyn Rogers, had a soft spot for the children, who called him 'Old Rodge'. He tilled a private plot for each of them on the premises of the rectory so that they could plant their own vegetables. He made them garden tables and chairs as well as bows and arrows to shoot with, and

Emily (left) and her sister Maud as young children.

Photo: Courtesy of Jennifer Hobhouse Balme

joined them in games of hide-and-seek. He took his meals with the family and flicked bread balls at Emily, when the parents were not looking, that she would catch in her mouth.

On one occasion, he and Emily played a game of badminton that lasted for two hours – to her father's frustration, as they were making a noise under his study window. By her count, their tally was two thousand strokes.[13]

To Emily, Rogers was like a father; her own father had been sickly since she was six years old. 'Old Rodge was everything to us, and my devoted slave in particular.' He was a part of the happiest times of her life.[14] In summer they went to the seaside for holidays or visited the Hobhouse family home Hadspen in Somerset.

At a young age Emily acquired the nickname 'The Missis'. The name was thought to have originated from a Valentine card she received from the family at the age of seven, which carried the message: 'Wherever I am, I will always be the missis.' Everyone thought that it suited her, and 'Missis' remained a nickname throughout her life.[15]

At the age of eight Leonard went to prep school at Exmouth and then followed his brother to Marlborough College, while the girls had to be content with inferior home education taught by governesses. Although they had a well-stocked Victorian home library in which Emily immersed herself, and she was taught skills such as sewing, singing, playing the piano and even how to speak

Fifteen-year-old Emily.

Photo: Courtesy of Jennifer Hobhouse Balme

French, this was not enough for her. An education of this type was the norm for girls of her social class but she yearned to study further and, like her brothers, equip herself for an occupation.

Emily turned fifteen and stood on the threshold of womanhood, but she found life perplexing. 'I looked in vain all my life for someone to talk to, and discuss things with, and explain things, but no one had time – the governesses were shallow and incompetent and I was but one of 'the little ones' and of no account.

'I envied the boys the special tutors they had, people whose brains they had the right to pick; of whom they might ask questions. I never had anyone to cut my mental teeth upon. So school lessons always bored me because they were (as taught to us) so superficial. They never told me the thing I wanted to know. If you asked, you were told: "Little girls should not ask questions." '[16]

At sixteen, Emily was sent to a finishing school in London where Maud was already a student. Blanche was also there, but had become very ill. The finishing school did not offer the kind of education Emily desired. She was still eager to learn, but instead she was given horse-riding lessons and too little food. She was taught how to entertain and be a good wife to a husband some day. It left Emily bitter. Her inadequate education 'has been the root cause of many of my mistakes,' she wrote years later.[17]

In the winter of 1876 the parents took the three younger daughters – Blanche, Maud and Emily – to Menton in the south of France, shortly after the marriage of Caroline. The main reason for the visit was to give Blanche, who probably suffered from tuberculosis, an opportunity to recover. The family spent the entire winter in Menton and then slowly started making their way home. But Blanche's health failed to improve, and she died at the age of nineteen in the French city of Toulouse.[18]

After their trip there was no longer enough money to send Emily back to the finishing school. Instead, she had to be satisfied with painting and violin lessons in the neighbouring town of Liskeard.[19]

Almost everything in Emily's life had changed. Her sister Carrie, as they called her, was married. Blanche was dead, and her mother's 'spirit' was 'crushed'. Her father increasingly worked in the parish, away from home. With no outlet for her intellectual abilities, Emily sought fulfilment in dreams and thoughts. 'I lived with heroes in this imaginary world and fell ardently in love with these fabulous beings.'

Emily went on long walks in the surrounding countryside. She felt the urge to embrace and explore far-off and wide worlds and meet many people, and she 'dreamt of their universal conversion to goodness (which for me meant then the Church of England) and a lift to material well-being'. Finally Emily came to a crucial realisation: what mattered to her was not the same as what mattered to everyone else, 'and that you can't make a silk purse out of a sow's ear'.

She realised that the parish was but a small world, far removed from a greater reality beyond its confines.[20] She also did not share her father's view that religious dissidents – those who did not agree with all aspects of the Anglican Church – had to be ostracised, and visited such people regularly.[21]

She became critical of her father's sermons, 'The trouble rather was that he had so little to say – not that he could not say it. He lived too much apart from ordinary humanity to understand it well, and strictly ruled out all that was modern in thought and science from his reading. His preaching never modernised.' Only once did she hear him preach from his heart, and then he cried.[22]

In 1880 Emily's mother developed a brain tumour and died within a few months. Emily was twenty years old, her brother Leonard was a student at Oxford, and Alfred had long since left home and moved to New Zealand. Only Maud was still at home with Emily, and the two girls looked after their father, whose health had deteriorated after his wife's death. He was now even more withdrawn and reclusive, and refused to let Emily develop her talents.

In 1889 Maud married one of the church's curates, Ernest Hebblethwaite, without her father's blessing, most likely to escape from the oppressive atmosphere at home.[23]

Emily taught Sunday school lessons, sang in the church choir and played the organ. Her life revolved around her father and the small population of St Ive. She read to him from *The Times* every day, thereby keeping abreast of what was happening in the world – it stimulated her interest in politics. Like her brother Leonard and her uncle, Lord Hobhouse, Emily had liberal political convictions, in contrast to her father's conservative views.[24] She did not dare to discuss her ideas with him, however.

In 1891 Leonard married Nora Hadwen in Oxford, where he lectured at Merton College and later at Corpus Christi College. Their first child, Oliver, was born a year later, and became one of the few joys in Emily's life.[25]

Emily's father was dead set against Emily meeting any young men. She had to care for him, and her chances of marrying and having a family of her own started to diminish. Loneliness and frustration drove her to 'morbid introspection and hysteria', since all she could do was sing and play the piano and the violin. 'I was so low that I took to illumination' – which was a kind of light therapy to treat depression. Finally she attempted writing, 'but never succeeded in that till my mind was released from the shackles of St Ive'.

Emily (thirty-three) with her brother's son Oliver
in 1893, when he was a few months old.

Photo: Courtesy of Jennifer Hobhouse Balme

Decades later she wrote about this time in her life: 'I find no
record of these years. They are recorded only on my spirit, and
fortunately will die with me. It was in a word a period of torture'.[26]

The circumstances must have been unbearable for someone of
Emily's intellect and spirit. For six years she lived alone in the rectory
with her father, apart from the servants. He died on 27 January
1895, a bitterly cold day. 'It was the end of our life as a family.'

All the family's possessions – from the animals to furniture,
paintings and a cello – were auctioned. Emily inherited £5300
from her father.[27] Two weeks after his death, Emily packed her
suitcases and left St Ive. She never returned to the village.

Emily at the age of thirty-four, shortly after her
father's death, when she left St Ive for good.

Photo: Courtesy of Jennifer Hobhouse Balme

***

The car's temperature gauge registers a low 2°C as I travel the
eight kilometres from Liskeard to St Ive. It is a tiny rural hamlet
you could easily pass through without realising.

A beautiful old church, more or less in the middle of the few
houses, is impossible to miss. I recognise the building from photo-
graphs I have seen of it. This is where Reginald Hobhouse was
rector for half a century.

Suddenly I am in the heart of Emily's early world. About a hundred
metres on is the rectory where she spent the first part of her life.

By prior arrangement, a few parishioners are waiting for me at the rectory. 'We're big fans of Emily's,' Dennis and his wife Doreen tell me.

We walk to the cemetery that surrounds the church. Emily's mother and father lie buried next to each other. Opposite the church the cottage still stands where her father had lived as a bachelor.

I walk around the church, along the pathway to the door through which Emily used to walk every Sunday for so many years, past the baptismal font of stone at the back of the church where she was baptised on 1 May 1860, down the aisle to the pulpit from where Reginald delivered the sermons his talented daughter found so dull.

On the wall next to the pulpit are separate bronze memorial plaques: for Reginald for fifty years' service; for Leonard, Emily, Alfred and Maud; and another one for Reginald, his wife and the other children.

One of the parishioners, Paddy, says that Emily sang in the choir and also played the organ. 'Those are the choir pews. The men sat here and the women opposite them; it has always been like that. Emily must have sat in that pew,' he gestures.

When I sit in that particular pew the pulpit rises in front of me, with church-goers to the left and lead-glass windows to the right. The organ Emily used to play is directly behind me. It feels to me as if Emily is there too, and I close my eyes to travel back 125 years in time and imagine myself in Emily's position.

Inching along a long flight of narrow steps on which I have to turn my feet sideways, I climb up inside the dark church tower. On one side there is a blue rope to hold on to. On the other there is nothing.

From the top of the tower there is a good view of the surroundings. Diagonally opposite is the rectangular old stone and red sandstone rectory of the Hobhouse family – a listed building that dates from 1852–54. The house has two storeys, with an attic and a cellar, set among several acres. It has a beautiful slate roof.[28]

Dennis and Doreen have assured me that it is virtually impossible to obtain permission to visit the house. Many journalists, TV crews and writers have failed in their attempts to gain entry. But four months earlier I made contact in a roundabout way with the owner who agreed grudgingly – and provisionally – to a visit. But will he still remember our conversation, and finally give his consent to a visit?

What do you know? He recalls my long story over the telephone, and kindly invites me in.

The front of the house in which Emily grew up and lived until the age of thirty-four, opposite the church in St Ive, Cornwall. Her parents had this house built before her birth in 1860.

Photo: Elsabé Brits

I cross the threshold and enter Emily's world. Above the door hangs the original bell rope, of which there used to be one in each important room – a kind of umbilical cord between employers and servants. When someone pulled the rope, a bell rang next to the name of the particular room on a board in the servants' quarters, so that the servants knew where they had to rush to.

The servants' area – including cellar, pantry and kitchen, with its spacious cooking area and separate scullery – is clearly cordoned off from the living area of the family members by a thick door, and here the wooden floor changes to serviceable tiles. An outside door gives access to the stables and other outbuildings.

There is the high drawing room, where the family would have sat reading or conversing. The fireplace is still there, encased in black marble. And also a study where all the books must have been housed.

Above the stairs are the bedrooms with thick, chamfered wooden ceiling beams. There are several bedrooms, with dressing rooms, and bathrooms with fireplaces, but it is impossible to say which bedroom was Emily's. The windows are big and look out over the huge property where the children would have cavorted to their heart's delight. This was also where Emily and Old Rodge used to play badminton and the children had their own little vegetable gardens.

The church sold the house in 1985 and since then it has been privately owned. We walk round the back, and I stand for a long time in the garden gazing at the charming old house, the outbuildings and stables. 'There is a pleasant shady garden around the house. It is a very good size, plenty of flowers and vegetables in their season, there are four fields and we have two cows, two pigs, and hosts of pets,' Maud wrote in 1873, when Emily was thirteen.[29]

After the death of their father Reginald in January 1895, 'two fat pigs, a horse, cows and calves' were offered for sale at the rectory. The enclosed horse carriage was fitted out stylishly with cushions and lanterns.

The windows of the spacious drawing room look out on the open land behind the house. I can imagine Emily and her sisters gazing out of this window, perhaps each with a book in her hand. When the Hobhouse family lived here, this room used to contain a small sofa and a piano, a writing table and piles of books. In summer they would hang white curtains lined with green gauze in front of the windows. In winter the room had crimson curtains and a bright fire glowed in the grate, Maud wrote.[30]

Sleet falls as I drive back along the narrow, winding road to Liskeard; I can hardly imagine a greater contrast than that between the green, muddy, wet fields of Cornwall and the glaring sun, heat and dust of South Africa that would colour Emily's blonde hair red.

2

Into the wide world

'I feel as if I were in fairyland or the Arabian Nights and pens won't tell adequately all I have seen and done . . .'
– Emily Hobhouse, New York, 1895

Emily had shaken the dust of St Ive off her feet and was intent on seeing the world – not just Oxford where she frequently stayed with her brother and his family, or London where Uncle Arthur and Aunt Mary, Lord and Lady Hobhouse, lived. She was not willing to wait longer than 1895 to chart her own course, albeit that it was unheard of for a woman of her social class to venture alone into the world at the age of thirty-five.

She still had no clear idea of the path her life should take, but of two things she was sure: she wanted to see more of the world, and she wanted to help people. Many miners from Cornwall – the 'Cousins Jacks', as they were called – had emigrated to America to make a new life there, and Emily resolved to follow the same route.

English miners, with their experience of mining tin, copper and china clay, had moved to the United States in their thousands. And it stood to reason that they would have social needs. With the help of the wife of the Archbishop of Canterbury, Edward Benson, Emily made contact with Archdeacon Appleby in Minnesota with a view to doing welfare work among the Cornish miners in that area.

In July 1895 she departed by ship to New York, where she stayed for a few days. She was enthralled with what she saw and experienced there, and wrote to Maud: 'I feel as if I were in fairyland or the Arabian Nights.'[1] After a visit to Chicago she travelled by train to the mining town of Virginia in Minnesota, arriving in August. She and her servant from Cornwall, Mary Scourney, found accommodation in Bodock House, a boarding house on Maple Street. Fortunately they had brought along their own bedding, as the boarding house was none too clean.

'My impulse was to run and flee,' she wrote to Maud, but they stayed there for the night.[2] Determined not to stay on, Emily scraped together a few pieces of furniture – two old hospital beds and some chairs – so that they could move into a cottage.[3] The first evening in the cottage, with the bed cleanly made with her own bedding, an exhausted Emily looked forward to a good night's rest. But the bed was crawling with lice![4] The cottage was infested with the bugs. She grabbed her clothes and a few personal possessions, and ran back to the boarding house in the dark – the lesser of two evils.

Miners and their wild habits were not a novelty to Emily; there were several mines near her village in Cornwall, and because of her father's work in the community she knew only too well how the men drank and gambled. In Virginia there were forty-two saloons and twelve mines in the area. It was bitterly cold and muddy in winter, and scorchingly hot in summer. The town had a saw mill, shops, a newspaper, electricity and five thousand inhabitants.[5] Emily started working in the community, but found only fifty-five people who hailed from Cornwall. Well, she decided, she had given her word that she would work here, and there had to be others who needed her services. Many people just sat around idly, she wrote. With two hundred dollars[6] that she collected among the residents she started a library, opened a recreation hall, founded a church choir and a Sunday school.[7] She opened her home to everyone, and she taught adults to read and write. In cases of need, she even allowed some of the people to sleep on the floor of her – now clean – cottage.

The doctor at the hospital was actually only a dentist. Emily decided to lend a hand there as well, as the patients were often neglected. She changed their bedding and sang to the sick.[8] She took a woman suffering from enteric fever to her home to care for her there, sacrificing her own bed.[9]

But she did not believe in only plastering wounds; she tried to uplift people through exposure to books, through singing, literacy and basic temperance programmes to lead them away from alcohol abuse. Her temperance campaign did not impress the saloon owners. 'All the riff-raff, the rag-tag and bobtail of society, the dregs of population' flocked there, she wrote. The police were inefficient, and the members of the town council owed their positions to bribery. There were 'four houses of ill-fame of large size', and people gambled day and night.[10]

She reached out to the men in the mining camps in the woods, walking long distances with Mary on Sundays in order to preach to them. The men received her warmly, even baked cakes for her and offered her tea in a tin mug. She sang to them, and would 'see the hard icy faces melt before me'. Soon she had won the trust of the hardened miners and the affection of the townspeople. Gifts were placed outside her door – a rabbit that had been prepared for the pot, vegetables and wood.

But it was not all plain sailing, and Emily had to learn the hard way that despite her good intentions and constructive work, she readily came into conflict with people in positions of authority who experienced her as a threat. And they were nearly always men. One of the first was the local minister of the Episcopal Church, Reverend James McGonicle – he subjected her to an hour-long lecture about the work she was doing. 'He did not think St Paul would approve of my holding mission services in a log camp. I said I should do it all the same.'[11]

The library was a great success, but the church was offended because it did not get the credit for this initiative. To Emily, it did not matter who received the praise. She wanted the library to be open on Sundays too, when the people were not at work, but was ordered to close it. Emily refused.[12] She felt too strongly about education and people's access to knowledge to let herself be dictated to in this regard.

Another point of dispute was that McGonicle wanted only people from his church to attend the temperance meetings, while Emily believed they should be open to all. He also didn't approve of her visits to women who were jailed for prostitution. Eventually their relationship soured to such an extent that he preached against her in his church.[13]

Under the banner of her Virginia Temperance Union, Emily held temperance meetings on her own in halls where she attracted audiences of up to three hundred men. She distributed cards on which they signed a pledge to abstain from alcohol. Here, too, she sang for the men.[14]

Emily received support for her work from an unexpected quarter in the person of John Carr Jackson, whom she had met earlier at the dirty boarding house. He had arrived in the town in 1893 and found employment as a clerk. Now he was the owner of Jackson & Co, a general dealer that also sold camp equipment.[15] He became the deputy chairman of Emily's library committee. One of the things that impressed her about him was that he had his eye on the United States Congress, and politics interested her. On top of that, he was elected the town's mayor in July 1896.

John and Emily saw much of each other, and before long she was in love. 'Mr Jackson consumes a great deal of my time . . . and I respect and admire him more every time I see him . . . We are sort of half engaged and expect to be wholly so in a short while,' she wrote to her aunt, Lady Hobhouse.

A few days later she informed her aunt excitedly 'that I promised Mr Jackson on Sunday night that I would marry him so now we are really engaged and I feel happy over it and quite at home with him, and as he has never known a home or comfort or happiness, he is quite dazed with joy.'[16] To Maud she wrote that John was very handsome, and that her pet name for him was 'Caro'.[17]

The town, however, was experiencing tough times. There was serious conflict between the mining bosses, and one mine after the other closed down. John found himself in financial difficulties because he had extended too much credit to people who were unable to pay.

John and Emily decided to leave Virginia, departing separately. He would stay behind for a while to wind up his affairs. The townspeople were sad to take their leave of Emily in September 1896, and a crowd came to see her off – with an orchestra accompanying her down the street to the station.

The train took her to Cleveland, Ohio,[18] where Emily spent some time with friends of her sister-in-law Nora, Leonard's wife, before continuing her journey to Mexico – a trip that took five days. Emily was to explore new possibilities for them while John was finalising his affairs in Virginia. In the end she used her inheritance money to buy a farm in Mexico with coffee, banana, pineapple and vanilla plantations, and had a house built on the property at a cost of eighty pounds. The farm was so remote that Emily never saw it.

Days, weeks and months went by, while Emily waited in Mexico City, but John failed to arrive.

Thanks to new friends Emily made, she was offered a government contract for John to supply fresh meat to Mexico City. Emily had only twelve hours to decide whether or not to buy the concession of twelve hundred pounds. With what was left of her inheritance money, she took this gamble.[19]

The entire winter of 1896 Emily waited for John in Mexico, learning Spanish and history, and painting occasionally. For months she kept hoping . . .

John was probably bankrupt by April 1897, as his shop with all its contents was sold and he left Virginia soon afterwards 'without a handshake and a parting word'. According to a report in *The Virginian* he was on his way to Chicago to meet Emily and marry her there; from there he would go to Mexico, where a new high position was said to await him.

But the reality proved to be less rosy: the man who had bought John's shop had to close it immediately, on account of lawsuits because John was insolvent. Moreover, Virginia's coffers were empty after his year-long stint as mayor.[20]

Emily was still hoping to be reunited with John, and travelled to Chicago to meet him. During her journey the train's boiler exploded and she saw the driver's body hurtling through the air. The burnt corpse of the stoker lay before the door of her compartment.

Was this perhaps an omen of what would follow? Emily kept believing that she and John would marry, presumably she dreamt of children of her own, but in the end nothing came of her hopes.[21] Orders were issued against John to appear in court because of bad debt.[22]

In 1897 Emily returned to England for a while to visit her family. During this period John visited her, but little is known about his stay.[23]

John Carr Jackson, Emily's fiancé; Emily; Nora, her sister-in-law; and Leonard, her brother, during Jackson's visit to Emily in London in 1897.

Photo: Courtesy of Jennifer Hobhouse Balme

Early in 1898, with the wedding dress still in her suitcase, Emily returned to Mexico as she and John had arranged. Meanwhile a letter from him was on his way to inform her that she had to delay her departure, but it failed to reach her in time.[24]

In Mexico there was no trace of John. Within a few weeks Emily was on her way home, heading for London and the home of Uncle Arthur and Aunt Mary.

Amid all this uncertainty and to-and-fro travelling, Emily lost the farm in Mexico too. It is not clear what had gone wrong, but there is a strong suspicion that John had abused Emily financially. Maybe he never really intended to marry her. Emily, however, had been genuinely in love, had wanted to marry him and had believed the marriage would take place. She never wrote about this pain in any of the documents I have found.

Yet there was one item that Emily preserved for the rest of her life: the bridal veil she never wore. It is made of the finest lace.

3

A vision that grows like a seed

'The constantly renewed picture of women and children home-less, desperate and distressed formed and fixed itself in my mind and never once left me.'
                    – Emily Hobhouse in her draft autobiography, 1900

'The case for intervention is overwhelming . . .'

According to a report in the morning paper from which Emily read aloud to Lord and Lady Hobhouse at the breakfast table, on a summer morning in 1899, these were the words of Sir Alfred Milner, governor of the Cape Colony and the British high commissioner in South Africa, in a telegram to Joseph Chamberlain, secretary of state for the colonies.[1] 'That means war in my opinion,' was Lord Hobhouse's sombre comment. Everyone at the breakfast table was upset about the 'dark cloud of war' that had been in the news in Britain throughout the summer.

The last year or so had been a period of calm and peace for Emily, during which she undertook long walks with her uncle

Emily Hobhouse. The photo is in a family collection
and has not been published before.

Photo: Courtesy of Jennifer Hobhouse Balme

and his dog Meg, and went on excursions with her aunt in the
horse-drawn carriage. The childless couple treated Emily like their
own child, but she wrote that she 'never found it easy to talk to
them very confidentially'.[2]

While Emily found the news of an impending war 'incredible', she realised that it seemed unavoidable. Because Lord
Hobhouse served on the Judicial Committee of the government's Privy Council, he was not at liberty to express his views
publicly – including his opposition to the looming war in
South Africa.

The tensions in South Africa had had a long run-up. At that

time South Africa consisted of the Cape Colony, which was first established by the Dutch East India Company in 1652 and finally came under complete British control in 1806, and Natal, which it annexed in 1843. In 1852 and 1854 Britain recognised the independence of the two Boer Republics, the Transvaal and the Orange Free State, but in 1877 it annexed the Transvaal as a first step to federate South Africa. This led to the First War of Independence (also known as the First Boer war). After this war the Transvaal's independence was given back when the Boers defeated the British at Majuba.[3]

However it was gold on the Witwatersrand in the Transvaal which made it a powerful threat. The Witwatersrand (literally, white water ridge) is also known as 'The Reef' – a thirty-five mile long stretch of hard rock with a plateau 1800 metres above sea level, with several rivers flowing over it. The area stretches from today's O.R. Thambo International Airport, to Johannesburg, to Krugersdorp in the west. Everything changed, and so-called Uitlanders (foreigners, most of whom were British subjects) flocked to the promised riches of the new town of Johannesburg founded in 1886. Before long they started demanding voting rights and a say in the mines,[4] and claimed that they were 'oppressed by the Boers'.[5]

Pretoria, just north of Johannesburg, is also in the Transvaal. It was founded in 1855 by the 'Voortrekkers' (Pioneers), who left the Cape Colony between 1834 and 1854 during a great exodus (the Great Trek), with their servants. They packed their wagons, and by 1840 some 6000 white Afrikaners (who also refer to themselves as Boers and Afrikaners) had left.[6]

Cecil John Rhodes, who dreamt of a united South Africa under the British flag, became prime minister of the Cape Colony in 1890. Rhodes sought control of the gold mines, and the only way of achieving this was to invade the Transvaal in the hope that the Uitlanders would be incited to rebel.

Rhodes's friend Leander Starr Jameson and his mercenaries, as well as a number of Uitlanders, invaded the Transvaal over the New Year period in 1895–96 via Bechuanaland (now called Botswana). The Boers defeated the invaders before they could reach Johannesburg, but the 'Jameson Raid' was a final blow to the trust between Boer and Briton.[7]

Although Rhodes had to resign as prime minister, his image was untarnished in Britain.[8] Chamberlain, the colonial secretary and an avowed imperialist, had evidently supported the Jameson Raid.[9] Annexing the Boer republics of the Orange Free State and the Transvaal and unifying them with the Cape and Natal in a South Africa under British rule would be the jewel in the imperialist crown, with the British flag flying from Cape to Cairo.[10]

In response, the Afrikaners became increasingly nationalist and started attaching greater value to their identity. More and more Afrikaners in the Cape Colony began to support their northern kinfolk in their anti-British sentiment. The Uitlanders, meanwhile, started giving stronger expression to their grievances. They claimed to constitute the majority of the white population of Transvaal, and through a petition they called on Britain to help them achieve equal rights, particularly voting rights.[11]

Chamberlain sent Sir Alfred Milner, the new governor of the Cape Colony and the British high commissioner, to meet the ZAR president, Paul Kruger, in Bloemfontein in May 1899 to discuss these problems. President M. T. (Theunis) Steyn of the Orange Free State, who wanted to avert war at all cost, had invited them to a conference in Bloemfontein to sort out their differences. But Milner was adamant; he wanted to force Kruger to grant Uitlanders the franchise after five years' residence.[12] Kruger refused, and insisted on a period of seven years. In addition, he demanded compensation for the Jameson Raid and that Swaziland be incorporated into the Transvaal.

On 5 June 1899 Milner broke off the negotiations[13] and subsequently sent the infamous and emotionally laden telegram to Chamberlain in which he stated among other things that the Uitlanders were little more than slaves: 'The case for intervention is overwhelming . . . The spectacle of thousands of British subjects kept permanently in the position of helots, constantly chafing under undoubted grievances, and calling vainly to Her Majesty's Government for redress, does steadily undermine the influence and reputation of Great Britain . . .'[14]

Chamberlain's intention had been to harden the hearts of the British at home against Kruger, so when the president did agree later to give the Uitlanders the franchise after five years' residence on condition that Britain refrained from further interference in the ZAR's affairs, Chamberlain conceded nothing.[15]

On 8 September 1899 England sent ten thousand soldiers to Natal. Chamberlain reckoned that the Boer forces were only a 'paper tiger', and that this show of force would trick Kruger into returning to the negotiating table. He considered it unlikely that war would break out, but if it happened, the British soldiers would already be in position.[16]

When Kruger heard about the troops the following day, he accepted that war was inevitable. Jan Smuts, the twenty-nine-year-old state attorney of the Transvaal Republic, shared his view. Later that month the press reported that a further forty-seven thousand troops were being sent from England to invade the Transvaal on 28 September. The Transvaal as well as the Free State, which threw in its weight with its natural ally, rapidly started mobilising their forces.[17]

On 9 October the ZAR issued an ultimatum to Britain: withdraw the troops who are already here from South Africa, those who are on their way may not disembark, and let there be arbitration. Britain was given forty-eight hours to respond. The British government, supported by the British public who were indignant about the ultimatum, rejected it.

Emily saw a poster of the ultimatum displayed on Trafalgar Square, and realised that the last hope of peace was gone: 'It sounded the death knell of tens of thousands of people completely innocent of its cause and it bore within it seeds of things worse than death for England,' she wrote about this moment on the square.

Behind it she saw a motive for the stoking of the conflict: an 'appetite for gold and territory'.[18]

The Anglo-Boer War[19] (also known as the South African War or the Second War of Independence, and as the second Boer War in Britain) broke out on 11 October 1899.[20] The next day, the first skirmish took place at Kraaipan in the Cape Colony between the towns of Vryburg and Mafeking when a Boer force of eight hundred men under the command of General Koos de la Rey captured a British garrison that had surrendered after a five-hour-long fight.

Three weeks after the outbreak of the war, the South African Conciliation Committee was launched in England by liberal Britons who opposed the war. The president of the committee was the sixty-seven-year-old Leonard Courtney, later Lord Courtney of Penwith, who was a seasoned politician and a former Deputy Speaker of the House of Commons.[21] His constituency was Liskeard in Cornwall, not far from St Ive where Emily had grown up. His wife Catherine (Kate), too, immediately became actively involved in the committee. The chairman of the executive was Frederick Mackarness, previously a judge in the Cape Colony and now a Liberal MP. Another prominent member of the executive was the Marquess of Ripon, a politician, while his wife Marchioness Ripon was a staunch supporter of their work.

Emily knew the Courtneys because Kate (née Potter) was the sister of her cousin Henry Hobhouse V's wife Margaret. Another one of Kate's sisters was the famous social reformer Beatrice Webb. Emily was soon drawn into the work of the committee, which aimed to distribute truthful information about the war and to advocate the necessity of friendly relations between people of Dutch and English extraction in South Africa. They wanted to see a peaceful settlement instead of the 'deplorable conflict' that had already started.[22] Emily 'committed herself wholeheartedly' to the anti-war cause in a country engulfed by 'war fever'. Several meetings took place at the London home of Lord and Lady Hobhouse at 15 Bruton Street, Mayfair. At that stage Emily had already been living for a few months in a flat in Chelsea, 21 Rossetti Garden Mansions.[23] Her flatmate was a young medical student from India, Alice Sorabji, whose family were old friends of Lord and Lady Hobhouse. The flat was very close to the Courtneys' house in Cheyne Walk, where many committee meetings were held.

On 15 January 1900 the committee's activities were officially announced. The members declared that they were pacifists and totally opposed to the war. Within a short space of time they received four hundred letters of support.[24] Emily was the honorary secretary of the committee's women's branch. The climate in which they strove to bring their views across was one where, Emily wrote, '[t]ruth and reason were obscured', and 'this excitability' about the war was 'fanned by the press and the pulpit'.[25]

'We are glad if we are but a light burning on a rock in the midst of the flood of jingoism – feeling that ours is the side of justice and of wisdom,' Kate Courtney wrote to Emily's brother Leonard.[26] The jingoes that they were up against were a section of

Lady Courtney (née Potter) and her husband, Lord Courtney. He
was the president of the South African Conciliation Committee
that was opposed to the war against the two Boer republics, and she
was also closely involved in the committee's activities.

Photo: Courtesy of Jennifer Hobhouse Balme

the British population whose understanding of patriotism was
that of 'my country, right or wrong'. A large proportion of the
British press supported this prevailing mindset.

In February, Emily attended the congress of the Liberal Party
in London. She enjoyed every minute of it. 'Liberals to the right
of you, Liberals to the left of you . . . with no cold Conservative
draught anywhere.'

What did irk her, however, was that they were such lukewarm
Liberals that they had not invited a single woman to address

them. 'Is it not to cut off their best arm?' Emily asked. The women supported the Liberal Party and did the hard work, yet they occupied the subordinate positions.[27]

She decided that women should play a more prominent role and organise a big protest meeting against the war. Kate Courtney agreed with her, and it was decided that a mass meeting would be held in the Queen's Hall. During the six weeks that they had to prepare for the meeting, Emily's flat in Chelsea became the headquarters where she and other women worked from 8 a.m. often to 11 p.m., to try and mobilise a general resistance against the war.[28]

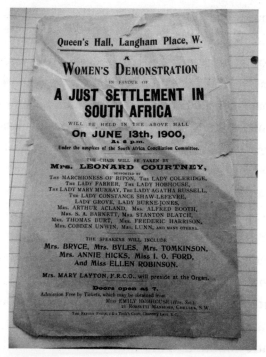

The pamphlet that advertised the women's meeting at Queen's Hall.

Photo: Elsabé Brits from Jennifer Hobhouse Balme Collection

On 24 May 1900 the Orange Free State was annexed by Britain, followed by the Transvaal on 5 June, and shortly afterwards martial law was declared.[29] The Boer forces did not regard these annexations as legitimate conquests, and embarked on guerrilla warfare to continue the struggle.

Lord Roberts, commander-in-chief of the British forces in South Africa at the time, warned in an announcement that Boers who continued fighting would suffer personal losses. If any railway lines or telegraph wires were damaged or disrupted, the houses in the vicinity of the place where the damage was done would be burnt down.

While this was the start of the 'scorched-earth policy' on paper,[30] houses had been burnt from as early as March 1900 on Roberts's instructions if they had been used to shelter Boer commandos.[31] In terms of this policy, farmhouses with their contents, as well as barns and outbuildings, were burnt down. Farm animals such as sheep, cattle, pigs and chickens were slaughtered. Farmlands and the veld were set alight, while in some cases entire towns were destroyed. By January 1901 this destruction was taking place indiscriminately, and hundreds of farms in the Free State and the Transvaal were left uninhabitable.[32] According to Roberts, it was a punitive measure for continued resistance against the new British regime.

Thousands of women from across the country attended the Conciliation Committee's mass meeting in London to protest against the war, including delegates of the Women's Liberal Federation. 'Our protest was more largely due to our proud desire for England's honour and our horror lest her rectitude be marred by an unjust act,' Emily wrote.[33]

That evening in the Queen's Hall the women passed four resolutions:

British soldiers burning a farmhouse as part of the scorched-earth policy. About 30,000 farms and farmsteads in the Transvaal and the Orange Free State were destroyed in this manner.

Photo: Anglo-Boer War Museum

1: That this meeting of women brought together from all parts of the United Kingdom condemns the unhappy war now raging in South Africa as mainly due to the bad policy of the Government – a policy which has already cost in killed, wounded and missing over 20,000 of our bravest soldiers and the expenditure of millions of money drawn from the savings and toil of our people, while to the two small States with whom we are at war, it is bringing utter ruin and desolation.

2: That this meeting protests against the attempts to silence, by the disorder and violence, all freedom of speech, or criticism of Government policy.

A burning farmstead.

Photo: Anglo-Boer War Museum

3: That this meeting protests against any settlement which involves the extinction by force of two Republics whose inhabitants, allied to us by blood and religion, cling as passionately to their separate nationality and flag as we in this country do to ours.

4: That this meeting desires to express its sympathy with the women of the Transvaal and Orange Free State and begs them to remember that thousands of English women are filled with profound sorrow at the thought of their suffering, and with deep regret for the action of their own Government. God save the Queen.[34]

It was significant that the last resolution had been drafted by Emily and was read out by her at the meeting. It contained words that were to gain new and concrete meaning in her life in the coming years: 'sympathy', 'women', 'sorrow', 'suffering', 'regret' . . .

She felt strongly that these views had to be placed on record as proof of the attitude of many of her compatriots towards the war.

The meeting attracted widespread attention, especially on the part of the jingo press which, according to Emily, 'excelled itself in virulence and inaccuracy' in its reports. Pro-war people wrote the names of the Boer leaders in big, white chalk letters on the pavement outside her flat.[35]

In July Emily went with Liberal MP David Lloyd George to Liskeard to propagate the objections to the war at a meeting. The town hall was packed that evening, with many of Emily's child-hood friends in attendance,[36] but the rowdy 'patriotic' pro-war contingent disrupted the meeting to such an extent that neither of the speakers could deliver a speech.

At least Emily managed to get a few words in: 'I think you will agree with me that if her majesty the Queen to whom you have sung, were present now, she would be heartily ashamed of her Cornish subjects. I have a great deal that I am anxious to say to you. Will you sit down for a few minutes and listen to me? It seems a strange thing to me that Cornishmen will not listen to a Cornishwoman.'[37]

The majority of the audience became even more disorderly, however, and when chairs and other objects where hurled at the stage, Emily and Lloyd George had to beat a hasty retreat.

***

It was sleeting as I walked towards the hall in Liskeard where Emily and Lloyd George had to face a barrage of insults. It looks like a typical school or church hall which can seat about eight hundred people. The stage is big and suitable for a town concert.

Up the narrow steps to the stage where Emily sat listening to the jingoes' songs, chants and shouts . . . To the side door through which they fled to escape from the riotous mob.

This was the beginning of the end of many of Emily's friendships. After this day in July 1900 in this hall some of her closest friends and relatives ostracised her.

***

'There followed a storm of abuse from relatives and acquaintances, some of whom even attacked me in the press. I lost the majority of the friends of my girlhood and it was a great loss. There was a divergence of principle at that time which broke many a bond, and taking up the work publicly I would not escape a painful severance of old ties.'[38] Emily increasingly learnt from reports out of South Africa that her country's troops, 'contrary to the recognised usages of war, were guilty of the destruction by burning and blowing up with dynamite of farm houses'. The news reached a few newspapers in England, but the British public were still in the dark about the extent of the destruction,[39] she wrote. Some letters from soldiers that appeared in the press described the 'horrible scenes which, to their honour, they for the most part found most distressing'.[40]

She was deeply upset about these events, and realised that they confronted her with an inescapable choice. 'Thus the constantly renewed picture of women and children homeless, desperate and distressed formed and fixed itself in my mind and never once left me. It became my abiding thought. The thought deepened to torture and by a kind of second-sight such as had often visited me in my life the whole became a vision of vivid reality wherein I saw myself amongst the sufferers bearing relief. I never doubted then that I should go and that, be the obstacles what they might, they would be surmounted.'[41]

She knew that some might ridicule this 'vision', but she had read in *Daniel Deronda* by George Eliot that this 'second-sight' was a kind of profound knowledge that eventually crystallised into an image of a new, alternative reality.

'Anyhow, explain it as you will, it was a curious and most solemn feeling that possessed me and nurtured in the quiet of the country, it grew into a definite plan when I returned to the solitude of my Chelsea flat. No one yet knew of my intention nor exercised any influence upon me. I thought out my plan.'[42]

And the plan was to be there – in South Africa. To make a difference there.

To achieve her aim she needed money, and she resolved to start a fund for this purpose. Leonard and Kate Courtney were the first people Emily told about her plan. Courtney paced the room, went to stand in front of the window and expressed his reservations: there was too little information about what was really happening in South Africa. How would the money be raised? How much would be sufficient? Would the government allow it? How would the money be distributed?

Emily tried to answer all the questions. She was in search of information – the facts about the war – in order to approach people for further donatations to enable her to travel. Without a proper fund she would not be able to act on her plan. Reluctantly, Courtney gave the project his blessing; this was all that Emily wanted at this stage.

The hardest for her was to finally gain the approval of Uncle Arthur and Aunt Mary. Armed with letters of support from prominent people from the Cape and London, she visited them in Mayfair. While they were sceptical, they supported her nonetheless. They would not prevent her from going, but they did not feel strongly enough about the cause to support her financially. Though Emily had not expected such a response, she resigned herself to it; just as long as she could rely on their emotional support.[43]

Aunt Mary, who nonetheless agreed to serve on the committee, used her influence and wrote to Joseph Chamberlain to obtain official approval for the fund. Known as the South Africa Women and Children Distress Fund, it was non-political, philanthropic and national in nature, and its object was to feed, clothe, shelter and rescue women and children, both Boer and British, who had been rendered destitute by the war. Membership included both men and women, she informed him.[44]

While Emily was working on this project, the first surrendered burghers – members of the Boer commandos who had decided to lay down their arms (called the 'hands-uppers') – and their families were placed in so-called 'protection camps' in Bloemfontein and Pretoria in September 1900. According to the British military authorities, this was done to ensure their safety, so they wouldn't be re-commandeered by their fellow burgers,[45] and to make provision for their livestock. Women and children who had nowhere else to go were sent to 'refugee camps' as well. Kitchener hoped that by putting the women and children in camps, the burghers would not be able to receive provisions from home. He hoped that would they lay down their arms and stop fighting, but this part of the plan was not successful.

However, there was no material difference between the 'protection' and 'refugee' camps and concentration camps.[46] The erection of concentration camps formed an important part of the British forces' tactics in an effort to outmanoeuvre the Boer forces' war effort. The homeless Boer women and their children who were homeless because of the scorched-earth policy, together with aged men who were unfit to fight, were transported to these 'refugee camps' where they soon by far outnumbered the 'refugees'. These people (the so-called 'undesirables') were not seeking British protection and had therefore been placed in these camps against their will. For this reason it is more appropriate to refer to these camps as concentration camps rather than 'refugee camps'.[47] Emily worked for six months to solicit support for her project among influential people in Britain and South Africa. She wrote as follows about the reaction of some: 'The chilling attitude of some accounted most saintly, the lack of imagination in others whose known gifts pre-supposed imagination – the feat of those with big reputations lest those should be marred – all left an indelible impression on my mind.'[48]

Her brother Leonard warned her of diseases in South Africa, but Emily was undeterred. 'For me life has no attraction,' she replied. 'The Boers are already dying.' What about all the gossip about her? 'I get that in England and am by long use too tough to mind it anymore.'

You are going too soon, Leonard cautioned. 'Destitution and starvation do not wait for opportune political moments,'[49] Emily retorted.

How would the Cape women view her plans? She wrote to Caroline Murray (née Molteno), wife of Dr Charles Murray, who was sympathetic towards the Boers. She had met the couple when they were on a visit to London and Caroline's brother, Percy Molteno, her sister Betty and her brother John Charles, a member of the Cape Parliament, were also involved in anti-war activities. Emily informed them that she was intent on coming to help the victims of the war, even though some were of the view that such assistance would cause the government to neglect its duty towards the women and children. Maybe such aid would 'soften the hearts of the sufferers towards us a little bit', Emily hoped.[50]

By the end of November 1900 Emily wrote to Caroline that she would soon be leaving for the Cape, and thanked her that she could stay with them in Cape Town. She was relieved that her departure was finally at hand – she could not wait for it to happen.[51] She had raised three hundred pounds for her fund; a reasonable sum, but small compared to the need she would find that had to be relieved. To save money, she travelled second class on the *Avondale Castle* that departed for the Cape on 7 December.

On board, Emily read books about South Africa and learnt as much 'Boer Dutch', as she referred to the emerging Afrikaans language, as possible from other passengers.[52] She had received lessons in London and had already developed a liking for 'the Taal' – the developing language – because it was capable of conveying such humour, tenderness and poetic sentiments.[53]

She was travelling on her own – a forty-year-old woman headed for a hot, dusty region of the world that was completely unfamiliar to her, radically different in all respects from her own country. Furthermore, a region where a war was raging.

To Emily this mission was nothing less than a calling: 'Deeply I had felt the call. Passionately I resented the injustice of English policy. Wholeheartedly I offered myself for relief to the distressed. Carefully step by step I prepared the way. Sternly I economised and saved. Greatly I felt the wrench and anxiety for my aged relatives. But never did the vision fade of those desolate women and children, nor the certainty that I must go to them.'[54]

The month before, Horatio Herbert Kitchener had been promoted to commander-in-chief of the British forces in South Africa after serving as Lord Roberts's second in command. Kitchener, who had just been promoted to the rank of general, had recently returned from the Sudan where he had been the Governor General; two years earlier he had won a celebrated victory at the bloody Battle of Omdurman in Khartoum in which about 10,800 Sudanese and 48 British soldiers died.

Kitchener, a fifty-year-old bachelor, was known for his antipathy towards women. After the death of his fiancée in his younger years he apparently allowed only unmarried men in his inner circle and never granted audiences to women.[55]

While Emily was still at sea, Kitchener issued a memorandum to his officers. The women and children that were sent to the concentration camps had to be divided into two categories: the families of surrendered and neutral burghers; and those whose husbands, sons, brothers or fathers were still fighting. The latter group would be known as 'Undesirables'. Preference had to be given to the first category in all respects, he ordered.[56]

Two days after Christmas Day 1900, the *Avondale Castle* sailed into the Table Bay harbour. The resolute woman who arrived in South Africa was intellectually cultivated and held strong views on many issues, especially where moral values were at stake. She was a tireless writer of letters and petitions in elegant, contemporary, often dramatic English that attested to a wide vocabulary with liberal use of quotations from writers and poets.

She had pale blue eyes and fair,[57] wavy hair that she combed away from her forehead and wore loosely gathered at the back. While her hair had distinct waves, it was not curly, and here and there it was already tinged with grey. Emily was nearly five foot eight and had a proud and straight bearing; she was poised, well dressed and conscious of her social class. She was by no means 'dumpy',[58] but rather of 'slight' build, with a distinctive slightly aquiline nose.[59]

Emily was overwhelmed by the beauty of Table Mountain and the 'rosy gold of early dawn'. The ship had arrived at four in the morning, but the port was so crowded with vessels that tugboats had to transport the passengers to the shore. Impatient to land, Emily took the first one she could find.

Owing to the war there was a confusion at the port during which Emily lost her luggage, which was only returned to her two days later. She stayed at the home of Caroline Murray and her husband Charles in Kenilworth, where various friends and acquaintances came to welcome her, among them Mary Sauer (née Cloete), wife of the Cape politician Jacobus Wilhelmus Sauer.[60] In the late afternoon, Emily sat eating figs and apricots on the stoep with a tame meerkat on her lap, 'as if I had known it always'.

Now the next challenge awaited her: How would she get to the north of the country? Accommodation would not be a problem, as she had received numerous invitations to stay on farms. Meanwhile she had received news of four thousand women and children 'in some kind of "Refugee Camp" in Johannesburg'. People informed her that another six hundred farmhouses had been burnt down in the past week.[61] This was the first time Emily heard of the existence of concentration camps, although this term was not yet in general use.

During the first days of January 1901 she began to get a picture of women and children who were being placed in 'refugee camps'. 'Terrible anxiety existed with regard to these camps' among people at the Cape who were concerned about the fate of relatives in the Free State and the Transvaal, 'but there were no clear knowledge of their condition. In England we heard nothing of the formation of such camps. More than ever I felt I must get to them.'[62]

At the homes she visited, she met women who had been deported to the Cape after their homes had been burnt and they had lost all their possessions. The stories she was told were 'humiliating and heart-rending', and having to listen sympathetically for hours on end was more than what she had thought humanly possible, she wrote on 6 January from Schoongezicht, the farm 'of the politician John X. Merriman. 'Perhaps in due time I shall grow hardened to it.' What was even more perturbing: 'The main fact learnt was that in many places large camps were now 'forming where women and children were crowded.' No one knew how many camps there were, 'but they are on the increase'.[63]

Emily wrote to Sir Alfred Milner, the forty-eight-year-old bachelor who was now the governor of the Transvaal and the Free State as well as of the Cape, and still the British high commissioner, and requested a personal audience with him. Her first attempt was unsuccessful when Milner's secretary indicated that 'the condition of women and children' would not get her close to the important man, and she would have to wait. Sooner than she had expected, however, she was invited to lunch on 8 January 1901.[64]

She had letters of introduction with her from her aunt, Lady Hobhouse, and her cousin Henry Hobhouse V,[65] a British MP. Henry and Milner had been friends since their student days together at Oxford.[66]

But Emily was 'in a blue funk' about the meeting, fearing that she might fail to put her case convincingly to Milner.

'I was well-nigh sick with terror lest I should prove incompetent for the ordeal. And as usual with me in moments of mental or emotional strain my heart beat so violently I could not breathe. If I failed in my presentment of the cause, the scheme for which I had toiled for months would fall on the ground and countless lives be lost that might be saved.'[67]

On her solitary train journey from Kenilworth to the governor's residence Government House (the later Tuynhuys) in Cape Town, she searched for something in her handbag from which she could draw comfort. In the bag was a letter from Kate Courtney, with a message her husband had written at the bottom: 'I add two words, be prudent, be calm . . .'

It put Emily in a somewhat calmer frame of mind, but this was short-lived; she had hoped to speak to Milner in private, and now discovered she was lunching with him and eight other men, none of whom she knew.

Milner started his discussion with Emily during lunch in the company of all the other men, but she cut him short and implored him 'to give me a few minutes afterwards'.

When Milner demurred, saying that he had too much work, Emily pleaded that 'this was part of the work and of great importance'. Milner then 'promised me fifteen minutes, not more'.

After lunch they sat down on a sofa in his living room and embarked on an animated exchange of views. 'We went at it hammer and tongs for an hour.' She made sure that Milner was left under no illusion about the spirit of the Boer women, as she had met many of them: 'How do you think will you govern thousands of Joans of Arc?' she asked.

She also requested rail trucks to take her relief supplies of food and clothing along to the interior, and asked that she be allowed to be accompanied by an Afrikaner woman.

Surprisingly, Milner acknowledged that the scorched-earth policy was a mistake. He had seen women being transported in open railway trucks, and it had left him 'uncomfortable'. 'Finally he agrees to forward my going around to the camps as a representative of the English movement and with me a Dutch lady whoever I and the people here like to choose as a representative of

South Africa . . .' There was a condition, however: Lord Kitchener, overall commander of the British forces, would have to agree.[68] Emily did not have much hope of obtaining Kitchener's approval. The chances were slim that the 'Butcher of Khartoum', and a 'women-hater' to boot, 'may welcome two women because of the difficulty he has created for himself of dealing with thousands'.[69]

On leaving Government House, Emily felt 'as if wings were attached to my feet', convinced that she and Milner had parted as friends. 'Everyone says he has no heart, but I think I hit on the atrophied remains of one. It might be developed if he had not, as he says he has, made up his mind to back up the military in everything. He struck me as amiable and weak, clear-headed and narrow.'[70] While awaiting Kitchener's response, Emily collected evidence from northerners who had managed to reach the Cape Colony. She also met eminent people such as the church leader Dr Andrew Murray, the chief justice Sir Henry de Villiers and his wife, and Sir William Bisset Berry, the speaker of the Cape Parliament.

On 17 January Emily received a letter[71] from Milner informing her that Kitchener had agreed per telegram that she could travel to the Free State, but on certain conditions. Two of these were that she could only go as far north as Bloemfontein, and that she preferably did not take a 'Dutch lady' along. This was bad news, as Emily had hoped to travel with Mrs Elizabeth Roos, a well-known community leader, who would act as interpreter in interviews with Boer women and assist Emily in locating certain towns and places.[72]

In Kitchener's telegram he referred to the 'Dutch Refugee women kept out of their homes by the Boers'. In terms of his logic, the situation was very simple: as soon as the last Boers surrendered, the war would be over and everyone could go home

Lord Kitchener, overall commander of the British
forces for the greater part of the Anglo-Boer War.

Photo: Anglo-Boer War Museum

– the women and children too. Hence the converse was also logi-
cal, albeit that he would not have admitted it openly: as long as
the Boers refused to surrender, their wives and children would
have to bear the brunt.

Emily preserved the telegram carefully, not because of its
contents, but because of the access it gave her. At the top she later
wrote: 'This was Kitchener's telegram which I carried everywhere
in the camps.'

She decided to pay Milner another visit. Couldn't something
be done to make it possible for her to also visit other camps that
were further north, she enquired.[73] Milner agreed to make a rail

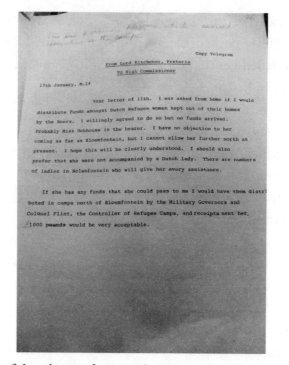

Copy Telegram

From Lord Kitchener, Pretoria
To High Commissioner

17th January. N.14

Your letter of 11th. I was asked from home if I would
distribute funds amongst Dutch Refugee women kept out of their homes
by the Boers. I willingly agreed to do so but no funds arrived.
Probably Miss Hobhouse is the bearer. I have no objection to her
coming as far as Bloemfontein, but I cannot allow her further north at
present. I hope this will be clearly understood. I should also
prefer that she were not accompanied by a Dutch lady. There are numbers
of ladies in Bloemfontein who will give her every assistance.

If she has any funds that she could pass to me I would have them distributed in camps north of Bloemfontein by the Military Governors and
Colonel Flint, the Controller of Refugee Camps, and receipts sent her.
£1000 pounds would be very acceptable.

A copy of the telegram from Kitchener to Milner that gave Emily
permission to visit the concentration camps in the Free State on
certain conditions. The £1000 he requested her to forward was not
sent because Emily simply did not have so much money.

Photo: Emily's scrapbook, courtesy of Jennifer Hobhouse Balme

truck available for the relief supplies she wanted to take along, but
this was the most he could do; Kitchener had the final say.

She set about purchasing food, clothing, blankets and other necessities, but the prices were high and she had only the three hundred
pounds she had raised in England. To Leonard she wrote that she had
bought six tons of clothing and six tons of food, but this would still
not be enough. She hoped that the Conciliation Committee could
send more money, as 'it will be horrible to be up there with empty
hands which would be the case in a very few weeks . . .'[74]

From early in the morning to late at night on Monday 21 January, Emily packed the rail truck at the Cape Town station, but it saddened her that the goods she had managed to buy left it barely half full.

In the meantime she had met Charles Fichardt[75] from Bloemfontein, in the Orange Free State, who was in the Cape 'on parole' (which meant that he had undertaken to return to Bloemfontein). He offered that she could stay at his parental home, Kaya Lami, when she arrived there.

The following evening, a large group of new friends came to see Emily off at the Cape Town station. They had packed a food basket for her that included a kettle, jam and bread, as well as fruit for the journey.

She was venturing on her own into the unknown, a depressing world of conflict and destruction.

Regarding the goodbyes at the station and the nocturnal train journey, Emily wrote: 'It was a glorious night. Their kindness had been unceasing and I felt I had in them a solid background in case of need. But as the train moved off towards the strange, hot, war-stricken north with its accumulations of misery and bloodshed I must own that my heart sank a little and I faced the unknown with great trepidation, in spite of the feeling that the deep desire of months which had laid so urgent a call upon me, was indeed finding accomplishment.'[76]

The journey she had embarked on would change her life dramatically.

4

Looking into the depths of grief

'Those truckloads of women and children unsheltered and unfed – bereft of home, bearing the vivid recollection of their possessions in the flames – and that mass of the 'sweepings' of a wide military 'drive' – flocks and herds of frightened animals bellowing and baaing for food and drink – tangled up with wagons and vehicles of all sorts and a dense crowd of human beings – combined to give a picture of war in all its destructive-ness, cruelty, stupidity and nakedness such as not even the misery of the camps (with their external appearance of order) could do.'

– Emily Hobhouse, near Warrenton
in the Cape Colony, April 1901

Emily was the only woman on the slow-moving troop train to Bloemfontein. At halts along the way she did not see a single woman. She found it difficult to buy food at stations because of the throng of soldiers crowding around the food outlets. The food

Emily Hobhouse's concentration camp journeys, 1901

1. **22 January:** Departs from Cape Town
2. **24 January – 1 February:** Bloemfontein camp
3. **2 February:** Norvalspont and Aliwal North camps
4. **21 February:** Back in Bloemfontein
5. **4 March:** Springfontein camp
6. **8 – 10 March:** Norvalspont camp
7. **12 March:** Kimberley
8. **13 – 18 March:** Kimberley camp
9. **19 March:** Departs for Cape Town
10. **24 March:** Cape Town
11. **5 April:** Back at Kimberley camp

12. **9 April:** Warrenton camp
13. **10 April:** Mafeking camp
14. **13 April:** Warrenton camp
15. **15 – 19 April:** In Kimberley
16. **21 April:** Stops at Springfontein
17. **22 – 30 April:** In Bloemfontein
18. **31 April:** Stops at Springfontein
19. **1 May:** Stops at Norvalspont camp
20. **5 May:** In Cape Town
    7 May: Departs for England
    24 May: Arrives at Southampton

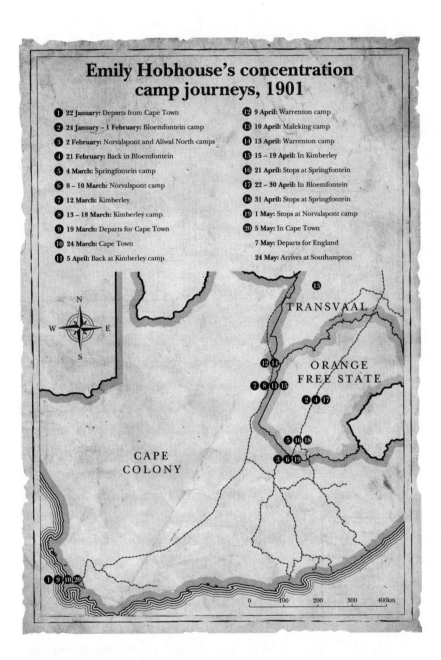

Bloemfontein concentration camp.

Photo: Anglo-Boer War Museum

basket from the Cape friends was her salvation: bread, apricot jam and drinks of cocoa. She would later survive on this kind of food for weeks and months on end, with the result that in time 'I could not bear the sight, much less the taste of an apricot'.[1]

She found the landscape strange, with its unfamiliar vegetation, the heat, dust and unusual rock formations; the solitude of the veld; the lack of trees and shade, and the exceptional silence.[2]

'As far as extent and sweep and sky go the Karoo is beautiful,' she wrote with regard to the completely new world that greeted her as the sun rose. 'On the second day there were horrible dust storms varied by thunder storms. The sand penetrated through the closed windows and doors, filled eyes and ears and turned my hair red, and covered everything like a table cloth . . . From Colesberg on it was a desolate outlook. The land seemed dead and silent, absolutely without life as far as the eye could reach, only carcasses of horses, mules and cattle with a sort of mute anguish in their look and bleached bones.'[3]

On Emily's arrival in Bloemfontein on 24 January, it struck her immediately that the entire city was controlled by the British military authorities.[4] Everyone's movements were under surveillance, and the city was crawling with soldiers. No one could do anything without the permission of the British.

The first night she spent in an inn after having found her rail truck with the relief supplies and arranging for the goods to be unloaded. The following day Caroline Fichardt, the mother of Charles whom she had met at the Cape, sent her carriage for Emily. With it came word from Caroline that they were already under surveillance in terms of martial law, and Emily could only stay with them if Major General George Pretyman, the military governor of Bloemfontein, gave his permission in writing. Caroline was worried that if she were to put a foot wrong, her two daughters and Charles would be punished. Emily went to see Pretyman forthwith.[5]

Major General George Pretyman, Military
Commandant, Bloemfontein.

Photo: Gallo Images/Getty Images/Print Collector

He nearly 'jumped out of his skin' when he heard that she intended to stay with Caroline, whose husband had died six months earlier, as she was supposedly 'a bitter woman', but Emily was ready with a reassuring explanation: 'My visit may have a softening effect upon her.'[6] Pretyman reluctantly granted her permission to stay with the Fichardts in their beautiful home, Kaya Lami. Emily used the opportunity to ask Pretyman for a permit to visit the camps south of Bloemfontein. She made it quite clear to him that she was not there to do the military authorities' work for them, but to give advice and to investigate the condition of the women and children in the camps and render assistance where she could. Everywhere she learnt that farms were being burnt down indiscriminately and that more concentration camps were being erected in the Free State and the Transvaal.

From his remarks, too, it was obvious that Kitchener despised the Boers and '[i]n general . . . had a low opinion of [them], describing them as "savages with only a thin white veneer." '[7] About the women he said that they 'were outstripping men in their bitterness and commitment to the war, and the only remedy to bring them to their senses would be to confine what he called the worst class to a camp.'[8]

It was only Emily's second day in Bloemfontein, and she was already disillusioned with the officers who had no plan for providing the women with clothing. She did not mince her words: 'Crass male ignorance, stupidity, helplessness and muddling. I rub as much salt into the sore places of their minds as I possibly can, because it is so good for them; but I can't help melting a little when they are very humble and confess that the whole thing is a grievous and gigantic blunder and presents an almost insoluble problem, and they don't know how to face it.'[9]

The permit Major General George Pretyman issued to Emily
to visit the concentration camps south of Bloemfontein.

Letter: Courtesy of Jennifer Hobhouse Balme

The concentration camp at Bloemfontein was about three kilometres from the city centre, situated on the southern slope of a
small hill in the barren veld without a single tree. In the camp
there were two thousand women, nine hundred children and a
few men – the 'hands-uppers' – these were men who had laid
down their arms voluntarily and in most cases had signed an oath
of neutrality. The Boers called them 'handsuppers'.[10] The first
woman Emily met there was Mrs P. J. Botha (née Stegman). There
was nothing in her tent – only flies, heat, her five children and a
black servant girl. Several other women joined them in the tent to
tell their stories too. They cried and even laughed together, and
'chatted in bad Dutch and bad English all the afternoon'.[11]

While they were sitting there, a snake slithered into the tent and everyone ran out. Emily, who 'could not bear to think the thing should be at large in a community mostly sleeping on the ground', attacked the creature with her parasol until a man arrived and finished it off.[12]

Over the next few days, the women each told Emily their personal stories: how their farmhouses and crops had been burnt, their livestock killed or injured and left to die; how they had been transported for days on wagons and/or trains and been forced into the camp . . . They were stories of loss, exposure, starvation, illness, pain and longing. 'The women are wonderful; they cry very little and never complain . . . Only when it cuts afresh at them through their children do their feelings flash out.'[13]

Within four days, Emily discovered the nature and extent of the misery in the camp. The most basic necessities of life were lacking. There were not even candles; they were only used when someone was seriously ill. There was no soap, and none had ever been supplied.

There was no mortuary tent; the dead lay in the heat among the living until they were buried. Flies lay thick and black on every-thing. Six people on average were crowded into one little tent, but in many cases a tent housed about nine or ten inmates.[14]

There was no school for the children. There was virtually no wood or coals to boil any drinking water or food, and the water of the Modder River was filthy. Typhoid was rife. Water was limited to two buckets for eight people – for drinking, washing and cooking. The food rations were not nearly sufficient to stave off hunger and disease.

It was 'murder to the children' to keep these camps going, which were probably housing fifty thousand people in total by this time, Emily realised.

Her suggestion to Captain Albert Hume, who had been designated to give her a hearing, was that a railway boiler be obtained and that all water be boiled in it. The fifty cows that were supposed to provide the camp inmates with milk were so starved that they produced only four buckets of milk per day. She was also concerned about the 'native camp' with about five hundred people who were in need of aid.[15]

Part of the reasoning of Lord Roberts' and later Lord Kitchener's scorched-earth policy was to destroy the Boer farms and all the food supply so that the Boers would not be able to continue without these resources. In order to clear the land, the black farm workers also had to be put in 'native refugee camps'. Their huts were destroyed and they were taken to camps. In some cases they went voluntarily in order to try and find refuge or their cattle.

'In August 1901 there were 53,144 black refugees in the refugee camps for black people. 22,795 in Transvaal and 30,359 in the Orange Free State, from a total population of 923,787 in both colonies . . .'[16]

'One of the main reasons for erecting these camps (the black camps) was to ensure they became self sufficient and they became an important source of labour for the army.'[17] There were ultimately fifty camps for white people and sixty-four for black people. In some instances, black house servants were in the white camps with the white women. Emily saw many of them, in the camps she visited.

Emily meticulously recorded the rations as they were measured out in the Bloemfontein camp on 16 January 1901:

Refugees
Flour or mealie-meal: 1 lb per day
Meat: ¾ lb per day

Coffee: 1 oz per day
Sugar: 2 oz per day
Salt: ½ oz per day

Undesirables
Mealie-meal (or samp, potatoes, flour, rice): ¾ lb per day
Meat: 1 lb, twice a week
Coffee: 1 oz per day
Sugar: 2 oz per day
Salt: ½ oz per day

Children under 6 years – Refugees
Flour or mealie-meal: ½ lb per day
Meat: ½ lb per day
Milk: ¼ tin per day
Sugar: 1 oz per day
Salt: ½ oz per day

Children under 6 years – Undesirables
Mealie-meal: ½ lb per day
Meat: ½ lb twice a week
Milk: ¼ tin per day
Sugar: 1 oz per day
Salt: ½ oz per day[18]

Emily's plan was to tell the 'other side' of the war story based on an eyewitness account, an alternative narrative to the one that the military authorities and the British politicians were presenting to the world. She started writing down individual women's stories, which would eventually appear in her book *The Brunt of the War and Where It Fell*.[19] She also aimed to use the evidence she was gathering to compile a report for the South African Conciliation Committee in England.

Day after day Emily walked from tent to tent, with people calling her from all over: 'Come and see, Sister.' (Many of the women regarded Emily as a nurse.) Among the sights that she saw were a baby of six months 'gasping its life out on its mother's knee'; children who were so weak from measles that they were unable to walk, lying there 'white and wan'; a dying twenty-four-year-old woman lying on a stretcher on the ground. Emily became exasperated with Captain Hume who considered her too sympathetic towards the camp inmates (she 'wanted to box his ears'), and sent him to fetch some brandy for the dying woman.[20]

A man came up and asked her to look at his son, who had been sick for three months. 'It was a dear little chap of four and nothing left of him except his great brown eyes and white teeth from which the lips were drawn back, too thin to close. His body was emaciated.' There had been no milk available for the dying child.

An appalled Emily called Hume to observe the scene.

'You shall look,' I said. And I made him come in and showed him the complete child skeleton. Then at last he did say it was awful to see the children suffering so . . .

I can't describe what it is to see these children lying about in a state of collapse – it is just exactly like faded flowers thrown away. And one hates to stand and look on at such misery and be able to do almost nothing.[21]

The British soldiers regarded her as if she were 'a fool, an idiot and a traitor combined'. The material destruction and bodily suffering were one thing, Emily wrote, but the worst aspect of war was the moral miasma that grew from it and infected everything.

It was during this time that she noticed Lizzie van Zyl[22] in the Bloemfontein camp's hospital tent. The English nurse told Emily that the seven-year-old Lizzie's mother was to blame for the child's condition, as she had starved her. Emily found this hard to swallow, and asked people in the camp about the case. She was told that the starvation allegations originated from the Van Zyls' neighbours, who were so-called 'refugees'. Lizzie's mother, on the other hand, was classified as an 'undesirable' because her husband was still on commando. As 'undesirables', the Van Zyls received less food than the 'refugees'.

Lizzie's mother subsequently removed her from the hospital tent because the child was being neglected there. Emily reported later that she 'used to see her in the bare tent, lying on a tiny mattress which had been given her, trying to get air from beneath the raised flap, gasping her life out in the heated tent. Her mother tended her, and I got some friends in town to make her a little muslin cap to keep the flies from her bare head. I was arranging to get a little cart made to draw her into the air in the cooler hours, but before wood could be procured, the cold nights came on . . .'[23]

Lizzie died in early May 1901, probably from typhoid. Other diseases that were prevalent in the camps included measles, whooping cough, scarlet fever, bronchitis, diarrhoea in babies, diphtheria and pneumonia. Few people in the camps were completely healthy.[24]

The atmosphere in Bloemfontein was so depressing that Emily felt paralysed and intimidated, 'like being in continual disgrace or banishment or imprisonment. Some days I think I must cut and run . . . The feeling is intolerable. To watch all these Englishmen taking this horrible line and doing these awful things . . .'[25]

She was concerned about the image of her country, and the devastation that England was causing; nevertheless, she remained patriotic. '[I]f only the English people would try to exercise a little imagination – picture the whole miserable scene and answer how long such a cruelty is to be tolerated . . .'

Appealing to Aunt Mary in a letter, she asked whether her aunt 'couldn't write such a letter about it in *The Times* as should make more people listen and believe and understand – which would touch their conscience? Is England afraid of losing her prestige? Well, that's gone already in this country.'[26]

The day before Emily left to visit the first of the other concentration camps, she met the wife of President M. T. Steyn, Rachel Isabella Steyn (née Fraser),[27] widely known as 'Tibbie', which was her Scottish nickname. Prior to their meeting Emily had seen Tibbie walking about in Bloemfontein, always followed by a soldier because the English did not trust her. 'A handsome woman, dignified and self-controlled,' Emily wrote later. The two women had a long and heartfelt conversation, and took an instant liking to each other.

Tibbie said about Emily: 'She was a beautiful woman, extremely intelligent and committed heart and soul to improving conditions in the camps. We owe her an incredible debt because if it had not been for her, the death rate among the women and children would have been much, much higher.'[28]

When she next saw Pretyman, Emily left him under no illusion as to what she thought of his camp. What horrified her most was the condition of the sanitation facilities. The slop buckets were not emptied regularly, and the stench at the tents that stood downwind was terrible.[29]

Pretyman was quick to cast suspicion on her. Emily had said beforehand that her mission was non-political, he wrote to Milner, but 'I hear that since her arrival the refugees in this camp have suddenly found out that they are very badly treated and ought to be supplied with many more comforts than at present afforded them ... I can see she is very much in sympathy with our enemies ... I fear this class of fanatic will not do the cause much good from our point of view.'

Yet Pretyman also made a surprising admission: 'But at the same time I could not help in my heart agreeing with her that this policy of bringing in the women and children to these camps, is a mistaken one.'[30]

On 2 February 1901 Emily set off on her own on a goods train for Norvalspont, about 195 kilometres south of Bloemfontein. She found herself in an alien, searingly hot, dusty world. In her letters to Aunt Mary, she gave her address as 'The Land of Nod' – the place east of the biblical Eden where Cain was exiled by God after he had murdered his brother Abel.

After what she had witnessed at Bloemfontein, Emily feared what awaited her at Norvalspont, where the camp housed fifteen hundred people. But she was impressed with the camp superintendent, Captain Du Plat Taylor, because the inmates did not have to use water from the Orange River but instead had access to piped water from a spring. The food was slightly better than at Bloemfontein and no diseases had broken out, although everyone who went to the hospital tent died there. There was also a school for the children, but clothes were urgently needed.

Most people in the Norvalspont camp were 'prisoners of war', as Emily referred to them, while 'refugees' were in the minority. She noticed in the camps she visited that there were in reality very few who fell in this latter category, and that they were housed in big marquees with furniture and other luxuries they had been allowed to bring along. But the military authorities still insisted to her that most of the inmates were 'refugees' who had come to the camps of their own free will.

Women and children plant trees at the
Norvalspont concentration camp.

Photo: Anglo-Boer War Museum

Snow in the Aliwal North concentration camp.

Photo: Anglo-Boer War Museum

From here Emily took the train to Aliwal North, situated about 155 kilometres east of Norvalspont. While the town had only eight hundred inhabitants, the concentration camp was home to two thousand inmates. Here, too, she was impressed with the camp commandant, Major Apthorp, who kept the camp neat and made sure that inmates received dried vegetables and potatoes twice a week.[31]

Emily distributed clothing. Like in all the other camps, there was no soap. 'This seems to have been due to a careless order from Headquarters with regard to the rations, and men don't think of these things unless it is suggested to them, they simply say: "How dirty these people are!" '[32]

While Emily was travelling from one camp to the other, the authorities increasingly took note of her activities. Major Sir Hamilton Goold-Adams, who had succeeded Pretyman as military governor of Bloemfontein, reported to Milner: 'Miss Hobhouse has been playing the dickens with the women in the camps.' She, Tibbie Steyn, Maynie Fleck and Caroline Fichardt were 'creating a great deal of unrest by impressing upon such people the hardships they are enduring'.

'I have it on good authority,' Goold-Adams wrote, 'that Miss Hobhouse is here on behalf of the Liberal Party to collect information for them for the usual purposes, and she has sent round circulars asking for information from various individuals as to their circumstances and whether their farms have been burnt.'[33]

Emily in turn described Goold-Adams as energetic, open and affable, but short on brains. She found it unbearable that such men were determining the fates of women and children. She did not seem to have much respect for their military abilities either, commenting that 'this army it is thought will never catch De Wet'. There was 'too much riding and shooting and picnicking and polo and golf playing for war to have much place ... All those Tommies asleep upon the line and all the badly kept offices. Oh dear it is dreadful ... it is remarked as a surprise when an officer does behave like a gentleman.'[34]

The people in the concentration camps informed her that they would never submit to British rule. The English, for their part, 'hate the Dutch and take every opportunity of shewing it and of saying so. But the Dutch women are aghast at the barbarities committed by what they believed to be a civilised nation.'

On 21 February 1901 Emily was back in Bloemfontein, where many letters from home awaited her. Aunt Mary recounted that Uncle Arthur had assisted at the swearing in of the new king, Edward VII, son of the late Queen Victoria. Kate Courtney informed her that the South Africa Women and Children Distress Fund Committee had met after receiving her letters; they would make a further sum of five hundred pounds available to her at a bank in Cape Town.[35] The money could not arrive soon enough, as the need in the camps was enormous.

Education had always been close to Emily's heart. She got the idea to select a few of the young girls with the most potential from the camps and send them to a good school. In Bloemfontein there was a ladies' institute (later renamed the Eunice High School) which, from what she had heard, was one of the best girls' schools in the country. She selected four girls: Hettie and Lizzie Botha, Eunice Ferreira and Engela van Rooyen, whose ages varied from fourteen to eighteen years. (The Botha girls were the daughters of Mrs P. J. Botha she had met on her first day at the Bloemfontein camp and who had assisted Emily diligently.) It cost one hundred pounds to keep the four girls at the school for a year; the money covered school fees, clothes and boarding fees.[36]

It took up to a month for letters between South Africa and England to reach their destination. The committee was still reluctant to send the news they had received from Emily to the newspapers for publication. At this stage they were only aware of the information she had gathered in the Cape; they did not know that she had already visited three concentration camps. Though there were suspicions in England that all was not well in the camps, information was very sketchy.

Meanwhile the death rates in the camps continued to rise. Emily compared the situation to the rural parish of her youth in St Ive, which had a population of about two thousand. While a funeral was a rare event there, 'here some 25–30 are carried away daily'.[37]

'They accused me of talking politics, whereas we could only talk of sickness and death, they objected to "shewing sympathy" but that was needed in every act and word. It was all kept very quiet; after a while the corpses were carried away at dawn, and instead of passing through the town approached the cemetery another way – many were buried in one grave.'[38] The death rate now stood at 200–390 per 1000 people, Emily reported.[39]

She went to see the new camp superintendent at Bloemfontein, Captain Trollope, about the high mortality figure. He replied sarcastically, asking why she could not just provide everyone in the Free State camps with clothing, and would she also donate money for the erection of a children's hospital?

Emily made it plain to him that it was the British government's responsibility to build a hospital. Because she had not been permitted to visit all the camps, she undertook to supply clothing to the women and children – not the men – in the camps she was allowed to visit.[40]

Meanwhile some of the Cape women, led by Caroline Murray, also sent food and clothing to the camps. Emily repeatedly called for the release of people interned in the camps who had relatives outside who could care for them, but nothing came of it. Her insistence on more nurses at least resulted in the arrival of four English women from the Cape, but one turned out to be a drunk and another's qualifications were falsified.

Every morning Caroline Fichardt's horse-drawn carriage transported Emily to the camp outside Bloemfontein, where she would walk from one tent to another in the heat and dust all day. In the evenings she returned on foot to the Fichardts' residence, a distance of two miles. This was her daily routine, also on Saturdays and Sundays. She hardly ever took a break. Slowly but surely the conditions in the camps improved somewhat, but Emily still wished that 'the jingos would come out here and have a good course'.[41]

Emily now regularly came across the Reverend Adrian Hofmeyr, who ministered to the spiritual needs of the camp inmates in his own way. He endeavoured to convince the 'undesirable' women that there was no hope that the Boers could still win the war. Likewise, Piet de Wet, a brother of General Christiaan de Wet, tried to persuade the women to convince their menfolk who were still on commando to lay down their arms. The women would listen to them patiently, but then turn their backs on them and walk away.

Kitchener now aggressively followed a three-pronged strategy to end the war: the scorched-earth policy was applied more ruthlessly (even churches were burnt and all forms of food were destroyed); the concentration camps were expanded and new ones were created; and systematic drives were used to herd the Boer commandos across the veld and trap them by means of barbed-wire fences between blockhouses.

In late February 1901 the British secretary of state for war, St John Brodrick, wrote to Kitchener and asked for a report on what was happening in the field and in the camps. From what he had heard, the wives and children of Boers who were still fighting were getting only half rations. Kitchener denied that half rations were given, but conceded that coffee and sugar rations were reduced for such people. 'Allowance is sufficient and families in camps satisfied and comfortable,'[42] he claimed.

During a debate in the House of Commons on 25 February, there were calls for an end to farm burnings, the destruction of private property and the internment of women and children in camps without adequate accommodation and food. In reply to questions, Brodrick stated that the women were free to leave the camps if they wished to do so.[43]

Three days later Lord Kitchener and General Louis Botha met in Middelburg, Transvaal, for peace talks at which Kitchener demanded that the two Boer republics surrender and relinquish their independence by becoming British colonies. Botha refused.[44]

In an effort to make the camps look less like a military operation, they were now taken over by a so-called civil administration. Henceforth officials, including soldiers who worked in the camps, had to wear civilian clothes instead of khaki uniforms.

Emily was not fooled by this change. 'So we play at pretending the war is over . . . It is hollow and rotten to the heart's core,' she wrote to her brother Leonard.

'To have made all over the state large uncomfortable communities of people whom you call refugees and say you are protecting, but who call themselves prisoners of war, compulsorily detained and detesting your protection. The whole object, of course is to enable Chamberlain to say in parliament that the country is settled and civil administration begun. It's a farce.'[45]

Emily became so exhausted as a result of the hard work in the camps, the emotional pressure of listening to people's stories and working even on Sundays when she sorted supplies, that she decided to stay in bed for a day and rest. Not for long; she took up her pen and wrote to her brother to ask if he could try to get someone to attend to the concentration camps for black people. She herself did not have time to focus on those camps too, but 'from the odd bits I hear it seems to be much needed'.

She also asked a Bloemfontein women's organisation, the Loyal Ladies League, to investigate the matter of the black camps. She did not have much hope in this regard, however: 'From odd bits I hear it would seem much needed and I dare not spare a moment to look into the question . . . But though they said they would I could see that they were not the right kind of person to be of any use and they were quite sure beforehand that there was neither sickness, suffering or death amongst those people. I hear there is much of all three.'[46] The *Bloemfontein Post* got wind of Emily's meeting with the Loyal Ladies and reported that some of the women were upset, especially because of this matter. From that point on all her letters were censored, but this did not prevent her from sending her brother photos taken in the camps.

The circumstances weighed more and more heavily on Emily, particularly the oppressive martial law provisions. She was frustrated and angry about what she was witnessing in the interior, and the failure of people at home to take note of it. And even worse: that the Liberal Party did not seem to be doing much about it.[47]

Her sense of duty trumped her frustrations and exhaustion. She wanted to visit more camps, such as those at Kroonstad and Kimberley, as well as the 'large and important ones in the Transvaal'. But Kitchener refused to permit her to travel further north than Bloemfontein. She wrote twice more to obtain permission for this; in both cases he refused.

This letter was sent to Emily by Kitchener's private
secretary on 28 February 1901 to confirm that she was not
permitted to travel further north than Bloemfontein.

Letter: Courtesy of Jennifer Hobhouse Balme

Early in March 1901 Emily set off again to the southern camps
in the Free State after leaving her relief work in the Bloemfontein
camp in the hands of a small group of women. Although she
had been granted a permit for the Kimberley camp, she was
not allowed to go south of Norvalspont, so to get there she
first had to travel to De Aar and then north again to reach
Kimberley. Emily did not indicate how she obtained the permit
for Kimberley, as the town is 165 kilometres *northwest* of
Bloemfontein.[48]

On 4 March she was at Springfontein, about 145 kilometres south of Bloemfontein, where she stayed at the home of the Reverend Sandrock, a German missionary, whose family was also battling to keep body and soul together. The camp at Springfontein was comparatively small, and the inmates 'poorer and more utterly destitute' than any she had yet seen.

Emily had brought along three cases of clothing and sat on the Sandrocks' stoep where some of the camp inmates came shuffling up to her in groups. She had enough supplies to clothe about sixty people every day.

'Some are scared, some paralysed and unable to realise their loss. Some are dissolved in tears, some mute and dry-eyed, seem only to be able to think of the blank, penniless future – some are glowing with pride at being prisoners for their country's sake. A few barely clothed women had petticoats out of the rough brown blankets so-called khaki blankets.'[49]

The blouses that had been sent from England were unsuitable as they were much too small for 'the well-developed Boer maiden, who is really a fine creature'. Could they please send any 'out-out women's sizes', she asked Aunt Mary.

At Springfontein there was no fuel for fires and although the people were given meat and mealie-meal, they were unable to cook anything because the veld was bare and the vegetation sparse. 'I thought Kitchener was considered such a great organiser, but is it good organising to have so little forethought and make so little preparation that thousands of people find themselves dumped down in strange places where there is nothing ready for their reception?'[50]

Next on Emily's itinerary was a second visit to Norvalspont. As usual, she wrote letters during her train journey – always with plans aimed at finding solutions. Again she raised the need in the

The concentration camp at Norvalspont, one of
the camps Emily visited more than once.

Photo: Anglo-Boer War Museum

black concentration camps with the Distress Fund Committee, and
appealed to the committee (in the same letter to her aunt) to send
people to investigate the conditions there. From what she had
heard, there were many large 'native' camps where the death rate
was also high. Shouldn't the Society of Friends – the Quakers – that
already had people in South Africa who provided relief aid, send
someone? Or the Aborigines' Protection Society, she suggested.[51]

As a liberal by conviction, Emily considered it self-evident that no
distinction should be made between the distress of whites and that of
blacks. 'In my camps there are many kinds of nationalities. They are all
suffering alike and it is not always possible to pick out the pure Boer
and leave those mixed or intermarried. Often there are little black servant girls whipped up and carried off with their mistresses and these
need clothing. Decency demands that all should be provided . . .'[52]

Families dressed up for their pictures to be
taken, Norvalspont concentration camp.

Photo: Anglo-Boer War Museum

In the camp at Norvalspont (where Emily arrived on 8 March) she soon clashed with the camp doctor, as he was of the kind 'who cannot open his mouth without using invectives against the Boers'. She felt 'ashamed in the name of the English'. In her view he was 'an insufferable cad', and she told him so to his face.[53]

At this camp the authorities had succeeded in persuading twenty-eight Boer men to fight on the English side. Emily was disgusted as she believed it to be unworthy of an English officer to sink so low, especially because these men had taken the oath of neutrality. 'I long to escape from this network of lies and horror,' she wrote.[54]

Two days later she tried to continue her journey by train via Noupoort to Kimberley, but she had to spend the whole day in the station's waiting room as conditions were too unsafe for travelling. The sounds of gunfire could be heard, and, according to rumours, the Boers were in the vicinity. By ten o'clock that evening the train had still not arrived, and the only solution was to sleep on the floor of the railway staff officer's office.[55]

When she stepped outside later to get some fresh air, the railway officer – a Mr Pates – followed her. Shyly he suggested that she could spend the night in the conductor's carriage, which he had fitted out as his sleeping quarters. He himself would sleep elsewhere. Overwhelmed by relief at this kindness, she collapsed on the small bed and started crying.

When she looked around her, she saw that he had prepared a bath for her and made the bed. Oh, it was a wonderful night, she wrote. To her, Mr Pates seemed almost like a saint.

The following day the train finally departed for De Aar, where they again had to wait for hours. She rested in the station's waiting room but was thrown out by the guard. The train to Noupoort only arrived at four o'clock the following morning.

Emily saw several trains that were on their way to Cape Town. She was sorely tempted to board one of them and end this interminable waiting in the middle of nowhere. She forced herself to look away because the temptation was almost irresistible.

The journey to Kimberley was a melancholy one for Emily; besides feeling unwell, she knew that their line would take them through a succession of battlefields: Belmont, Graspan, Modderrivier, Magersfontein . . . In the distance she saw trenches and graves.[56]

On 12 March she finally reached Kimberley, where she stayed in the Queen's Hotel, twenty minutes' walk from the camp. The camp commandant was a Major Wright who Emily quickly sized up as a 'coarse, lazy, indifferent old man'. There was no nurse in the camp, the tents were overcrowded and dirty, and measles and whooping cough were rife.

Among the unfortunate inmates was a Mrs Louw, who had been captured on her farm with her children, including a seventeen-day-old baby, by General Paul Methuen and his troops. She had pleaded with Methuen to allow them to take the donkey along, as the baby could drink only donkey's milk. Methuen had given special commands that the donkey had to accompany her, but once they reached the Kimberley camp the donkey disappeared. They had tried to give the baby cow's milk, but the child kept wasting away.[57]

When Emily arrived at the camp a new donkey had been found, but the baby was already so weak that it was past recovery. 'It was still alive this morning when I called,' Emily wrote, 'but in the afternoon it was dead. They beckoned me to see the tiny thing laid out – with a white flower in its wee hand. A murdered innocent.'[58]

In an attempt to soften the grief, Emily bought Mrs Louw black material for a mourning dress; 'Don't think that foolish or extravagant. You would not if you knew how much these people think of a bit of black and it seemed to me the best way of shewing some sympathy . . . the Boers are like our Cornish folk in the importance they ascribe to black clothes; so I understand their feeling exactly. Cornishwomen would spend their last shilling on a piece of crape. So Mrs. Louw's mourning will be a present from England.' She wondered how Methuen's wife would have felt if it had been her baby.[59]

The women at Kimberley were more bitter and antagonistic than those she had encountered in the other camps; not towards her, but as a result of what had happened to them. She wished that she could send six of the young girls to England so that they could tell the British Cabinet what was being done in South Africa in the name of England; 'you couldn't beat them in argument – or anything else'.

The women told her that some of them had been brought to the station at Vryburg by large groups of armed black men who were fighting on the English side. They had experienced their treatment as 'terrible'. She heard more and more accounts of farms burnt by black people, sometimes without a single British officer being present.

In a long letter to her brother Leonard, Emily wrote: 'You must not think that I pick out bad cases to send home. I never pick out at all. The tents are entered at random and I note what they say and often leave a camp without having seen people who have had the worst experiences.'[60]

Emily wanted to return to Bloemfontein but did not have a permit to do so, and Pretyman, who was now stationed in Kimberley, did not make it easy for her after she had confronted him about the child deaths in his camp. He was angry. Ignorant mothers were causing their own children's deaths with their home remedies, was his defence. No, he decided, she could get a permit for a trip to De Aar or Cape Town, but not to Bloemfontein.

Emily now had to decide on her next move. Maybe back to Cape Town to collect another rail truck full of clothing? But in the meantime she had heard that a camp had been opened at Warrenton, and that the need there was terrible. Perhaps she should go there as well as to Mafeking? In the end she opted for Cape Town; without supplies she could not really help alleviate the need.

The South African Conciliation Committee had met at the home of Lord and Lady Hobhouse in Mayfair, London, to read out Emily's letters, while she was again alone on a train full of sick Tommies on her way to Cape Town. She cared for the sick soldiers, cooked food for them, and took walks with them in the veld when the train stood waiting somewhere for hours.[61] On the way she saw rail trucks full of armed black men and told herself, it's naive to think that they are not part of the war.

On 24 March Emily arrived in Cape Town, where she stayed once more with Caroline Murray. She addressed a large meeting in the city for an hour and a half, explaining in detail what was happening in the camps. She was probably the only person who had personally visited so many of the camps.[62] The packet of letters to her that she received in the city had been 'mostly censored, some doubly censored'.[63]

Emily met with Sir Walter Hely-Hutchinson, the new governor of the Cape Colony, who gave her the necessary permits to visit both Warrenton and Mafeking. He was also very cooperative in arranging for tons of clothes, which the Cape women had helped to collect, to be sent by train to the various camps. This time Emily had the supplies delivered directly to the camps in question. The journey from Cape Town to Kimberley took five days, but she was determined to assist the distressed people in the Kimberley camp once more.

The train journeys were exhausting and lonely; there was no one Emily could talk to about her real thoughts and feelings. Invariably she fell back on pen and paper and wrote lengthy letters to the family in England, albeit that they would first be scrutinised by the censors. Despite buying a first-class ticket and being at the station hours before a train's departure, she seldom managed to get a seat in first-class carriages. The English officers simply shoved her aside and sat wherever they wanted to. 'First class here is about equal now to third class at home so that anything below is very dirty, smelly and disagreeable.'[64]

Four days later she was again on her way to Mafeking, visiting Warrenton along the way. Here she found 310 women who had been 'pushed' into the church and the school because there were no tents for them. And hundreds more women and children were on their way here after all the Boer commandos of Hoopstad had also been captured, a young British captain informed her on the train.[65]

After Warrenton, Emily witnessed a scene next to the railway line that would stay in her memory for the rest of her life, the result of the British forces 'sweeping' of the countryside:

And there, in a great mass by the railway line I saw his [Kitchener's] sweepings, thousands of animals, carts and wagons, soldiers and horses, crowds of human beings both black and white. And I happen to know there is not tent at Warrenton to put them into!

. . . Those truckloads of women and children unsheltered and unfed – bereft of home, bearing the vivid recollection of their possessions in the flames – and that mass of the 'sweepings' of a wide military 'drive' – flocks and herds of frightened animals bellowing and baaing for food and drink – tangled up with wagons and vehicles of all sorts and a dense crowd of human beings – combined to give a picture of war in all its destructiveness, cruelty, stupidity and nakedness such as not even the misery of the camps (with their external appearance of order) could do.[66]

Emily was shocked to the very fibre of her being; things would only get worse for all of them. Moreover, it was 9 April 1901, her forty-first birthday.

The next day she arrived in Mafeking for the first time: '. . . a lonely, lonely spot. Mafeking itself feels like the end of the world and the camp seems like driving six miles into space.'[67]

The camp had been in existence for almost a year, and was the oldest of the camps she had visited. Its nine hundred inhabitants were very surprised that an Englishwoman had arrived at this remote spot and seemed to care for them and their suffering. She spent three busy days at the camp, interviewing people, recording what was happening and trying to convince the military authorities to improve the conditions.[68]

Here, too, there was no soap, and many people had no blankets. Emily distributed clothing and formed a committee of seven camp women to help her with all the work. A certain Mrs Coetzee ('a real character'), after lamenting her fate for almost an hour, ended with solemn thanks to the Lord that the English people cared enough to send someone just to look upon the Boers' misery.

Emily was still haunted by the scene next to the railway line outside Warrenton. Passing through this town again on her way to Kimberley, where she wrote on 13 April, 'I have just returned. At Warrenton I found about 150 people left, the rest were being sent on. At the station were two train-loads full of them, quite half in open coal trucks – all piled up and wedged-in with such goods as they had been able to bring. They were tired and hot. I went and spoke to several of them. There were 240 packed in . . .'[69]

They followed Emily's armoured train to Kimberley. From her enquiries there it was clear that no one had known that these people were supposed to arrive there. No one could help, and no one knew where to get hold of fuel or kettles late on a Saturday night.[70]

When Emily returned to the Kimberley camp two days later, she heard that seven children had died during the few days she had been away. The rain kept pouring down and it was cold inside the tents, most of which were leaking. The meat the people received was maggotty, and those who complained did not get meat again.[71]

On her way to Bloemfontein, Emily got off the train at the Springfontein camp. She was shocked to find that the camp population had increased from five hundred to three thousand since her previous visit. At the station she found another six hundred women and children who were forced to sit waiting in open trucks with no shelter from the sun, wind and rain. They had been there for two days. This was even worse than what she had witnessed at Warrenton.

It was a Sunday morning. Clara Sandrock, the daughter of the German missionary at Springfontein, had seen Emily's train arriving and had run down to the station with a can of hot coffee for her. Emily did not drink any of it herself and gave the coffee as well as all the food she had on the train with her, a 'twopenny loaf' and some tinned meat, to the women in the open rail trucks.

The children were crying from hunger because they had not eaten anything for three days. Emily gave Clara money to buy all the food she could find and told her to take it to the women, with a further instruction: 'Leave the church today.'[72]

It pained Emily that she could not see to the alleviation of the people's plight herself, but her permit did not allow her to break her journey to Bloemfontein. With a heavy heart she jumped back on the train, just in time for its departure. The women and children in the open trucks she had to leave to the mercy of the elements. Even though she was wrapped in her thick grey shawl, it was still bitterly cold.[73]

Just because Emily stayed at the home of Caroline Fichardt in Bloemfontein, Caroline's permit was withdrawn so that she could no longer ride out to their farm Brandkop to visit her husband's grave.

At the Bloemfontein camp Emily found that the number of women and children had almost doubled in the six weeks she had been gone;

Emily glued this photo of the Bloemfontein camp on a sheet of paper and preserved it in one of two scrapbooks she compiled on South Africa. At the bottom she wrote: 'We are orphans and futureless, our mothers are as widows. Lev. 5:3.'

Photo: Emily's scrapbook, courtesy of Jennifer Hobhouse Balme

the population now stood at four thousand. 'My camp work grows so fast and so rapidly that I feel it is almost impossible to cope with it.'[74]

'It is endless and hopeless,' she wrote to Aunt Mary. 'I feel paralysed in the face of it. I feel money is of little avail and there are moments when I feel it would be wisest to stop trying and hasten home to state plain facts and beg that a stop may be put to it all.'[75]

The camp would only increase in size, Goold-Adams assured her after she had gone to talk to him again. Meanwhile sixty-two people had died there while she was away. The doctor himself was sick, and two of the Boer girls who had been trained as nurses were among the dead.[76]

There was still no soap in the camps. The official answer Emily got was that it was a luxury, and that the soldiers were not given soap either. According to the authorities, feed for the emaciated cows – her solution so that they could produce more milk for the children – was too precious to be used for this purpose. And, no, railway boilers could not be procured for the boiling of water. Boilers could be built from bricks, but this was too expensive.[77]

Emily was appalled at the condition of many of the people in the Bloemfontein camp who had been hale and hearty during her earlier visit. 'Disease and death were stamped upon their faces.'[78]

Emily was convinced that unless there was a constant influx of doctors, nurses, other workers, food, clothing and bedding, nothing would improve. The death rate had now risen to about 20 per cent, and there was no hope that it would decline. She pleaded with Goold-Adams that he should try to improve conditions in the camp, but he informed her that inhabitants of the Transvaal and the Free State were now being placed in camps on an increased scale; 'a new sweeping movement has begun'.[79]

She made a last attempt to visit the northern camps, such as the one at Kroonstad. Again she requested Goold-Adams's permission, and again he refused. This time he was very direct and told her the reason for his refusal was that she 'was showing personal sympathy to the people'.

Astonished, Emily replied that that was exactly what she had come to do – as well as to help in 'personal troubles'. Goold-Adams was of the view that 'gifts could be dealt out in a machine-like routine' without personal involvement. 'I said I could not work like that, I must treat people like fellow-creatures and share their troubles. He believed this unnecessary.'[80] It dawned on Emily that her personal sympathy was being confused with political sympathy with the Boers' cause. 'It was no question of political sympathy. On that score I always maintained a negative attitude.'[81]

She was shocked when she read Kitchener's claim in a newspaper that the families in the camps 'had a sufficient allowance, and were all comfortable and happy'.[82] She knew that they were 'all miserable and underfed, sick and dying',[83] and realised that the British public was being sold lies.

This brought Emily to a point where she had to take an important decision: 'To stay among the people, doling out small gifts of clothes, which could only touch the surface of the need, or return home with the hope of inducing the Government and the public to give so promptly and abundantly that the lives of the people, or at least the children might be saved.'[84]

After much reflection she decided to tackle the evil at its root, with those who had started it and had the power to end it. Please book me a passage on a ship to Southampton, she wrote to Caroline Murray.

On the way to Cape Town, the train stopped once again at Springfontein. To Emily's horror, the same group of about six hundred women and children she had seen when passing north ten days earlier were still stuck at the station.[85] There was neither water nor toilets, and very little food.

She also came across the elderly uncle and aunt of President Paul Kruger at Springfontein. Despite the cold, the old lady was half naked. Emily took off her own petticoat and draped it over the woman. Some of the other women clung to Emily in the hope that this angelic figure would deliver them from their misery. 'The picture photographed in my mind can never fade,' Emily wrote of the episode later.

Though it was bitterly cold, there was no shelter for the women and children. Some tried to sleep under the rail trucks. Others had found some sailcloth from which they constructed makeshift shelters. Emily was called to one of these shelters where a woman sat with her fast-fading child on her lap.

In a last-ditch effort to save the child's life Emily sent a message to Captain Gostling, the camp commandant, to request a few drops of brandy, but he let her know that their supply was limited.

Emily was present when the child died in silence.

The mother neither moved nor wept. It was her only child. Dry-eyed but deathly white, she sat there motionless looking not at the child but far, far away into depths of grief beyond all tears. A friend stood behind her who called upon Heaven to witness this tragedy and others crouching on the ground around her wept freely.

The scene made an indelible impression upon me. The leading elements in the great tragedy working itself out in your country seemed to have gathered under that old bit of sailcloth whose tattered sides hardly kept off sun, wind or rain.[86]

After this gruelling morning she still had enough stamina left to brave the concentration camp, to which she had to walk. Captain Gostling followed her like a shadow, engaged her in seemingly innocent chitchat and kept steering the conversation in a political direction. But Emily was nobody's fool, and avoided saying anything that smacked of politics. Late that night she boarded the train again as it slowly made its way southwards. The next day she got off at Norvalspont and, as usual, headed straight for the concentration camp where she spent the day.

Late that afternoon she returned to the station on foot, only to hear that the train to Cape Town would only arrive the following day. She had nowhere to sleep, as all the available beds in the town were occupied by the troops. Trudging back to the camp was her sole option. It was pitch dark when she arrived at the tent of an old acquaintance, a Mrs Boshoff, who was overjoyed to see her. Early the next morning Emily crawled out of the tent, in time to catch the train just after seven o'clock.[87]

When Emily finally reached Cape Town, on 5 May, she had not washed for six days. She was indescribably dirty, covered in red dust from top to toe. On some days she had not even been able to wash her hands. There was little time to rest, however, as she had to decide at once whether to leave for England on the *Saxon* in two days' time, or wait a while longer. All the ships were packed to capacity.[88]

Within an hour she decided to embark on the voyage as soon as possible.

To Emily's great surprise, Sir Alfred Milner – now administrator of the Transvaal and the Orange Free State – was a fellow passenger on the *Saxon*.[89] 'There also on a little raised dais sits His Excellency alone in the upper deck. He has told the captain he does not wish to mingle with anyone nor speak with any lady.

However he came and spoke to me as soon as waves and wind allowed and I plunged into my subject, but a noisy windlass cut us short,'[90] Emily wrote to Caroline Murray.

Learning 'the Taal'[91] from fellow passengers was pointless, Milner's private secretary Walrond informed her, as she should not be allowed to visit South Africa again. Emily suspected him of spreading malicious gossip about her on the ship because many passengers turned their backs on her. Nevertheless, she got another opportunity to speak to Milner when the ship stopped at Madeira and everyone was admiring the view from the deck.

Emily knew somehow that military spies had watched her in Bloemfontein and provided Milner with all kinds of falsehoods about her, such as that she had caused trouble in the camps. He told her that he'd received 'some sixty-four reports on me'. Now she had the chance to confront him about it. She pointed out 'the low class sort of people that were willing to be informers', and that he had to be spending a lot of money on them.[92]

She emphasised again that she was not in South Africa for political reasons, and also told Milner how Captain Gostling had tried to provoke her into making political statements. She had the impression that he believed her.

'There were two Alfred Milners – there was the charming, sympathetic, gracious and cultivated man, whose abilities and culture found rather a desert in South Africa, and whose liberal leanings were in contrast to the military men surrounding him. And there was the politician who had given his word to carry out the ideas of the English statesmen and felt bound in honour to do so. The clash must have given him many dolorous moments of agony.'[93]

Emily parted from Milner with these words from the writer Macrobius when a Roman knight had been censured unfairly by

Augustus Caesar: 'Caesar, when you make inquiries about honourable men, see that you employ honourable men to do it.'[94]

On 24 May 1901 Emily was back in England after having left for South Africa five and a half months earlier. She still had no idea of how exactly she would bring the need in the concentration camps to the attention of the English public in a way that would engender sympathy instead of giving offence.

What she did know was that her experience of the conflict in South Africa had imbued her with an intense aversion to war and everything it entailed. She had seen clearly what war did to people:

'You can no longer be an individual, you are one of a herd – and that herd preserves itself by the reversal of the principle of virtue. Untruth, lies, hatred, inhumanity, destructiveness, spying, treachery, meanness innumerable, suspicion, contempt, unfair dealing, illegality of every kind flourish and become as it were the "virtues of war".

'The atmosphere thus created is a moral miasma.'[95]

5

Reviled, but not defeated

'You know we were called pro-Boers. It was purely a nickname and never seemed to fit though for convenience we adopted it ourselves. From the first, and indeed all whom I knew had been concerned primarily about our own country and whether or not she was acting upon the highest principles of justice and humanity. We had thought comparatively little of the Boer side.'

– Emily Hobhouse, 1900

Emily had enough insight into the workings of politics – and experience of important men's egos – to know that she had to use her evidence of the conditions in the concentration camps judiciously and in a way that would have the greatest possible impact.

She did not rush to the British papers with her story or immediately hold public speeches. First she approached the politicians, mostly members of the Conservative Party, which was in power in a coalition with the Liberal Unionist Party.

Emily had a powerful weapon in her arsenal: the irrefutable fact that when she left South Africa a short while ago, 343 people out of every 1000 were dying in the camps.[1] At this rate, one out of every three people taken into the camps would perish there.

However, the Secretary for War St John Brodrick tried to paint a totally different, more rosy picture for the public. He had recently declared in the House of Commons that women came to the camps voluntarily 'for food and protection against the blacks – 20,000, 30,000, 40,000 women who had placed themselves under our protection,' and that they and their children were not in want of anything.[2] Emily could not believe her ears, and sought a personal meeting with Brodrick. She explained in a letter that she wished to provide him with a first-hand account of the diseases, deaths and lack of adequate food and other supplies in the camps.

Brodrick knew well who Emily was, not only because of her camp visits; they were distantly related through marriage.[3,4] On 4 June 1901 Emily was granted an hour to speak to Brodrick. What upset her most about their conversation was his extreme ignorance regarding the situation in South Africa and her impression that he did not listen attentively to what she said. She found him 'slippery and pleasant – mediocre and agreeable, ready to listen, ready also to drift', and 'did not feel I got my claws into him anywhere'.[5]

At least Brodrick asked her to put her recommendations for improvements in writing. She delivered her response to the War Office the same afternoon. Among others, she recommended the release of camp inmates who had friends and relatives in the Cape Colony they could stay with, as well as of those who had houses in towns or who were able to maintain themselves; that those who had applied to leave the camps be permitted to do so;

that people should be allowed to go to the towns to work there; that no new internees should be taken up in the camps; that bilingual matrons be appointed; and that the government should take heed of the report of the Bloemfontein camp doctor. Clergymen should also be allowed into the camps to minister to the people and to conduct funerals.[6]

Without Emily's knowledge Brodrick immediately forwarded her report to Milner, who had apparently already referred to her as 'pro-Boer and a screamer'.[7] He now responded in the same vein: 'I should advise her not returning [to South Africa] and nobody else being sent. Of course, there will be a howl, but the pro-Boers will howl whatever we do . . . I have myself to write to Miss Hobhouse and tell her whether she is allowed to return. If she does not she will doubtless make all possible mischief in England . . . As long as she is working in the camps she will not be able to carry on a crusade in England, though of course she can write mischievously.'[8]

As Milner's biographer put it, he considered that 'she was unable to refrain from displaying political bias on an avowedly non-political mission . . . The effect of her visits to the camps, too, had been to stir up discontent among the refugees.' Nonetheless, he 'gave careful consideration' to her suggestions.[9]

Meanwhile the Distress Fund decided that Emily would address a meeting in the Queen's Hall in London and report on what she had seen, heard and experienced in South Africa. They rented and paid for the hall in advance.[10] While Emily was very excited at this prospect, the authorities were of a different view. The booking of the hall was withdrawn without reason and the Westminster Chapel, too, refused to make their facilities available. They then attempted to arrange a public meeting in York, but the police refused to give their permission for fear of public unrest.

To Emily, 'this showed the determination on the part of the Government to prevent my appeal to the national sentiment . . . To me the great disappointment was that I was prevented from adequately keeping my word to the Boer women viz that I would tell the English people of their sufferings and if they knew would set things right.'[11]

Emily made an appointment to see Sir Henry Campbell-Bannerman,[12] leader of the Liberal opposition and future prime minister. He was shocked at what he heard from Emily in the course of their two-hour conversation and whispered repeatedly: 'Methods of barbarism'.[13] He was deeply moved, and Emily got the impression that he would do everything possible in order to arrive at the truth.[14]

On the same day, the National Reform Union held a dinner at the Holborn Restaurant[15] where Campbell-Bannerman delivered a speech: 'A phrase often used is that "war is war", but when one comes to ask about it [the Boer War] one is told that no war is going on, that it is not war. When is a war not a war? When it is carried on by methods of barbarism in South Africa.'[16] This momentous phrase – 'methods of barbarism' – would continue to reverberate in the years and decades to come.

Three days later, a long and fiery debate was held in the House of Commons after David Lloyd George, a Liberal Party MP who had shared the podium with Emily on the riotous evening in Liskeard, had called for a discussion on the conditions in the camps and the alarmingly high death rate.

This was the first occasion on which Emily was recognised at a high level as the one who had investigated the conditions in the camps in person and in detail.[17] Herbert Lewis, another Liberal Party MP, declared: 'Fortunately we have evidence at first hand, taken from a considerable number of the camps by a lady whose word will command implicit confidence from everyone who knows her.'[18]

He added a prophetic statement: 'I would venture to say, looking at these 40,000 children in the camps, that we are only sowing the seeds of discontent, and that we may reap a terrible harvest someday – not perhaps this year or the next year, but in time coming a nation will grow up which will remember all these iniquities.'[19]

Previously, War Secretary Brodrick had presented Lord Kitchener's version of the conditions as fact, including the notion that most of the 'refugees' were black, but in light of Emily's revelations he had to change his tune. Now he admitted that there were about 64,000 white and black people in the camps, and that the death rate was high.

To this, Lloyd George replied that the answer provided by Brodrick proved that the deaths were not due to temporary circumstances, but were in fact increasing. Why was war being waged against women and children, he asked.[20]

The following day, 18 June 1901, saw the appearance of Emily's forty-page printed report, which included her recommendations to Brodrick. In addition, a condensed eighteen-page version, a summary of her letters, was distributed to the members of both Houses of Parliament.

Her report caused an outcry in England and gave the Liberals more ammunition. Lloyd George accused the government of following a 'policy of extermination' in South Africa. Brodrick retaliated with the defence that 'war is war', and that the concentration camps were places of refuge for destitute people.[21]

Emily found herself at the centre of a political war, which was by its nature one with few rules. Many Britons resented her for her 'unpatriotic conduct', the jingoes denounced her as a traitor to her country, and most newspapers wrote scathing reports about

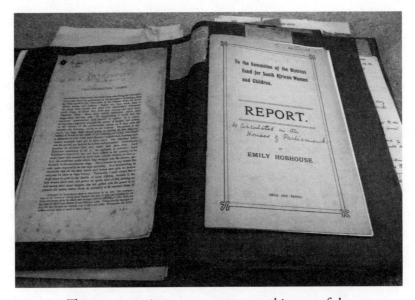

The concentration camp report pasted in one of the
three scrapbooks Emily compiled. On the front she
wrote: 'As circulated in the Houses of Parliament.'

Photo: Emily's scrapbook, courtesy of Jennifer Hobhouse Balme

her. To her great shock, the majority of the English public
showed no sympathy for the destitute women and children in
the camps.

According to an article in the *Cheltenham Looker-On*,[22] Emily's
report was geared to sensation and the people in the camps did
get enough vegetables, but the Boers, 'not being used to such a
diet, showed no inclination but to waste it'.

The Times ripped her report apart and said that instead of
conducting a proper investigation, she had simply taken the
women's stories at face value. Why did *The Times* not rather
publish the full medical report of Dr Henry Becker, the camp
doctor in Bloemfontein? Then the readers would be able to draw
their own conclusions, Emily suggested in a letter.[23]

The reply of the Secretary for War St John Brodrick,
to Emily, in response to her recommendations
regarding the concentration camps.

Photo: Emily's scrapbook, courtesy of Jennifer Hobhouse Balme

A member of the Guild of Loyal Women of South Africa,[24] Mrs K. H. R. Stuart, attacked Emily in *The Times* for deliberately denigrating 'the brave British soldiers'. Stuart wrote that the Boer women themselves would testify that their houses were full of flies and snakes. Families frequently camped at the seaside, and then they would all live together quite comfortably in such tents. The women were the ones who had insisted on their children living in such unhygienic conditions.[25]

As on many other occasions, Emily with her insight and articulateness made short shrift of her critic: 'Mrs Stuart, I understand, is in England collecting money to put gravestones over the victims of the war fallen on either side. Hers is a sacred task. She cares for the dead, I care for the living. I do not interfere with her work, why should she criticise mine? The great fact of the death rate she totally ignores.'[26]

Mrs Stuart referred to a political agitator the Reverend Adrian Hofmeyr – whom Emily had encountered in the Bloemfontein camp – who was now writing letters in the British papers in which he claimed that Emily did not know what she was talking about. He alleged that she had promised people in the camps that the Liberal Party would soon come to power and alleviate their plight. Also, according to him, Emily failed to understand that many Boer children tended to die of measles and diphtheria in any case because the parents did not listen to doctors. As a 'gentlewoman' she was shocked by conditions that were, in fact, normal for these women in peace time. This was the usual way in which the Boers lived, he claimed.

More and more people snubbed Emily and ostracised her in the London drawing rooms, the gathering places of the upper-class society to which she was accustomed. Still, she said, 'I survived to tell the tale. Lived also to sum up Governments as poor things more careful of their own prestige than of justice and right. And always when the conduct of war is in question devoid of conscience.'[27]

Emily embarked on a speaking tour – addressing twenty-six public meetings in four weeks – in order to inform more people about the true state of affairs in South Africa. One of the first meetings took place on 25 June at Balliol College in Oxford where her father and many other male members of the family had studied. She was received most kindly by the Master, but also attracted widespread criticism.

The criticism was either aimed at her as an individual, or was driven by justifying the existence of the camps. In many places she was reviled as 'a traitor and rebel' and 'a disseminator of inaccurate and bloodcurdling stories', while her report, Emily said, 'was described as a weapon used wherever the name of England was hated'.[28]

In cities such as Leeds and Manchester she was received warmly, but in York there was such an uproar that the meeting had to be moved to one of the Quakers' halls. It was clear that many people believed that the Boer women and children were dirty simply because they were backward and did not wash themselves.

Emily explained that this was untrue; there was no water and soap in the camps. Some of the camps had no clean drinking water, or too little of it. She had to explain this over and over again. She herself had only been able to bath once during her visits to the camps: it was in the Norvalspont camp when a hole was dug in the ground, lined with waterproof sailcloth and then filled with cold water, but this was an exceptional luxury.[29] In Leeds a journalist described her as someone who left the impression that that which she had seen weighed heavily on her mind. 'It was nearly an hour before she smiled. Her face is full of charm and sweetness when it is thus lit up and she drew the audience a good deal nearer after this . . . Miss Hobhouse is very earnest but she has a good sense of humour.'[30]

Brodrick had evidently taken some of Emily's revelations seriously, but as a politician he would rather die than admit to a mistake. On 21 June he sent three telegrams to Kitchener and requested that the death rates of white and black people be sent to him on a monthly basis. (Later he asked that he be provided with these figures every second week.) He also forwarded Emily's list of recommendations to Kitchener, but without mentioning that they came from her.[31]

As for his response to Emily, after three weeks he informed her that the government was considering her recommendations and that they had been forwarded to Kitchener. Yes, some of the camp women could go home if they had somewhere else to go, but only if there was no 'military objection'. There was also objection to great numbers of 'refugees' entering the Cape Colony. Permits were already being granted to people to leave some of the camps; there were matrons and clergymen; they were trying their best to avoid overcrowding in the camps, and they would take her advice into consideration if it should be decided to erect more camps.[32]

The government still had not seen the report of Dr Becker from the Bloemfontein camp, Brodrick said, although Emily had long had it in her possession.[33]

While some of Emily's recommendations were adopted in essence, she received no official recognition for this. The government did not acknowledge the extent of the diseases, the fatality rate and the causes of the camp inmates' grief and suffering. There were still excuses and denials.

'The government have made me various concessions,' Emily wrote to Caroline Murray, 'but they are furious at me I am told and regard me as a thorn in their side . . . Have had some splendid meetings but still have to be very careful in my presentment of the subject.'[34]

Caroline comforted her in an empathetic letter: 'Most people live only on the surface of life and are the unconscious instruments of good or evil in the hands of the few who really think and plan and sway the conscience of most as they will. To go counter this wave of popular opinion means a struggle for which few are fitted and therefore one cannot but find many well-meaning people considering you an enemy.'

She added that Emily did not rate herself highly enough. She did not realise how much she had already done for so many people in South Africa.

On 18 July Emily again had a meeting with Brodrick to impress upon him the distress in the camps. But later that same day he informed her that the government would not accept her services for further camp visits. He also levelled the accusation at Emily that her actions had prolonged the war.

He had already come up with another plan, which he announced publicly soon afterwards: a commission made up of other women would be sent to South Africa to investigate conditions in the camps. 'We are sending out no one specifically identified with any form of opinion . . .'[35] This was clearly a barbed reference to Emily and her alleged pro-Boer sympathies.

The commission would be headed by Millicent Garrett Fawcett, a prominent advocate for (limited) suffrage for women, who had earlier refused to meet Emily, an advocate of universal suffrage.

Fawcett was hardly an impartial choice without 'any form of opinion', as she had written in a book that the Boer women and children often accompanied the men on commando and would then arrive at the camps already in a worn-out and starved state. Emily took offence at this allegation because it was untrue; the women and children who survived on their own in the veld, sometimes along with servants, were in good health when compared to the camp inmates.[36]

The other members of the commission were Dr Jane Waterson, a medical doctor and the daughter of a British general; Alice, Lady Knox, wife of General William Knox who was serving in South Africa; Katherine Brereton who did nursing duty at the

Imperial Yeomanry Hospital in Deelfontein, South Africa; Lucy Deane, an expert in welfare and sanitary services, and Dr Ella Scarlett, a medical doctor.

What these women had in common was the conviction that the war against the two Boer republics was justified, and that 'certain unpleasant measures' aimed at the civilian population were therefore condonable.[37]

It was a bitter pill for Emily to swallow that these particular women were to conduct the investigation and that she was not allowed to be part of the commission. However, she had no choice but to accept it.

The Cape politician John X. Merriman wrote to Leonard Courtney that he could not express his shock at the appointment of Dr Waterson too strongly because of her 'absolute unfitness . . . for the task of forming an unprejudiced opinion on the camps'. His alarm stemmed from the fact that, shortly after her appointment to the commission, she had written a letter in the *Cape Times* stating that:

We ordinary Colonial women who have been through the stress and strain of these last two years are not very favourably impressed by the hysterical whining going on in England . . . It would seem as if we might neglect or starve our faithful soldiers . . . as long as we fed and pampered people who have not even the grace to say thank you for the care bestowed upon them.

This war has been remarkable for two things – first the small regard that the Boers from the highest to the lowest have had for their womenkind, and secondly the great care and consideration the victors have had for the same, very often, ungrateful women.[38,39]

'Did ever a woman pen such nonsense?' Emily asked when she heard about Dr Waterson's remarks. Was she unaware of the Hague Convention and the rights of prisoners of war that were entrenched in it? The care to which inhabitants of camps were entitled had to be similar to the care given to soldiers, but this was not the case in South Africa. Besides, children and babies required care of a totally different kind than that given to adults.

Ella Scarlet, in turn, wrote to the War Office before she had even disembarked in South Africa: 'The refugees are ungrateful, dirty beyond description and never speak the truth, they have heard something of the pro-Boer agitation at home, and try to be impertinent.'⁴⁰

Some members of the Ladies' Central Relief Committee – Emily's friends in South Africa who by August had already spent twenty thousand pounds to help the women and children in the camps – met Fawcett and her delegation at the Mount Nelson Hotel in Cape Town on 12 August. Lady de Villiers, wife of the Cape chief justice, Caroline Murray and Anna Purcell were present. After the customary pleasantries, they asked whether one of the Relief Committee members could accompany the British women to the interior. Fawcett refused bluntly.

The meeting ended on a stiff note, and shortly afterwards Lady de Villiers informed Fawcett by letter that the Cape women wished to have no further contact with her and her commission.

To Emily, the news from South Africa was heartrending: There were now, in August, 93,940 whites and 24,457 blacks in camps. And the fatalities were rising – previous figures were, May: 505; June: 782 and July: 1675.

As Parliament was in recess, Brodrick could not be called to account publicly for a number of months. Accordingly, Emily resorted to writing an open letter to him on 29 September. It was her last appeal to Brodrick:[41]

'Three months have passed since I approached you on the subject of the concentration camps in South Africa, three terrible months in the history of these camps . . .' By this time the number of whites in the camps had risen from 85,000 to 105,000. In August alone 1878 people had died, 1545 of whom were children.[42] A total of 3245 children had died in the three months since her first conversation with Brodrick.

'Daily children are dying and unless the rate is checked a few months will suffice to see the extermination of the majority. Will nothing be done? Will not prompt measures be taken to deal with this terrible evil?'

She pleaded for the children in particular: 'For the men of either side I say nothing. They have chosen their part and must abide by it. For the women also I do not now plead, they are always strong to endure. But I do ask in the name of the innocent and helpless children that England's humanity may triumph over the policy so that the sacrifice of the children may be stayed.'[43,44]

After Emily was again pelted with vegetables at a meeting in Portsmouth, she went to stay for a few days with Lord and Lady Ripon at Studley Royal. The visit provided her with an opportunity to reflect on the events of the past months, particularly the hostile reception she had had in her mother country, as well as on the future.

Not only was Emily controversial on account of her identification with an enemy of the British Crown, she had also acted in ways that conflicted with what was expected of a Victorian woman of her social standing. These women were supposed to stay at home, do needlework, play the piano, paint, learn more than one language, read edifying books and serve on welfare committees.

Emily had done all of that – but also much more. She had challenged the status quo and that was unheard of, especially for a woman. Women were not supposed to be leaders. Or to embarrass high-ranking politicians and the military elite by pointing out their mistakes. Such conduct was regarded with disgust, albeit that the changes Emily had proposed were for the good and in England's best interest.

After much pondering and 'very full discussions' with Lord Ripon, she arrived at a decision: to return to South Africa, more specifically to the Cape Colony – although sadly not to the camps because they were forbidden to her. She still wanted to help to ameliorate the painful consequences of the war, but she would now have to do so in other places and on behalf of other groups of people.

Hundreds of people had been deported to Durban, Port Elizabeth, East London and Cape Town. There were many British refugees among them. All the deportees 'were in sore need'.[45]

Emily immediately started making arrangements for the voyage and informed her Cape Town friends that she was coming. She did not want her arrangements and movements to become known prematurely, and asked that her name be omitted from the official passenger list.

But for how long would she be able to keep her plans secret?

6

'I feel ashamed'

'You are disgracing your uniforms by obeying such an order. A Higher Law forbids you. The laws of God and humanity forbid you.'

– Emily Hobhouse to soldiers who removed her forcibly from the *Avondale Castle*, 1901

The Cape waters were deceptively calm when the *Avondale Castle* sailed into Table Bay on 27 October 1901 after a voyage of twenty-two days. The four hundred and fifty passengers, including the one whose name was missing from the passenger list, were excited at the prospect of going ashore.

Emily could not wait to disembark after the exhausting voyage. Not only had the past year been emotionally gruelling, she had injured her hip in a fall during the voyage. She also suffered from a weakened heart and other health problems – lumbago and neuritis (inflammation of a nerve in her arm) – which started around the age of forty-one.

An undated portrait study of Emily.

Photo: Courtesy of Jennifer Hobhouse Balme

Undiagnosed, her heart condition was the reason why she was at times so weak, tired and out of breath that she could barely walk, and why she had trouble climbing stairs. Emily was accompanied by a nurse, Elizabeth Phillips.

Although she had been refused permission to visit the concentration camps again, no mention had been made of her being forbidden to visit the rest of the country.[1] Her plan was to visit friends in Cape Town and then travel to Durban, East London and Port Elizabeth, where British and other war refugees were situated. She intended to investigate their living conditions and see what aid she could provide. While this was her own initiative, the South African Women and Children Distress Fund had undertaken to assist with the distribution of food and clothing.[2]

It was late afternoon. When Emily saw the men in khaki uniforms in the steam tug that appeared alongside the *Avondale Castle,* she knew at once that this did not augur well for her. All passengers would be examined one by one, a Lieutenant Lingham informed them after he had boarded the ship.[3] When he heard Emily's name, he ordered her to wait until he had finished with the other passengers.[4]

In Britain, a nosy journalist had ferreted out the name of the anonymous passenger on board the *Avondale Castle* and made it public.[5] The Colonial Office in London, in turn, informed Joseph Chamberlain, colonial secretary. Although he agreed that the authorities in South Africa should be notified, he was blasé – and sarcastic – about this snippet of news: 'The Empire was not threatened by a hysterical spinster of mature age. She would have to have a permit to visit the camps anyway. It was foolish to take any note of her,' he replied patronisingly, but conceded 'that the Army is terribly afraid of women'.[6]

Finally it was Emily's turn. She was told to accompany Lingham to the cabin of the ship's captain, Captain Brown. Suddenly Lingham turned to her: 'You are placed under arrest and would not be allowed to land anywhere in South Africa.' She was prohibited from communicating with anyone. And she and the nurse were placed in the charge of Captain Brown, who would be held responsible for her.[7]

Emily demanded to know why she had been arrested, what the charges against her were and who had given the order. The order came from Colonel H. Cooper, the military commander of Cape Town, was all that Lingham told her.

She was appalled and disgusted at her arrest, by her own compatriots at that. She had been brought up to obey laws, and to her

A snapshot of the *Avondale Castle* by Margaret Clark.

Photo: Courtesy of the Alfred Gillett Trust

anything illegal was a disgrace. 'The shock was to find oneself – a law-abiding, free Englishwoman – arrested and imprisoned.'[8] Immediately after her arrest Emily demanded to be watched over by a guard because she knew 'how soldiers hate guarding women'.

That night she did not sleep a wink. 'All night I lay awake, shuddering from head to foot with the effects of the shock, for oddly enough it was a shock and unexpected in that form. Then I began to see my way and brace myself to the battle. I shall be very polite, very dignified, but in every way I possibly can a thorn in the flesh to them,' she wrote to her brother Leonard.[9]

She wrote a stream of letters to the authorities – to Cooper, Kitchener, Milner, the Cape Colony governor Hely-Hutchinson – to which they were required to reply. They had to be delivered by Lingham. (Kitchener, incidentally, was well aware of Emily's presence. From Pretoria he sent a telegram to General Arthur Wynne, the officer in command of the Cape Colony district: 'High Commissioner and I are agreed that Miss Hobhouse should not be allowed to land.')[10]

Monday 28 October 1901 was a long day for Emily, her first in imprisonment while the other passengers went ashore. To make matters worse, the southeaster started blowing and the ship was tossed about, so she could not read. She did manage to do some

A copy of the scathing letter Emily wrote to Kitchener after her arrest and deportation in 1901. Her handwriting is unusually scratchy and uneven.

Photo: Free State Archives Repository

A copy of the equally biting letter Emily wrote to Milner.

Photo: Free State Archives Repository

painting, and 'did two little oils of Table Mountain and the Lion's Head'. As the gale prevented the ship from docking, she made another painting: a panorama scene of the mountains. The wind was so strong that she had to pin her paper to the deck and paint while lying flat on her stomach.[11]

On that day she found herself thinking in particular of one of her famous and distinguished ancestors on her mother's side, Jonathan Trelawny, who had been appointed the bishop of Bristol in 1685. When King James II ordered in 1688 that the Declaration of Indulgence (which granted free exercise of their religion to all faiths) be read in every church, Trelawny and six other bishops refused to do so. They were arrested and imprisoned in the Tower of London.[12] Their arrest sparked widespread revolt; in Cornwall, the inhabitants were ready to march to London. A song was even written to give expression to their feelings: 'And shall Trelawny die? / Then 20,000 Cornishmen shall know the reason why . . .' The bishops were eventually acquitted after a trial.[13]

But these thoughts did little to resign Emily to her treatment, and feelings of anger and humiliation regularly got the upper hand. Meanwhile, her family and friends in England became increasingly concerned about her as they did not know where she was and had received no communication from her.

Emily pleaded with the authorities that a washerwoman be sent to help her with her washing. 'Or is uncleanliness part of the regime to which I must submit?'[14] But nothing came of this request.

At last the ship was able to dock on the Wednesday afternoon after the southeaster had started abating. Cooper came aboard soon afterwards. 'I am sorry to make your acquaintance under these circumstances.'

'I am sorry too,' Emily replied, upon which an uncomfortable silence followed.[15]

Cooper informed her that it would be best if she returned to England on the *Carisbrooke Castle* that same afternoon. Emily refused. She felt tired and sick; she was still waiting for replies from Milner and Kitchener to the letters she had sent them, and she would rather be detained in a prison on land.

Cooper left the ship without having accomplished anything. Later that evening he sent Lingham to Emily to ask whether she would give her 'parole' – a promise or undertaking – that she would not escape.

'Giving my parole not to escape was tantamount to keeping myself in prison, and why should I do that? I was detained at their wish, not at my own.' Besides, the authorities did not want to trust her word on land, why would they so at sea?[16] However, Emily undertook not to escape, at least not before Milner and Kitchener had replied to her letters. She assured an embarrassed Lingham that she 'attached no blame to him, regarding him merely as the mouthpiece of a tyranny and injustice higher than himself'.

On another occasion she told Lingham in no uncertain terms that the military authorities should not think they would get away with this. She promised him that 'England would ring with the infamy of my arrest'.[17]

Emily's Cape friends knew she was on board the *Avondale Castle*; they had long been expecting her arrival, but 'for fear of difficulties that might arise in the present atmosphere', they decided not to speak to anyone about it. They were extremely concerned about her.[18] A Miss Steedman, who had befriended Emily on the ship, informed them that she was in detention.

Caroline Murray managed to board the ship with some female friends and take Emily flowers and food, despite orders that Emily was not allowed to receive any visitors. They were shocked at how thin and worn she looked.[19]

The next day, Betty Molteno obtained permission at the Castle in Cape Town to visit Emily again – Caroline's similar request was refused. At noon Betty boarded the ship and found Emily reclining in a deck chair. Her eyes were closed and she looked exhausted. She startled when Betty gently touched her arm.

On Emily's lap was a large official envelope. Emily wearily informed Betty of its contents: an order from the military authorities that she had to return to England on the *Roslin Castle* that same afternoon.[20] Betty spent the rest of the day at Emily's side, mostly in silence.

Betty (Elizabeth) Molteno, left, with her life-partner
Alice Greene. South African friends of Emily.

Photo: Courtesy of Robert Molteno

Suddenly Lingham was there, instructing Emily that her nurse
Elizabeth had to pack their luggage for the voyage that would
start in a few hours.

Emily refused point blank and forbade Elizabeth to pack
anything. But Lingham, with the power of the state on his side,
called a stewardess to pack Emily's trunks. Emily insisted that she
was too ill to undertake the weeks-long voyage to England. Besides,
the *Roslin Castle* was a troop ship, with hundreds of men on board.

'Why not take me on shore and hang me? Why torment me
so?' she asked Lingham, who decided to call a doctor.[21]

Lieutenant-Colonel J. F. Williamson of the Royal Army
Medical Corps arrived to examine Emily. At first she resisted and
insisted on her own doctor, but finally agreed when her request
was denied. Williamson examined her in the ship's smoking room.
Betty was present as he listened to Emily's heart, inspected her
tongue and took her temperature. There was nothing wrong with
her heart, he found; all she needed was a stimulant such as cham-
pagne or brandy.

'I never supposed I had a diseased heart. What did he expect to find? It was my nerves and the exhaustion and the shock I had that I am suffering from.'[22]

By this time Emily's luggage and bicycle had been unloaded and were waiting in the horse carriage that would transport her to the *Roslin*. She dug in her heels: 'They can take my luggage, but they will not take me.' Williamson warned her that unless she came voluntarily, she would be forcibly removed. She was still hoping that such conduct would be beneath the dignity she expected from English officers. 'I can't believe that any English gentleman would carry out such an order.'[23] It became a protracted war of words between Emily and the military authorities of her beloved England, during which she tried to convince the officers and soldiers of the injustice and inhumanity of their actions, first through reasonable requests, then fruitless threats, and finally an appeal to higher values and morality.

The hours ticked past. The *Roslin Castle*'s departure was immi-nent. Williamson ran out of patience. 'Madam, do you wish to be taken like a lunatic?'

'Sir, the lunacy is on your side and with those whose commands you obey. If you have any manhood in you, you will go and leave me alone.'[24]

Two soldiers then stepped up to take her away by force. 'You will not treat your mothers and sisters so. There is a higher law, you cannot, you dare not obey these orders.' Nonetheless, the soldiers took hold of her shoulders. Williamson cautioned them not to hurt her.

'You are disgracing your uniforms by obeying such an order. A Higher Law forbids you. The laws of God and humanity forbid you. Colonel Williamson, you will rue this till your dying day. You will all rue this,' Emily called out.[25]

But her protestations were in vain. The power of the state triumphed over Emily's resistance, regardless of how noble her intentions were.

Williamson himself tied Emily's arms down with her shawl. The men then picked her up and strapped her down on a stretcher with a black cord 'like a baby'. They carried her down from the ship to the carriage.

Emily turned around and called out: 'Goodbye, Captain! Goodbye, officers! Goodbye, stewards! Thank you all for your kindness.'

Betty ran to the carriage with a basket of fruit for Emily. At the *Roslin Castle* she had to be carried into the cabin allocated to her as she refused to walk.[26]

Apropos the episode on the ship, Williamson later remarked to Caroline Murray that Emily was 'a very charming woman he could not but admire'. She 'had the face of a Madonna, but she fights like the devil'.[27]

It was an uncomfortable twenty-four-day voyage that awaited Emily and Elizabeth. The only two other women of Emily's social class on board, officers' wives, snubbed her and never spoke to her. The hundreds of other passengers were all men, mostly soldiers, who smoked incessantly. The food was unpalatable. Emily had only a few shillings with her as she had not had the opportunity to get to a bank.

'The dirt and disorder were indescribable, and the smell sickening . . . We heard later that it had carried a cargo of rotten onions . . . The cold was dreadful as we came north, for we had no winter clothes with us . . . This was a slight realisation in my own person of what tens of thousands of your [South African] countrywomen endured and still were enduring torn by military force

from home, belongings and comforts to meet exposure unprepared',[28] she wrote years later to Tibbie Steyn.

Table Mountain was barely out of the *Roslin* passengers' sight
when Emily turned to two faithful companions – pen and paper.
She wrote to her brother Leonard, recounting her experiences in
detail. The sharp edge of her tongue she saved for Kitchener and
Milner in words that probably stuck in their memories for the rest
of their days.

To Kitchener:

Your brutality has triumphed over my weakness and sickness.
You have forgotten so to be a patriot as now to forget that you
are a gentleman. I hope that in future you will adopt greater
width of judgement in the exercise of your high office. To carry
out orders such as these is a degradation both to the office and
the manhood of your soldiers. I feel ashamed to own you as a
fellow countryman.[29]

She did not spare Milner either, albeit that they had got on
fairly well earlier:

Your brutal orders have been carried out and thus I hope you will
be satisfied. Your narrow incompetency to see the real issues of
this great struggle is leading you to such acts as this and many
others, staining your own name and the reputation of England.

I liked you first and would have helped you. But now I see
you more clearly as you really are. I can believe it is true what a
man once said to me: That you have the 'soul of a spy'. Perhaps
that is necessary in a despot. At least you should try in the
words of Burke, to be a patriot is not to forget you are, or ought
to be, a gentleman.

You have lost us the heart of a fine people; beware lest that is not the prelude to the loss of their country also.[30]

In the Cape Colony, too, the British sympathisers and jingoes saw in Emily's deportation an opportunity to express their allegiance to the Empire. *The Owl*, a Cape paper that was evidently unaware of its own racism, wrote as follows about her resistance to deportation:

> As a matter of fact she kicked, scratched and yelled worse than any coloured woman ever run in for drunkenness in District 6 and used language to Dr Williamson and Lieutenant Lingham which proved, that in her time, she must have frequented places just as filthy and quite as crowded as she alleged the concentration camps were.
>
> It is to be hoped that we have heard the last of this woman. No sewing-machine agent ever lied like she did, and if notoriety was her object she certainly succeeded for her falsehoods were printed in all the civilised languages of the world.[31]

Emily's Cape friends were very upset about these comments, and tried in vain to extract an apology from the paper.

Meanwhile, Emily's family were still in the dark about her whereabouts. The only news they received was a cryptic telegram that Alice Greene had sent from Cape Town to a distant relation of Emily: 'Tell Nora Gained Prize.'[32]

It was obviously a message in code to say something that the censors would not understand – the family nearly did not either. Leonard did managed to decipher it, however, and found that it contained the key word 'DEPORTED'.[33]

Lord Hobhouse, Emily's uncle, wrote to Brodrick and the War Office, who enquired from General Wynne. He took five days to reply: on account of 'the attitude she has taken',[34] she had not been permitted to disembark in Cape Town.

Even before her relatives were informed, Emily's arrest and deportation made headline news in the press, even as far afield as Australia. Aunt Mary received a telegram Emily had sent when the *Roslin* stopped at St Vincent: 'Prisoner. Penniless'.[35]

It was a debilitated, sick Emily that disembarked at Southampton on 24 November 1901. She had been aboard two ships for forty-eight days. Her clothes had not been washed in all that time. The food had been barely edible. She had been without anyone she could really talk to. To crown it all, she had been humiliated by distinguished compatriots in the name of her country.

To her, the personal consequences of this experience were far-reaching, lasting and incredibly disillusioning: 'To this day I feel its effect physically, while mentally it could not fail to change my outlook upon life and henceforth I reckon the boasted English liberty and justice at its real value,' she wrote more than twenty years later.[36]

7

Vindicated

'We all feel that the policy of the "Camps" was a huge mistake which no-one but these unpractical ignorant Army men could have committed. It has made the people hate us . . .'

> – a member of the Ladies' Commission
> that investigated conditions in the
> concentration camps, December 1901

Towards the end of 1901 it finally started dawning on the British government and its military commanders in South Africa that the concentration camps were not what they – the politicians and the officers – claimed them to be. On 12 November Brodick wrote to Kitchener: '[Ladies] Commisson death rates higher than those in reports thus far published – why?'[1]

In a letter of 20 November to Major Hamilton Goold-Adams, Milner made an astonishing admission by saying that 'the government would evidently shrink from no measures, however costly, to mitigate the evil of the camps'.[2]

Did the conversations between Milner and Emily, her irrefutable revelations and also the accusation that he had the 'soul of a spy', which was 'necessary in a despot', perhaps contribute to this change of judgement on his part?

Two weeks later he followed this up with a letter to Joseph Chamberlain in which he expressed delight at the British military successes yet conceded: 'The black spot – the one very black spot – in the picture is the frightful mortality in the concentration camps ... I entirely agree with you in thinking, that while a hundred explanations may be offered and a hundred excuses made, they do not really amount to any adequate defence.'³ A few days later, on 12 December, the members of the Fawcett Commission (also known as the Ladies' Commission) finished their report in Durban, but it was only published as a Government Blue Book at the beginning of February 1902.⁴

It was a hefty three-hundred-page report, based on the commission's visits to thirty-three camps in the Free State and the Transvaal to which, according to Emily, they had 'travelled *en luxe* – each had a private compartment, their house for their sole use, a cook and a saloon-servant'.⁵ The report noted improvements to be made at all the camps they visited. They also described the high mortality rate due to insanitary conditions caused by the war, causes within the control of the inmates and causes within the control of administrations. They noted the lack of clean water, insufficient milk for children, the outbreak of disease and the 'thin, non-nutritious meat'. That there was also a lack of wood for cooking and boiling water and that a number of camps are not suitable due to the location. In some of the camps they found extremely impure water. They did not approve of the tradional medicine the Boer women used. They made numerous recommendations to improve the conditions, including better and more food, increased fuel, disinfection, clean water, proper medical care, housing. They also asked that camp matrons should be appointed, and for at least 100 teachers to be sent from Britain to assist in the schooling.

The report and Emily's arrest and deportation from the Cape Town harbour gave rise to a heated debate in the House of Commons. Brodrick was not prepared to accept responsibility for any of it, but nevertheless endorsed Kitchener's decisions in that regard.[6] Broderick was also taken to task for his refusal to accede to Emily's request to limit the intake of newcomers so as to prevent overcrowding in the camps. And what steps had he taken to prevent the outbreak of disease, which he had been warned was imminent?[7]

The Boers were to blame for overcrowding in the camps, according to Brodrick, because they kept blowing up the railway lines and 'the difficulty of moving large numbers of persons in the African winter, made it impossible to fix limits to the number in particular camps'. But he gave the assurance that even before Emily's return steps had been taken to deal with the outbreak of measles.[8] In June 1901 he said, 'It is urged that we have not done sufficient to make these camps sanitary, and to preserve human life. I deny it altogether.'[9]

The Fawcett Commission had evidently not closed their eyes to what they encountered in the camps, and their report confirmed some of the findings Emily had made about nine months earlier. They also came up with an array of practical recommendations to improve the quality of life in the camps: that more tents and toilets be provided as a matter of urgency; that boilers be procured urgently to purify drinking water; that a water inspector be appointed to test the water quality on a regular basis; that lime juice and vegetables be added to the camp inmates' diets; that firewood or coals be made available to enable people to prepare their food.

In addition, the Commission criticised the lack of medical care and found that more teachers, medical staff, medicine, beds, mattresses, blankets, washing facilities and toilets were needed.[10]

Some improvements had already been made earlier thanks to Emily's report and campaigns. And, in the course of the women's visits to the camps, they made certain suggestions to the camp authorities, some of which had been implemented swiftly. Inspectors were appointed and, in particular, more doctors and nurses were sent to the camps, where the hospitals were also improved.[11] These recommendations were implemented by November 1901, when the mortality rates started falling, especially after Milner took over the administration of the camps.

A personal letter by Lucy Deane (which was not included in the official report) was a clear sign that some of the Commission's members had changed their opinion on the camps after visiting them in person:

> We all feel that the policy of the 'Camps' was a huge mistake which no-one but these unpractical ignorant Army men could have committed. It has made the people hate us, it is thoroughly unnatural and we were not able to cope with the hugeness of the task, at any rate the muddling of the War Office wasn't. I believe it has lengthened instead of shortened the war ... Even those of us who approved at first are now of another opinion on the policy of them.[12]

Fawcett, however, had no time for the average Boer woman, albeit that the members of the Commission had been received kindly and their questions had been answered patiently although they had not brought along gifts. She wrote in her diary, the women had a 'horror of ventilation', their sanitary habits were exceptionally unhygienic, and washing oneself was considered a dangerous luxury only for those who enjoyed robust health.[13]

In response to the report, Emily said that the months that had elapsed between her visits and those of the Ladies' Commission had given the authorities the chance to do some rapid 'white washing'. The ladies had not seen the camps as she had seen them; around two thirds of the camp inmates had no beds, water had been in short supply, and the camps had been hopelessly overcrowded – nevertheless the Ladies' Commission still found grave conditions.[14] Like Emily, the Commission did much to alleviate the suffering in the camps. Brodrick himself wrote an official letter to thank them for their good work. The tragedy is that so many more lives could have been saved if he and the British authorities had heeded Emily's findings and advice at an earlier stage. The Commission's recommendations were very similar to those Emily made months before to Brodrick.[15]

When it became apparent that the Ladies' Commission had not paid attention to any of the camps for black people, Emily contacted Henry Fox Bourne, secretary of the Aborigines' Protection Society, and asked for assistance.

Bourne in turn wrote to Joseph Chamberlain[16] and said that, although the information was patchy, he had nonetheless obtained figures indicating that by November there were 43,594 black people held in camps in the Free State and 39,323 in the Transvaal. About five sixths were women and children. The death rate was about 363 per 1000 people. He requested that the British government investigate the matter.[17]

Chamberlain replied that the mortality figures at his disposal showed that the conditions had improved considerably; out of a

An undated, handwritten note in which Emily recorded the death
rates of the Anglo-Boer War. The figure of 27,927 deaths in the
white camps was the earliest official figure.

Photo: Courtesy of Jennifer Hobhouse Balme

camp population of 40,000 in the Transvaal there had been 'only'
800 deaths in January 1902, 550 in February and 400 in March.
(These figures are still disputed, and thought to be much higher.)
Captain Wilson Fox of the Native Refugee Department had
informed him that 'the natives are generally content'. The death
rate 'appears high, but under the circumstances, I think it can
scarcely be called excessive'. According to him, food was scarce but
great quantities of milk, sugar and medication were distributed.[18]

In the black camps there was no nursing care, however, and
enteric fever claimed many lives. There were only a handful of
'bedside attendants', which contributed to the death rate. In various respects, black people in the camps were severely neglected.[19]

Ultimately, approximately 30,000 white people and as an estimate about 25,000 black people died in 50 and 64 tent camps respectively that together had to accommodate around 285,000 people.[20]

A total of 21,144 soldiers lost their lives on the British side, 7,894 on the battlefield and the rest as a result of diseases. On the Boer side there were 9098 'military deaths', of which about 4000 (or 6100, according to some sources) occurred in battle.[21]

There were at least also some small surprises for Emily, and tokens of appreciation – albeit that these did not come from her compatriots. In particular, for Christmas 1901 she received a ballad from

The cover of the ballad and sheet music that Edmond Rostand wrote and composed for Emily. The ballad was later translated from French into English, Italian and Dutch.

Photo: Emily's scrapbook, courtesy of Jennifer Hobhouse Balme

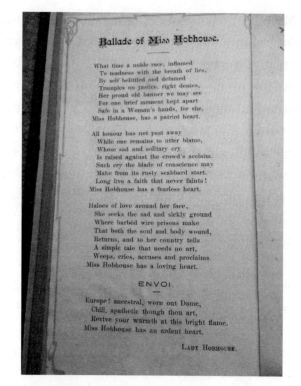

The text of the ballad that the Frenchman Edmond Rostand dedicated
to Emily. Her aunt, Lady Hobhouse, translated it into English.

Photo: Emily's scrapbook, courtesy of Jennifer Hobhouse Balme

the French poet and playwright Edmond Rostand, the author of
Cyrano de Bergerac, which was dedicated to her. He also included
the sheet music for it. Emily was evidently touched by the gift
and preserved it in her scrapbook. The ballad was eventually
translated from French into English, Italian and Dutch.

In the spring of 1902 Emily realised that she was in need of sun
and silence. Quiet repose was an unlikely prospect in England,
where she was constantly involved in heated public debates.

She packed some of her papers, letters and books and travelled
to a solitary spot on Lake Annecy, near Talloires in south-eastern

France. She was the only guest at the Convent Inn, an old Benedictine abbey. For eight weeks she spoke to hardly anyone except occasionally to the local peasants.

'I am the sole monk and there is no sound but the echo of my own footsteps and the lapping of the lake against the garden wall. I have everything lovely outside from snow-capped mountains to flower carpets and walks innumerable.'[22]

Here she worked in peace on her book for which she meticulously wrote down the women's accounts of the war and life in the camps. She also recorded the number of people in both the white and the black camps, and the death rates; the exact rations, and how they differed for the various groups: whites, blacks, refugees, undesirables . . .

There was little mention of the personal trauma she had experienced in far-off South Africa. She let the emphasis fall on the women and children. It was their story.

She made no secret of the perspective from which the book was written: 'This book is designed to give an outline of the recent war, from the standpoint of the women and children.'[23] Published later in 1902, she called it *The Brunt of the War and Where It Fell*, and dedicated it to the women of South Africa 'whose endurance of hardship, resignation in loss, independence under coercion, dignity in humiliation, patience through pain and tranquillity amidst death kindled the reverent appreciation of the writer and has excited the sympathy of the world'.[24]

She made her total aversion to war and commitment to pacifism abundantly clear:

To the plain man and woman, outside the political and military worlds, it seems as though in war an arbitrary line is drawn, one side of which is counted barbarism, the other civilisation.

May it not be that, in reality, all war is barbarous, varying only in degree? History shows that as nations have advanced in civilisation this line has gradually been raised, and watchful care is needed lest it slip back. None of us can claim to be wholly civilised till we have drawn the line above war itself and established universal arbitration in place of armaments.[25]

The first of June 1902 was 'a lovely morning', and Emily sat working on her book by the lake. The newspaper was delivered, with momentous news: 'BRITAIN AND THE BOER REPUBLICS HAVE MADE PEACE!'

Emily could hardly believe it. During the two months she had spent in France, there had been little news from South Africa. She had been unaware of the peace negotiations and that they had already reached such an advanced stage.

Peace in South Africa! Peace on the plains and in the mountains! Peace in the camps?

She tried to imagine what was now on the horizon. No more battles in the hills and on the plains. No more railway lines being blown up. No more concentration camps! Women and children being released. Who had to return to the burnt farms and their worn-out menfolk. But still: Peace!

The paper reported that the Peace of Vereeniging had been signed the day before – 31 May 1902 – in Melrose House in Pretoria by ten Boer leaders on the republics' side, and Milner and Kitchener on the British side.

Milner described the settlement as a surrender, but the British government was more tactful[26] in referring to it as a negotiated peace.

It was agreed that all prisoners of war could return from places overseas such as Ceylon (current Sri Lanka) and St Helena, an island in the South Atlantic Ocean. The burghers of the defeated republics would retain their property. Britain would pay three million pounds in reconstruction aid. Victims of the war would receive compensation for their losses. Interest-free loans would be made available.[27]

But for the Boers there was also a bitter flip side: all burghers had to surrender their arms and swear allegiance to the British Crown.

> Till that moment which brought the news of its end, I had hardly realised the strain which the war had been. The sudden release from that tension seemed too much . . . The peace news was mingled. On our side – just that it was over – and not another life need be sacrificed was all joy, but I could not forget how bitterly the brave women and children in the camps would feel its terms and the crushing of the hopes that had borne them up through loss and pain. For them it contained sorrow.[28]

Emily was overwhelmed by conflicting emotions: torn between loyalty to England and empathy with the Boer women and children, reproaching herself that she had not done more for them, relieved that an end to all of this was in sight . . .

She started crying uncontrollably. Far from both England and South Africa, she cried her heart out sitting there alone next to the French lake.

8

Peace – and loss

'We have done all that we can afford to do and I think that it would be undesirable that the Generals should press us any further in the matter.'

> – Secretary of State for the Colonies Joseph Chamberlain on the Boer generals' requests for financial help after the war, 1902

In the milling crowd of people and soldiers in the port of Southampton there were three men who, in Emily's eyes, stood out above the hubbub. A striking trio. This was not only due to the similarity of their clothing and beards but particularly to their bearing – while they were nonetheless quite different as individuals.

Louis Botha was 'a kingly man' with a commanding presence. Christiaan de Wet, with his 'enigmatical' face, reminded her of a lion caught in a net. Koos de la Rey was a 'patriarch, very gentle and quiet'.

Generals Christiaan de Wet, Koos de la Rey and Louis Botha.

Photo: Gallo Images/Getty Images/ The Print Collector

To Emily, the three Boer generals were not just soldiers but also great men whose dignity had been impaired. They were on a visit to England, and Emily was 'the first English person to welcome them on English soil', in the heartland of the Empire. Alongside her was Caroline Murray, who was there to welcome her sister, Betty Molteno, a fellow passenger of the generals on the *Saxon*.

They arrived only a few days after the coronation of King Edward VII and Queen Alexandra on 9 August 1902. As Emily had watched the spectacle from a grandstand next to St Margaret's Church, another famous/infamous general on horseback had caught her attention: none other than her old adversary Lord Kitchener.

This was the first time she had seen him in person. His full title was now 'Viscount Kitchener, of Khartoum and of the Vaal in the Colony of Transvaal and of Aspall in the County of Suffolk'. Though Kitchener was part of the impressive procession, Emily was unimpressed: 'He seemed quite unable to manage his horse; the animal would only walk sideways or backwards. It was very funny and undignified.'[1] Emily despised him as a leader and as a man, and to him she was 'that bloody woman'.[2]

The Boer generals were in England to raise money for the tens of thousands of destitute women, children and men who would soon have to leave the concentration camps in the Transvaal and the Free State: widows, orphans, the sick and the wounded.[3] Another aim of the trio was to plead for an amelioration of the terms of the peace treaty.[4]

Though they were granted an audience with King Edward VII and also met Colonial Secretary Joseph Chamberlain, the meeting with the latter did not go well. When the generals demanded greater financial support for the defeated Boer republics, Chamberlain's reaction was: 'We have done all that we can afford to do and I think that it would be undesirable that the Generals should press us any further in the matter.'[5]

From England the generals travelled to the Netherlands and Germany, among others, while an appeal for financial contributions appeared in several European newspapers under the heading, 'Appeal of the Boer Generals to the Civilised World'. The campaign was largely based on anti-British sentiment. It was only modestly successful, but a sum of at least of £105,000 was raised.

On their return to London, Emily invited the generals one by one to a meal at her flat in Chelsea. She was worried about how the conversation would go as she still thought her knowledge of 'Boer Dutch' was rather patchy.

How could she make the generals feel special, she wondered. Cigars! She was sure they would enjoy such a treat. As it was considered improper for a woman of her class to be seen in a tobacco shop, she asked a male friend to buy 'three large, fat cigars'. But to her surprise and disappointment each of the men kindly declined the proffered cigar. Secretly she was relieved, however, as she detested smoking.[6]

Emily revealed nothing of the substance of their conversations, only a few impressions: Louis Botha had exceptionally good manners; Koos de la Rey was the quiet patriarch; Christiaan de Wet's face was 'stamped with the responsibility and sorrow of war'. She was surprised by De Wet's friendly company as he tended to be quiet and withdrawn among other people, probably because he usually required the help of an interpreter.

It was clear that the dignity of all three men had been dented, but 'to me they were perfectly sweet'.[7]

To Emily, meeting the generals was very different from her encounters with the Boer women she was used to. She heard from the men's perspective how the treatment of the women had affected them. 'The women themselves would turn off their troubles with an "I don't care" or an occasional joke – not so the men. It has created in them a feeling stronger.'[8]

***

On a visit to London in early March 2015, I tried to get a look at Emily's flat in Flood Street, Chelsea. Rossetti Garden Mansions, which was built in 1889–90, was named after the painter and writer Dante Gabriel Rossetti who lived around the corner in Cheyne Walk. It is still an affluent neighbourhood.[9]

Emily Hobhouse's flat – on the left-hand corner – 21 Rossetti Garden Mansions, Chelsea, London, as it looked in March 2015.

Photo: Elsabé Brits

To Emily, who travelled constantly, Flat 21 was one of her most long-standing abodes – she stayed in the corner flat from 1899 to the middle of 1904, when she was not elsewhere. The building is still beautiful, with an exterior that is more or less unchanged. The front door has charming white pillars, and an old-fashioned lamp shade hangs above the entrance.

I stood gazing up at this flat that she transformed into a work space for the South African Conciliation Committee in 1900 and where the arrangements were made for the first big meeting in the Queen's Hall. It was on this very pavement that people had scrawled the names of the Boer generals to try to intimidate her. This was also where she had hosted three of these generals two years later.

Here she had devised her plans to go to South Africa, and this was the place to which she had returned to expose the conditions in the camps. This was her only private refuge where she could reflect on the appreciation of the Boer women – and could sorrow over her vilification by her own people. Her only other emotional home was the house of her uncle and aunt at 15 Bruton Street, Mayfair, which no longer exists.

***

For Emily, the end of the war did not mean the end of her relationship with South Africa. She still regularly received letters from there – and in most cases the news was not good.

Mrs Edith Dickenson, whose husband was a camp doctor at Bethulie, informed her in October 1902 – five months after the peace – that there were still two thousand people in the camp at Bloemfontein and two thousand five hundred at the one in Bethulie, and although there were now few instances of disease and everything was considerably cleaner, poverty was taking its toll.

Emily felt that it was her duty to follow up on her work.[10] 'It is not so easy to convey this fact to others whose experience of a devastated country was nil.' Before long she had made up her mind and paid her passage.

In late April 1903 she left for Cape Town on the *Carisbrooke Castle*. Once again she tried to keep her identity secret but it leaked out nonetheless, and as soon as some of passengers heard who she was they would 'turn their backs on me', she wrote later to her sister-in-law Nora.[11]

The chief engineer on board the *Carisbrooke* told her that when he heard about her arrest, his first reaction had been: 'Serve her right.' Why? Emily asked.

'I simply believed the newspapers, but as soon as I saw your face I knew you were genuine.'

'Don't you think I might wear a card with the words "I am genuine"?'[12]

At the customs office in the Cape Town harbour Emily encountered similar preconceived ideas about her. 'Miss Hobhouse, tell me ... Tell me the real truth, have you got any firearms?' the official inquired.

She burst out laughing.[13]

But the opposite happened too. An official who searched her luggage enquired: 'Beg pardon, but are you the original Miss Hobhouse? Sorry to ask, but you see I've read your book.'[14] Emily confirmed it hesitantly, uncertain of his reaction. Whereupon the man removed his cap out of respect, and thenceforth 'served me promptly and with marked docility'.

It was a beautiful autumn morning in Cape Town, with the sun rising in the east while the moon was setting over the Atlantic Ocean in the west.

Her faithful friend Caroline Murray was at the harbour to meet Emily. This time she stayed in Gardens, at the home of Sir Henry de Villiers, chief justice of the Cape Colony, and his wife Aletta, Lady de Villiers.[15]

The news of Emily's presence soon became known, and a stream of Afrikaans-speaking women came to visit and sat conversing with her on the stoep.

But it was not for this that Emily had come so far; she wanted to get to the Free State and the Transvaal to see and hear at first hand what the state of affairs was. For that she needed a permit. 'I had to answer all kinds of questions and fill in forms and seeing I was English the official was most hearty and said there was no difficulty – I could go anywhere.'[16]

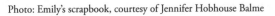

The permit that authorised Emily after the conclusion of peace to
travel unhindered in 1903 to the Transvaal and the Free State.

Photo: Emily's scrapbook, courtesy of Jennifer Hobhouse Balme

When he read the form and realised who she was, however, his
attitude changed. She was told to return the following day. Emily
suspected that her name was on a list,[17] but three days later she
was given the green light nonetheless.

Emily visited the Home for Girls in Wynberg, a refuge for
unmarried pregnant women, which had been opened by Emmie
Murray, daughter of church leader Dr Andrew Murray.

Here Emmie told her about the terrible consequences of
the massive influx of soldiers into the country. 'Her information, as noted down, is serious, but cannot be here repeated.'

Emily wrote to Leonard. 'If someone would write a book on the effect of war on public morality her experiences should find a place.'[18]

As a guest of Sir Henry de Villiers Emily attended the opening of the Cape Parliament on 5 June and had lunch with him, John X. Merriman, J. W. Sauer and other MPs.

She also spoke to 'Onze' Jan Hofmeyr, leader of the Afrikaner Bond, who showed her packets of telegrams that had passed between himself, Paul Kruger and Theunis Steyn, and by means of which he had tried to prevent the war. He told her that during a recent meeting he had had with Joseph Chamberlain in Cape Town he had pleaded that at least ten million pounds was required to reconstruct the devastated interior. Chamberlain refused to consider this, however.[19]

Hofmeyr was one of many people who saw her off at the Cape Town station later on 5 June. She was on her way to the north, but would first pay a visit to a new friend, Olive Schreiner, in the Karoo. Two months earlier Schreiner had written to her to congratulate her on her book. She was extremely flattering about Emily's work in the camps:

> I consider you did more effective and useful work in the cause of humanity and justice in South Africa than any other individual has been able to do. You saved not hundreds but undoubtedly thousands of lives.
>
> I fear your work must have told heavily and permanently on you. One does not pass through such a time of combat with injustice ever to be quite the same again . . .[20]

This was the start of their friendship.[21]

A young Olive Schreiner.

Photo: National English Literary Museum

Emily met Schreiner in person for the first time in Beaufort West. Betty Molteno and her life partner, Alice Greene, were also visiting her at the time. They sat talking in the winter sun. Olive could talk incessantly at times, despite suffering badly from asthma. Emily wrote to Tibbie Steyn:

Few understood the enigmatic character of her genius. Perhaps it was not understandable. English critics have attempted to compress her into the European mould and judge her so, forgetting she was South African born and bred and belonged to the vast spaces and simple life of the veld, and was subject to its strange influences. South Africans, I think, try to judge her by their standards alone, forgetting that her mind and spirit had burst all frontiers and racial bonds and embraced the world.[22]

Emily also met many people in this town with its six thousand inhabitants from all population groups. 'But no words of mine can portray the attitude of mind towards England. Every atom of respect and love has vanished. It is a deep disdain both for the policy and the methods by which the policy has been carried out,' she wrote to Aunt Mary.[23]

For all that, Emily heard that many people here had bought her book, *The Brunt of the War*, and kept it next to the Bible and the hymn book on their shelves.

The most pressing problem was that no rain had fallen for eighteen months. Some days not even the trains could run because there was no water. Thousands of head of cattle had been herded into the Free State where there was at least some grazing left. Nevertheless, when she was about to leave for Bloemfontein, she received a basket with hard-boiled eggs, sandwiches, a tin of biscuits and a bottle of milk as provisions for the journey. Schreiner gave her raisins and oranges, and an old man sent his cart and horses to take Emily to the station.[24]

On the way to Bloemfontein the train went past Springfontein, where she had seen the mother cradling the dead child on her knees. This time she saw about a thousand graves in the distance, row upon row upon row . . .

One after another, people told her that nothing had come of the three million pounds for 'reconstruction' that had been promised to the Boers. They had handed in some of the receipts the British officers had given them to receive compensation for war damage, but nothing had happened. Allegations of corruption were rife.[25]

The Treaty of Vereeniging lay down that three million pounds would be apportioned among Boers who, owing to war losses, were unable to provide for themselves. An additional three million pounds would be granted as interest-free loans,[26] while about two million pounds was allocated to local British subjects, black people and neutral foreigners.[27]

The treaty also provided for Repatriation Boards with offices in every district that had to apportion the money to people who had lost their farms and homes. The payout of these funds, however, was a protracted bureaucratic process. In some cases the British officers had given people receipts during the war as evidence of goods they had seized. These receipts could now be submitted in order to receive compensation.[28]

To Milner, the repatriation of all displaced persons, which also included the settlement of British immigrants, was a priority. The logistics of repatriation and resettlement was daunting: 31,000 prisoners of war (with the majority in overseas camps), 116,000 white and 115,000 black inmates of concentration camps, 500 Uitlanders, 21,000 Bittereinders (Boers who had continued fighting to 'the bitter end') and 5400 members of the National Scouts (Boers who had fought on the British side).[29]

The inhabitants of the two former republics regarded the three million pounds for 'assisting the restoration of the people to their homes and supplying those who, owing to war losses, are unable to provide for themselves' (as it was formulated in the treaty) as reparations. Milner ensured, however, that preference was given to the loyal Uitlanders and National Scouts and the handsuppers.[30]

Jan Smuts wrote to Emily's brother Leonard that Joseph Chamberlain's visit to the Transvaal had brought bitterness rather than reconciliation. The Boer leaders had asked that no war debt be imposed on the two impoverished and devastated former republics, but Chamberlain 'did not even deign to reply to us'. Britain had determined that the Transvaal and Free State colonies should pay a war debt of three million pounds, but it was later written off. The colonies had also been given a loan of thirty-five million pounds, which was mainly used to improve and expand the railways.[31]

Chamberlain's 'great taunt' was the Boers' 'ingratitude and non-recognition of the fact' that the British government was spending fifteen million pounds (in the end more than sixteen million) on the reconstruction of their country. 'Everybody then and since has been wondering and asking where and how and on whom this vast sum of money has been spent, for there is certainly no public evidence of it, except perhaps in the Blue Books which are sent to the Colonial office for home consumption,' Smuts wrote.[32]

Emily was now even more determined to see for herself what the post-war Free State and Transvaal looked like. Kitchener had been able to stop her two years earlier – not this time.

9

A country of skulls and bones

'If we could have you for ever among us, to bind the wounds which even time could scarcely heal, to be our priestess of suffering and sacrifice, how many more happy hearts there would be in this land of sorrows how we would look up to you and give you that which is sweetest to the human heart, which no other people on earth would give you.'[1]

– General Jan Smuts to Emily Hobhouse, 1903

If the English people could clearly see and know the appalling aftermath of their war, then their hearts would soften and they would help to get these people, with whom they had ties of blood and religion, back on their feet. This was Emily's firm belief, albeit that 'to tell England things is like dropping water into the ocean' – she was well aware that what she envisaged was by no means the general sentiment of her compatriots at that stage.

Emily's travels through the scorched earth after the Anglo-Boer War, 1903

1 **12 May:** Arrives in Cape Town

2 **6 June:** Beaufort West

3 **10 June:** Bloemfontein

4 **12 June:** Departs on first leg of journey through the devastated districts

5 **14 June:** Boshof

6 **17 June:** Hoopstad

7 **18 June:** Bultfontein

8 **21 June:** Brandfort

9 **Returns to Bloemfontein, stops at Thaba 'Nchu and Tweespruit, arrives on 27 June**

10 **30 June:** Koppies

11 **1 July:** General De Wet's farm (Roodepoort)

12 **2 July:** Heidelberg

13 **4 July:** Pretoria

14 **8 July:** Middelburg

15 **12 July:** Witpoort and Roos Senekal

16 **13 July:** Dullstroom

17 **14 July:** Belfast, departs for Pretoria

18 **21 July:** Warmbaths and Nylstroom

19 **23 July:** Pietersburg

20 **25 July:** Back in Warmbaths

21 **29 July – 1 August:** Heilbron, Lindley and Reitz

22 **2 August:** Frankfort

23 **3 August:** Pretoria

24 **10 August:** Johannesburg

25 **22 August:** Klerksdorp

26 **23 August:** Hartebeestfontein

27 **2 September:** Pretoria

28 **8 September:** Potchefstroom

29 **12 September:** Lichtenburg

30 **17 September:** Schweizer-Reneke

31 **20 September:** Wolmaransstad

32 **30 September:** Kroonstad

33 **1 October:** Ventersburg

34 **4 October:** Bloemfontein

35 **25 October:** Paarl

36 **8 November:** Stellenbosch

37 **23 November:** Tulbagh

38 **30 November:** Stellenbosch (Uitkijk)

39 **22 December:** Departs from Cape Town for England

Knowing, as I do, that England is comfortably feeling that the Boers have now realised their mistake and are rejoicing in the peace and the flag and the good rule and forgetting the camps and singing 'God Save the King' and are also thinking how generous a conqueror she has been with her millions . . .

It is too curious to find how different the attitude here really is and that the Boers, silent to the outer world, are shaking their sides with laughter at England, her complacency and her mistakes. So they let her go her own way and out of these mistakes will come their opportunity.

For one thing, they know perfectly well they are not conquered . . .[2]

It was not only her faith in the English nation that motivated her, but the faith she had in the Boers: that they would regain their self-respect and rise from the ashes.

Once again Emily wanted to see for herself what the true effects of the war were – and what practical measures could be taken to ameliorate them. She intended taking 'a speedy trip into the country districts', but in the post-war conditions there were virtually no carts, horses or mules available. Moreover, she failed to realise that the vastness of the country made a 'speedy trip' impossible.

'Yet it is the country districts to which I must get and where such great destitution prevails,' she wrote to Aunt Mary.[3] At this point she had only enough money to travel for ten days.

In Bloemfontein she stayed again at the home of her old friends the Fichardts. Caroline's son Arthur Fichardt suggested that she travel with a Mr Enslin, a pedlar who had just returned from the farms.[4] He had been a prisoner of war on Ceylon, and Arthur knew him well enough to trust him. Seeing that it was Emily, Enslin agreed, after first having consulted his wife, 'for no Boer acts without consent of Mrs Boer'.

Emily waving goodbye to the Fichardts in front of their home in
Bloemfontein, about to embark on her journey through the devastated Free
State and Transvaal. Her companions on the first leg of the journey in the
wagonette drawn by four mules were a Mr Enslin and a helper called Jacob.

Enslin provided the wagonette, which was big enough for the relief food supplies for destitute people as well as their own supplies and bedding, four mules, feed and a black helper, Jacob.

At ten o'clock on the morning of 12 June 1903, Emily, Enslin and Jacob departed from Bloemfontein on their journey through the scorched earth of the Free State, and later of the Transvaal too.

The two men sat in front and Emily at the back. As usual she was dressed smartly, a hat on her head in true Victorian fashion. She had taken along a food basket, a blanket, clothes and her materials for watercolour painting. She was exchanging the luxuries of Kaya Lami with its electricity, fireplaces and soft beds for a lantern and a bed roll.

Enslin knew the area well, and presumably Arthur Fichardt had also advised them on the direction they could take. Just before sunset the trio arrived at the farm of the Rheeder family, Bultfontein, eighteen miles outside Bloemfontein. Before darkness fell, Emily made a watercolour painting of the ruins of the burnt farmstead.

One half of the family lived in the burnt wagon house and the other in patched-up rooms in the burnt, roofless house. 'Not a penny has been received in compensation; the question, I notice, raises an incredulous smile.'

At least there was food. That evening Emily had a meal of bread, biltong, fruit jam and coffee with the family.[5] Mrs Rheeder, who had spent twenty-three months in the Bloemfontein camp gave Emily her and her husband's bed for the night.

By eight o'clock the next morning Emily was ready to leave, but the mules had escaped and were evading – it was only by eleven o'clock that Jacob and Enslin managed to get them inspanned. Emily used the time to make another watercolour painting, this time of a farm on the side of the Modder River.

The painting Emily made of the farm Bultfontein shortly
after she and her companions arrived at the farm.

Painting: Anglo-Boer War Museum

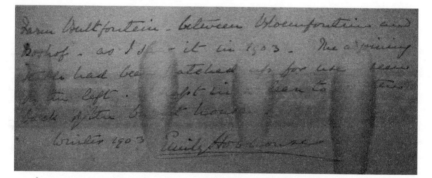

The back of the painting, on which Emily had written: 'The Farm
Bultfontein – between Bloemfontein and Boshof – as I saw it in
1903. The adjoining stable had been patched up for use as seen
on the left. I slept in the lean-to at the back of the burnt house.'

Painting: Anglo-Boer War Museum

Along the way they stopped at the Van Aswegen's farm. The
family was in such dire straits that they did not even have coffee.
There were no cows, and the hens were so starved that they no
longer laid eggs.[6] Emily ate some of her own provisions.

154

By five that afternoon they outspanned on the Strijker farm where the children took a keen interest in her. 'It is very difficult to write with a row of Boer children watching me.'[7] The people were very hospitable and put a bedroom at her disposal, while the entire family – six children in all – 'squeezed themselves I don't know where'.[8]

Early the next morning she was woken by the family's devotions; Dutch prayers and hymns resounded from the 'dining room'.

An icy wind bit through Emily's cloak as they rode off. After a mere two days in the sun and open air, she already felt like a 'piece of dried biltong'.

At Piet Nel's farm Palmietfontein they stopped for a rest. Nel was fairly well off and the house had already been rebuilt, but there was other tragic news. When the English had arrived to burn the house, the family was fired upon as they tried to flee to the hills. The Nels' daughter Christine was wounded in the head. While she was dying, the house was burnt down.

More than four thousand sheep and twenty-eight horses had been killed. Emily went to inspect the scene of the slaughter 'masses of white skulls and countless bones strewed thick over the wide kraal and piled in heaps upon the veld outside'.[9]

Emily heard from more and more people that when they submitted their receipts for compensation, their claims simply went missing. Others received as little as a tenth of what they had claimed. In another case, two families had claimed fifty and ninety-six pounds respectively, yet both had received only fourteen.[10]

The second planting season was already past but the soil still lay barren. How could the people plough and plant when they lacked oxen, seed and implements?

*

At the town of Boshof Emily discovered that the rations Chamberlain had promised had only been given to the most destitute people – and also only up to the end of May, the previous month. Moreover, the rations were even more skimpy than those in the concentration camps had been: just bully beef and meal. No coffee, sugar, salt or even some condensed milk for the children.[11]

Many widows had been living solely on these rations for months. A woman recounted that she and her five children had to survive on half a bag of mealie-meal and forty-eight tins of bully beef per month. Emily had some coffee and rice to give her.

She and Boshof's minister put their heads together to assist some of the poorest people. The town had six hundred residents, all of them impoverished and many destitute.

With the help of the town's lawyer she visited a number of farms in the district. 'I have not yet met a single instance in which a man has received payment of his receipts from our military, but I have heard of a few cases in which a small proportion of the money due has been paid. All feel it would have been far better to pay the receipts and let the further loss lie forgotten rather than have raised hopes for nothing.'[12]

While the minister and his wife were at church, Emily saw herself for the first time in a long while in a mirror.

'I laughed aloud for my trek had so altered me I did not know myself. I am like the raw Springbok biltong which is to be seen hanging in strings outside some farm house walls, and my hair is electrified and blazes when I comb it.'[13]

Her face had been burnt red by the sun. 'I was a complete Rooinek!' (In South Africa, 'red neck' was an insult used by the Boers to describe the sunburnt necks of the British Army soldiers, whose pith helmets did not give enough protection from the sun.)

Before their departure from Boshof, Emily left money for three of the poorest widows and a sick couple in the town.[14]

At Hoopstad dozens of people awaited Emily on her arrival, as a telegram had been sent in advance. Everyone wanted to talk to her and tell their story. Out of necessity she decided to listen to no more than twenty people a day. It was simply too exhausting; although she understood 'Afrikaans-Dutch' reasonably well, trying to follow it was a strain. She also had the endless bumping in the wagonette to contend with. The group that required most attention were the *bijwoners*, subfarmers or tenant farmers, who had nothing; they were 'penniless and stripped bare'.[15]

To her, the poverty-stricken, dry, barren landscape seemed covered with death. It reminded her of Ezekiel's Valley of Dry Bones:

'The hand of the Lord was upon me, and carried me out in the spirit of the Lord, and set me down in the midst of the valley which was full of bones, And caused me to pass by them round about: and, behold, there were very many in the open valley; and, lo, they were very dry.' (Ezekiel 37:1-2)

At the town of Bultfontein a local resident took Emily to visit some of the farms. They drove through an endless landscape of sand. After travelling for hours, they stopped for lunch at a lonely farmstead. She walked to a row of aloes in the distance to stretch her legs. The aloes had been planted in such a way that they formed a kraal, an enclosure, and when she peered through the plants, she saw that it, too, was full of bones. Emily started counting the skulls but stopped when she reached five hundred.

'The sheep gazed at me reproachfully through their hollow eyes. Beside the hedge was the black ruin of the house.'[16] The occupants had started rebuilding it thanks to a loan of three hundred pounds from the Repatriation Board.

The rations had just about run out and the little food that was left in the pack stores was not being distributed by the English, she was told. The people were scared to complain or write letters since the Peace Preservation Act[17] prohibited criticism of the government.

It was difficult to get out of Bultfontein, as there were no horses left in the town. After two mules had been obtained, an 'English-Afrikander' supplied a suitable harness but when he heard it would be used for Emily's journey, he took it back on the spot. 'So it was late when a less political harness was found, and we started.'

Piles of tents lay rotting on the terrain where the concentration camp at Brandfort used to be. When the Boers asked whether they could have them, the English refused – they had to buy them.

On this Sunday morning Emily walked to the camp's cemetery while the local people went to church. The church was really all that was left of 'the old life', and there seemed to be a spiritual revival among the people. 'They cling passionately to it and the minister has more power than ever. I wonder if any priesthood ever had such complete power over a people.'[18]

While this may sound like an innocent observation, the central position of the ministers in the community was a phenomenon that Emily would later harness ingeniously.

She also observed that 'there is an abnormal number of marriages since the war and the widows and widowers won't remain lonely much longer'. In Brandfort alone there had been thirty-eight marriages in two months, while there were usually about twenty per year.[19]

Emily became exasperated with the 'bijwoner's daughters, big strong girls with nothing to do and eating their parents' heads off', who were in her view extremely lazy. In England women of their class would immediately have gone into service, working as servants in wealthy households, but the *bijwoners* refused to do so. They regarded that kind of work as exclusively for black people.[20]

'These people I wholly refuse to help, because I am sure their old customs must be altered owing to the great upheaval the country has undergone and the pressure of circumstances must drive them to take service . . . I have begged the dominees' (minister's) wives to use their influence to inculcate this idea.'[21] But she did not get much help on that front.

By now Emily had used up three quarters of the money the Distress Fund had made available to her. As usual, she had distributed food at many places along the way.

Back in Bloemfontein for a few days' rest, Emily took the train to Koppies on 1 July 1903. On its arrival at the station just before three o'clock the next morning, two of General Christiaan de

A watercolour painting Emily made of General Christiaan de Wet's farm Roodepoort in the district of Koppies on 1 July 1903. On the back she wrote that she stayed in the new, empty building that had been erected after the farmhouse was first burnt and then blown up with dynamite.

Painting: Anglo-Boer War Museum

Wet's sons were waiting for her. She was very glad about the warm sheepskin that she had to keep out the Free State cold.[22]

Emily was shocked to see how thin General De Wet had become since the time she had hosted him in her flat in London. All he had left after the war was his gun and Fleur, his white horse who had carried him faithfully throughout the war. After the family's house had been burnt by the English, the ruins were then blown up with dynamite. 'Like all the other burghers De Wet is laughing. If he did not, he says, he should die. It makes him great fun.'[23]

The English and their soldiers were the constant targets of the gallows humour of De Wet's wife, Cornelia. Her anger was still raw after she had lost everything except her sewing machine and gone through hell in the Vredefort camp.

Emily left De Wet's farm at midnight for the station at Koppies. At half past two in the morning her train steamed out of Koppies towards Germiston, where she took the first available train to Heidelberg, to attend General Louis Botha's national assembly; the first large Afrikaner public meeting since the war.[24] Along the way, more and more Boer men boarded the train. 'On all sides across the veld I could see them collecting, specks of dust trending towards Heidelberg.'[25]

At times she amused herself by talking to Boers who were unaware of her identity. This gave her an insight into their attitude towards the English: conditioned politeness coupled with icy aloofness. As soon as she told them who she was, however, the Boers' manner changed in an instant and they radiated kind-heartedness.[26]

In Heidelberg, the Boers of the Transvaal colony were holding their first organised meeting since the war to protest against the colonial government of the British Crown – particularly the planned importation of Chinese labour. Milner had announced this plan at a conference in Bloemfontein four months earlier after a commission had found that there was a shortage of 129,000 unskilled labourers on the mines.[27]

At this meeting she met the thirty-two-year-old Jan Smuts, the former state attorney of the ZAR and now an attorney in Pretoria.

Men came pouring into the town from all sides: on foot, on bicycles, on wagons of all kinds and by train. They were poor, their clothes were threadbare and they looked hungry. 'I had never seen such a mass of Boer men before and certainly was deeply struck by this strange procession of impoverished men – their seriousness, their silence, their orderliness, their perfect good-humour and their deep sense of the importance of the occasion.'[28]

About two thousand people walked in a cloud of red dust to the market square where General Botha delivered a speech from the church steps. They adopted three resolutions, which Milner had to send to the British government: the Boers rejected the plan to import Chinese labour; they demanded that English and Dutch be given equal status and wanted local control of education; and without the approval of any legislative authority they rejected any debt[29] that might be placed on the Transvaal.[30]

Coffee and sandwiches were carried in after the meeting, and when the men heard that the refreshments were for everyone, they broke their silence with loud cheering.[31] Emily sat at a table with eight generals but felt extremely unwell. Perhaps it was due to the altitude; her heart was giving her trouble. 'Everything was swaying around me.'

A group of orphans formed a tableau. The children pinned flowers to each of the generals' lapels, and the two smallest ones presented Emily with a basket of flowers. As General Botha introduced her to the crowd, she had to concentrate to stay on her feet. She thanked everyone in a short speech, in Afrikaans, which was greeted with tremendous applause.

The following day a number of people came to see her off at the station. 'We got dreadfully snapshotted at Heidelberg station,' Emily wrote to Aunt Mary.[32] There were handshakes and hugs aplenty.

On her arrival in Pretoria, Emily was received by a large group of women, all elegantly dressed in their Sunday best. Emily, on the other hand, had been travelling for days, and her clothes were still red from the Heidelberg dust. She heard someone say at the

The garden party that the Boer women held for Emily in Pretoria. She stands in the middle, in a white dress. Next to her are General Christiaan Beyers (left) and General Jan Smuts (right).

Photo: Courtesy of Jennifer Hobhouse Balme

station: 'We can't think what the Boers can see in Miss Hobhouse, she can't even dress.'[33] Again she was given roses and violets by orphans, and she had to leave immediately to attend a garden party. Her friends had planned to hold the party in Burghers Park, but when the government heard that it was in honour of Emily, they refused permission. 'Another little snub for me – and not the way to conciliate the Dutch or make them believe the English forgive and forget.'[34]

The women moved the event to a private garden, even with a carpet and sofas under the loquat trees. One by one the women were introduced to Emily. 'It was a long day, but the day was perfect and the people all so pleased that it was impossible not to enjoy it, which I did thoroughly.'[35]

From everything she was told, it was clear that the 'repatriation' scheme was a woeful failure, albeit that Milner reported on the success it was achieving. The Repatriation Boards that had to pay the Boers' claims were still travelling around the country, but were wasting the 'free grant' of three million pounds that was supposed to be apportioned among the poorest Boers.

Emily wrote that she had not yet come across a single person in the Transvaal that had received money from the Repatriation Board. Some of the Boers were even asked to provide security before they could receive a free grant.

Louis Botha sent a long letter to Leonard Courtney for publication in *The Times*, in which he gave an account of the 'dismal failure' of Chamberlain's visit and how the latter had hinted that the Boers were ungrateful for the fifteen million pounds England was spending on the reconstruction of the country.[36]

On this visit to Pretoria Emily met Lily Boshoff (née Rautenbach) on 7 July 1903 and wrote down her story. It was published in 1924 with photos and sketches, along with the war memories of other women, in *War Without Glamour: Or, Women's War Experiences Written by Themselves, 1899–1902.*

The accounts had been written by the women themselves – about half of them in Afrikaans, which Emily translated, and the others in English. 'Nearly all the writers I met personally and saw their ruined farms and homes,' Emily wrote. 'Besides their value as historical records these accounts are in my belief a real aid to the cause of permanent peace, for they depict war in simple unvarnished language, with complete unconsciousness disclosing its squalid and ghastly details, thus making clear to unbiased readers its effects on the children, the old and the sick. The universality and similarity of experience is striking.'[37]

The exception was the story of Lily, who was no longer able to write. She recounted that she had worked as a nurse at the Bezuidenhout's Drift camp near Harrismith. She wore an armband marked with a red cross, and this flag also hung above the hospital. On 9 January 1902, however, between thirty and forty British soldiers arrived there and simply started firing through a window at the wounded Boers in their beds.

Lily was hit in the neck while one of the Boer patients was wounded as well. As a result of her injury, she lost the use of her hand and arm and was unable to do sewing. Her letter to the authorities had gone unanswered. Emily could at least give her fifteen pounds.[38]

On her arrival in Middelburg, Emily wanted nothing more than to relax on the stoep. She had grown fond of this typically South African custom. But there was no rest for her; the parsonage where she was staying was bustling with people, all perched on straight-backed chairs and all hoping to speak to her.

Emily headed for the concentration camp cemetery as the sun was setting. Row upon row of children's graves lay before her. Most of them had died during 'that fatal July' of 1901 after her meeting with Brodrick. Each child's name had been 'written on a bit of paper and put in a glass bottle' that now stood on the grave.[39]

The long journey was 'trying, tedious and painful but I hope useful',[40] she wrote to Aunt Mary. In this country where only sunshine and goodwill were left, her heart sank at night when she had to face the cold and the uncomfortable sleeping arrangements.

And then in the morning she had to be on the road again, enduring the 'jolt of the wagon' on dusty tracks. The neuritis in her arm was becoming acute.

Moreover, she went hungry. 'The Boers partly by custom, party largely now by necessity, eat so much less than we do, that I am underfed, and though I carry some food with me I am ashamed to have to confess I must supplement their meals. At night I chew a little biltong and crack up some bread which has dried in the air beyond cutting with a knife.'[41]

Everywhere Emily went people wanted to shake hands with her, 'even the tiniest mortal'. It led to her referring to South Africa as 'this handshaking country'. Even babies who had just learnt to walk would come up to one and solemnly put out their 'wee hands', which, Emily observed, might not be clean: 'I find it wise to keep my gloves on till I am well ensconced in a house.'[42]

The following day Emily travelled with the *predikant*, minister, to Roos Senekal. While it was less dry here, there was neither a boerbok (a type of goat) nor a sheep to be seen. The four mules that pulled the ramshackle wagon struggled to get up a hill, and Emily decided to get off and walk for a while.

That night they slept at the house of the Haupt family who had been ordered by 'His Highness the Predikant' to house her.[43]

Emily wanted to sleep outside on her bedroll, but this caused great consternation. Mrs Haupt insisted that she sleep in the stable, together with all their other visitors. The house itself had been burnt down.

'I have no longer a large house and large rooms, but I still have a large heart and I cannot bear you to sleep outside,' Mrs Haupt told her.[44]

Emily did not sleep a wink in the crowded stable. Before sunrise she set off to a nearby hill to do a painting of the farmstead. On her return she found that everyone was up; they were raising the roof with their praying and singing, thanking the Heavenly Father for food, clothes and a roof over their heads. Roos Senekal was virtually a tent town, as almost everything had been destroyed in the war. The congregation was gathered there for a *nachtmaal*, a communion service, and they had erected a private tent for Emily. To her astonishment, a bed, chair, table, washing utensils, candles and a mirror were carried into her tent.

As the pews of the gutted church had been burnt, the people brought in chairs and boxes to sit on. The windowpanes were broken, and only some sections of the roof were still in place. Emily did not attend the communion service; she sat to one side in the sun, preferring to listen 'to the long tuneless hymns at a respectful distance'.[45]

After the service she shared a meal with the congregation in the ruins of the church. Here people told her that they did receive food from the Repatriation Boards, but accounts had been issued for what they had received. It turned out that these were not donations: everything had to be repaid.

Next, they travelled 'break-neck roads through the mountains'. In distance Emily saw a white garment. As they came closer, they came upon a destroyed house. Behind the house stood a nine-year-old girl and her even younger sister. The mother, a Mrs Britz, was sick and bedridden. The father had gone to look for work. Emily gave them rice and flannelette for clothing for the children.

At Dullstroom Emily was too hungry to talk to the people and asked for a respite to first eat something while resting outside the burnt church. After the breathing space she felt refreshed and ready to listen once more to the outpouring of stories and memories. Emily was the ear for England and its soldiers' war offences.

She stayed overnight, at some distance from the town, at the farm of Piet Taute, a former field cornet – the equivalent of a lieutenant. The house had been burnt three times; he was now trying to rebuild for the fourth time. His wife 'was stamped with the Camp look'.

The next day, when Emily was about to leave, she called Taute aside and presented him with money to get back on his feet. He burst into tears.

At Belfast the schoolchildren sang for her, tea was served, and people came to tell their individual stories. Once again she listened patiently to each account. She tried to arrange transport to visit the towns of Ermelo and Carolina, but there was not a single horse or mule to be found.

The pain in her arm grew worse by the day, and she still felt malnourished. The neuritis was like 'hell-fire within you'.[46] She decided to return to Pretoria to rest before continuing her journey any further.

This was the first time Emily stayed at the home of Jan Smuts and his wife Isie, in Sunnyside, Pretoria. She soon became besotted with their baby, Santa. But there she also received the sad news of the death of her good friend Caroline Fichardt from Bloemfontein, with whom she had stayed only recently.[47]

This visit was the start of a long and close friendship between Emily and Jan Smuts. Her letters to him are filled with emotion and compassion and attest to her intelligence and wide reading. But she did not hesitate to take him to task when she deemed it necessary.

She was a pacifist, a humanist and a feminist. He was a statesman, a field marshal, a nature lover and a philosopher. What they had in common were a good education, high intellect and liberal values.

Emily found him very charming, cultivated and clever, not embittered like his wife. He was open-minded, and neither hopeful nor without hope about the country. Yet he did not feel part of the country in its current state, Emily thought.[48]

Because he had studied at Cambridge he understood the English. Under his skin, she noticed, there was sadness about the war, yet at times it seemed as if he was completely uninvolved in current affairs.[49]

Emily saw in him a future statesman: 'I prophesy a great future for Smuts, hopeless as he now is I feel sure he is the man respected by all parties and feared by Milner, and one day the English and all will look to him to get them out of the muddle into which the country is drifting. But Smuts will work, not only side by side, but behind Botha loyally, till someday his superior education will force him to the front.'[50]

After a few days of relaxation, first at the home of the Smuts family and then with friends at Warmbad, Emily made her way to Pietersburg, where she stayed at the parsonage. She was surprised to find such a big town. There was no meat here, however; the people lived on mealie-meal and vegetables. The Boers had had to hand in their guns and were no longer able to shoot small game for the pot.

She met Commandant Swemmer, who had been a medical officer of the Boer commandos and now served as a deputy chairman of the Compensation Boards. The Boers were being paid out fixed amounts, irrespective of the damage or the extent of the claim, he told her. The most that people would get in compensation was a 'shilling per pound'.[51]

By his estimation, between 85 per cent and 89 per cent of the districts on the Highveld and up to 50 per cent of those in the Western Transvaal could no longer sustain themselves. Around Pretoria the figure was about 25 per cent.[52]

To Emily, the traditional black people in the area were an unusual sight; they wore adornments of beads and copper bracelets, and their tribal chiefs lived in the hills around the town. She visited one of the black villages in the vicinity of Pietersburg and saw the 'evidence of their terrible work as English instruments during the war'.[53]

These people still wore their khaki uniforms and they had herds of cattle; there was no shortage of mealies. Time and again Emily heard the same story: that black men had herded the Boer women and children along to the concentration camps 'with never a white officer amongst them'.[54]

Numerous accounts of atrocities perpetrated by black and white soldiers were told to Emily, and she wrote them all down. One that touched her deeply was the story of the Van Stadens: a father and his two sons who had surrendered. They were shot and thrown into a hole by Harry 'The Breaker' Morant and his guerrilla band. Despite that fact that the younger boy, a fourteen-year-old, was not dead, the men left him there.

His attempts to dig himself out were fruitless as he had been shot in both knees. Three days later a black man heard soft crying as he walked past the spot, but the boy died before he could help him. The people wanted Emily to visit these graves, but she simply did not have the strength to do so. This story kept haunting her.[55]

Reaching the town of Louis Trichardt would be difficult, she was told, as there was little water along the way. It would cost her thirty pounds to get there, and this money could be better spent on food. She decided to send a wagonload of mealie-meal to the people there, as well as one to the people in the Lowveld. 'The meal is better than myself.'[56]

Good news was that the Distress Fund had deposited five hundred and sixty pounds[57] in her account. She would need every penny of that money.

Back in the Free State, it was one o'clock in the morning when Emily arrived by train from Pretoria at the station in Heilbron. There was neither a waiting room nor lamplight, but fortunately a young man, Willie Steyn, turned up after a while to take her to town in a coach in the dark.[58]

There a group of people were waiting for her at half past eight. It took all her strength to remain friendly and emphatic while listening to the most gruesome tales. She also heard about people who had taken their own lives. On top of it all, the people of Heilbron expected her to deliver a speech.

It was no joke making an encouraging speech to people who were dying from hunger and living in the ruins of their former homes. 'A Dutch audience is dreadful to speak to, for it makes neither sign nor sound to intimate its feeling. Absolute silence and bared heads and then, when over, it melts silently away. A week later they may have something to say on the matter.'

When Emily slept over at the home of an elderly couple, the Koks, in Lindley, she realised: not only had they lost everything like everyone else, they were too old to rebuild their lives. They would die in poverty, whereas they had been comfortably off before the war. 'A large poor class which never existed before is being created' she observed.[59]

On her departure from the town, she left thirty families a bag of mealie-meal each. 'We drove away from the ruins early, trying to shake the depression which hung upon the place.'[60]

As she and her driver Jasper Theron drove on, they came across a twelve-year-old girl who was riding a debilitated horse. The child stared at Emily with a motionless face.

Did they have food?

'No, we have nothing.'

Maybe not meat, but other food?

'No.'

Did they have any vegetables?

'No.'

Any bread or potatoes?

'No.'

What did they eat?

'Only mealies.'

With tear-filled eyes the child told Emily that they had very few mealies left. And they still owed money to the government for their horses.

Emily gave her the loaf of bread she had with her. A flicker of a smile passed over her face. Hugging the loaf, the girl on horseback 'trotted away over the veld, a solitary blue speck in the vast brown expanse'.[61]

Further on they came to a farm named Plezier. No one came out to receive them, not even after she had knocked.

She entered the house. There was no furniture inside, only wooden boxes, and a woman with eleven children. It was clear that they had nothing, probably no food either.

Emily did not have the heart to eat anything in this house, albeit that the food was her own. But she was so thirsty that she boiled water for herself on the fire – even that felt unfair to her. 'I hated myself afterwards to think I had made my tea at their table.'[62]

The husband had gone to look for work. One of the children took Emily by the hand to talk to her in private: We actually have nothing to eat, the child pleaded.

What about the government's rations? Apparently they had already been discontinued; the relief rations were only available for a year after the war.

Emily took the oldest boy along to a shop a few kilometres from the house. She bought food for the family and ordered more supplies of mealie-meal from Lindley. At this shop, too, Emily was swamped by destitute people.

A pregnant woman came up to her. 'We have nothing, do you understand? We have nothing.'

Although the words were spoken in Afrikaans, Emily understood better than the women realised. She gave her a shawl and some flannelette for the baby, a tin of mutton and other groceries.[63]

In Reitz, too, hungry people flocked into the town. Emily stayed at the parsonage of the Reverend Viljoen and his wife. This was where people came to request help.

The minister's wife could no longer cope with the pressure and asked Emily to assist. She saw an eleven-year-old girl who had reportedly walked more than sixteen kilometres that day without anything to eat. The child sat motionless on a stone outside the shop. Emily bought a two-penny loaf (yet it cost a whole shilling) and a tin of sausages. She fed the girl.

She fed many people that day. A nineteen-year-old woman, her eyes swimming with tears, came up to Emily. Her face was pale and tinged with blue. She tried to speak, but was so weak that Emily first had to give her some food before she could say anything.[64]

While Emily was at the Reitz parsonage, a black man came to the kitchen door looking for her. He had heard that the English 'Missis' was here to look at the destruction. This was how she met the evangelist Alexander Tschwangtwe.

To the surprise of the whites, she stood up immediately to pay a visit to the black people. Emily and Tschwangtwe walked side by side down the street; he with his long brown coat and walking stick, and Emily smartly dressed as always.[65]

She enjoyed Tschwangtwe's company, and met his wife and baby. The tiny school that had been burnt, he had rebuilt himself. A teacher was busy teaching seven children. They sang English songs for Emily. The blackboard had also been burnt, but Tschwangtwe had made a plan and painted a blackboard on one of the walls.

He told her he had been in the Harrismith concentration camp where up to fifty inmates had died per day. 'My heart aches, aches for my people,' Tschwangtwe said.[66]

That evening she was at a gathering in the school hall, where she encouraged the white people and the minister prayed. There were only four candles lighting up the room. 'I could see the hopeless look on the seamed, wrinkled faces of the men,' Emily wrote to Aunt Mary. Perhaps Emily saved some people from death that day in Reitz, perhaps not. But she certainly put new heart into them with loaves of bread and tinned sausages, bags and bags of mealie-meal, with flannelette for babies. And showed thereby that at least one person from the enemy's camp cared about them.

On the way to Frankfort and in the town itself, the conditions were no different. Again Emily supplied bags of mealie-meal but she knew that this was only a temporary solution. Could something not be done that would save people from imminent starvation and at the same time ensure food for the future she wondered.

She decided to use her influence with prominent people in England once more. As a first step, she sent a telegram to Leonard Courtney along the following lines: 'The distress is most alarming in certain districts. Get friends at home to make representations for repatriation food to recommence and continue till summer crops. People need cash to buy beyond charity. The Govt aid is imperative. Boer representations to the govt authorities have failed.'[67]

Without this aid, Emily believed, many people would not survive the winter.

Secondly, she requested help from her friends in the Cape again. Her first letter was addressed to Sir Henry de Villiers, chief justice of the Cape Colony.

What Emily did not know was that these telegrams were intercepted by the military authorities in South Africa who made sure that they ended up on Chamberlain's desk. Their codeword for Emily's messages was 'Psoriasis'.[68]

Meanwhile she had got hold of an idea, one that had apparently not occurred to any official, politician or minister of religion. What if the Boers were able to plough and plant again?

The people in England felt assured that the defeated colonies were being treated generously by the British government. Surely three million pounds was more than enough! 'Unfortunately, the press or the authorities never let England know the extent and completeness of Kitchener's destruction. In addition there was Mr Chamberlain's promise to support the widows and orphans. So of course, all was well!' Emily wrote caustically.[69]

Emily was closely watched by British military spies and her correspondence was monitored. This telegram was sent in September 1903 from London to Immanuel in Bloemfontein, the code name for Sir Hamilton Goold-Adams, Lieutenant-Governor of the Free State, to inform him of the contents of Emily's telegram to Leonard Courtney. Their code name for her messages was Psoriasis.

Document: Free State Archives Repository

Writing about the failure of the repatriation scheme as she experienced it, Emily noted that almost everywhere in the world people have difficulty in understanding each other's languages, customs and world views. The Repatriation Boards, which issued slips of paper for the food they distributed, could not understand that the Boers thought the slips were an acknowledgement of debt. Many people were so afraid of this debt – and others too proud – that they would rather die than collect some of the rations. Besides, the lack of mules and horses made it impossible for most people to get to the mealie-meal supplies in the towns.

Emily read in the *Rand Daily Mail* (29 July 1903) that only one million pounds' worth of relief supplies had been distributed, but that the related administrative costs had amounted to one-and-a-half million![70]

'Above all the psychological condition of the people was never taken into account,' she wrote later. 'The trauma of seeing your house and possessions going up in flames . . . your sheep, cattle, pigs slaughtered in front of your eyes . . . the hunger, diseases, exposure and deaths in the camps. And when peace came at last, there was nothing left to return to.'[71]

After her return to Pretoria, Emily visited the new orphanage in the Johannesburg suburb of Langlaagte that Abraham Kriel had opened in September the year before. It already housed two hundred and fifty children who had been orphaned by the war. There she was told that the female teachers who were sent out from England were very unpopular among the Afrikaners, who had started establishing their own Christian-National schools.

On 16 August, under the headline 'Widespread distress', the *South African News* published an urgent appeal in which Emily requested donations from the Cape colonists to aid the Boers.

The idea that had been simmering in Emily's mind for weeks had suddenly taken on a concrete form: the farmers had to plough and plant so that they could maintain themselves! But they lacked the means to do this. Ploughing teams were the solution, Emily had realised in a flash. Oxen! Mules! Even donkeys. That would move through each district in teams and plough where rain had fallen.

She had already made sums: one team would cost between £100 and £120. To start with, a team for every district. The local minister would be in charge of the arrangements (and would probably also have to keep the peace).

After giving an account of how thousands of people in the country districts were wasting away from starvation, she asked: 'How can it be otherwise? Lord Kitchener's work was done so well that the land was swept bare as the seashore.'[72] This was the aftermath of the war and the failed food relief scheme. 'Who is going to help? There is no doubt the government must feed the people and feed them freely.'

Emily set out the whole plan in her appeal in the paper. Donors could send money to her for the ploughing project – to the Standard Bank in Pretoria.

Before long, the Cape colonists had contributed two thousand pounds. It came just in time, as she was almost out of funds and wherever she went there were starving people. But she made sure that she kept some of the money in reserve to fund the ploughing plan.

Emily's journey continued. The farmer who drove Emily around in Klerksdorp and Hartebeestfontein had four fat mules. These were the first fat animals she had come across, but this was just because the farmer had chased them into the hills during the war and by a miracle they had survived there unharmed.[73]

At a farmhouse Emily shared her cheese and bread with a woman and four hungry little boys. At the next farm she gave her 'Boer biscuit' to a widow and her children. Another woman had only two pumpkins in her house, but 'they will never ask for anything'. 'The hungry look in these people's eyes speaks for itself . . . The black people are in as sore straits . . . those who were true to the Boers come back to the land and are suffering just as the Boers suffer.'[74]

At Klerksdorp a small reception had been arranged for Emily. A young girl presented a gift that her father, a jeweller, had made: one half of a Kruger pound in the form of a brooch. That evening, 22 August 1903, Emily delivered a speech in the church hall where she said:

Sorrow draws individuals together. And that is why studying your people, I made friends with them, for then I learnt the noble character they have developed which is of a far greater value than the gold in your country.

I came back to South Africa to renew my acquaintance with your people, for whom I have great sympathy. I have now been from ruin to ruin and from stable to stable, and I can state that I have eaten and slept with the people . . .

We in the towns have no idea how it is getting on outside. These people can't suffer any longer.

Good is born out of evil – that good is the completeness of character. But suffering can sometimes last too long, when the spirit lacks and becomes weak and then all is lost.

We can't forget the suffering. Those who live in happiness have to help in these dark days. When life lasts there is hope and it is our duty to cheer them up and maintain hope.

For those in the far outlying districts the English people at home have collected money and given me to distribute, and this is the reason I am passing through your town. This was an unlooked for and hearty welcome.[75]

On her return to Johannesburg, she heard that the papers were again calling her a 'hysterical woman' for claiming that there was distress in the country. Captain C. A. Madge, an inspector from the Repatriation Department, said it was totally untrue that these boards were incompetent, and that all was well. If Miss Hobhouse had come across any people who were suffering hardship, she should have brought it exclusively to the attention of the British government.[76] She was further attacked in an editorial in the *Transvaal Leader*: 'Miss Hobhouse's past record, the manifest absurdities of her statements about ploughing, the anti-British suggestions and omissions of her letter drives us reluctantly to the conclusion that mischief, not mercy, is the motive of her action.'[77]

Emily challenged the paper to prove that anything she had written about the concentration camps had been inaccurate. 'To call a woman "hysterical" because you have not the knowledge necessary to deny her facts is the last refuge of the unmanly and the coward. I always felt when termed "hysterical" that I had triumphed because it meant my arguments cannot be met nor my statements denied.'

Hartebeestfontein was where Emily met Alie Badenhorst. Emily described Alie as small, fragile and sadly invalided, but a woman with force of character and rare spiritual. She was to translate and publish Alie's account of her detention in the Klerksdorp concentration camp. By the time the diary was published as *Tant' Alie of Transvaal* in 1922, Alie had passed away. The impression she made on Emily was one 'that has never faded'.

In Pretoria Emily received a note from Patrick Duncan, the colonial treasurer of the Transvaal and head of the Repatriation Department, who wanted to meet her after all the reports about distress and suffering. She seized the opportunity to speak to him in his office and informed him of everything she had seen. They talked for two hours. Once again she pleaded with the British authorities on behalf of the Boers and the black people, interceding for people who were not her compatriots but for whom she had great compassion.

What had become of Chamberlain's promise of aid to the widows, she enquired. Duncan showed her that 930 women in the Transvaal had applied for these grants, but only 86 of them had received the full grant, probably because many applications had been incomplete. Emily wrote immediately to the ministers in these districts so that they could address the matter. The widows were supposed to receive a cow and a calf, three months' rations, ten pounds worth of wood and iron for a house, five pounds worth of pheasants or cash, as well as seed and having ten acres ploughed.[78]

Duncan assured her that seventy thousand pounds had been spent on the widows' scheme. Emily made her own sums: if eighty-six widows had received these goods at market prices, the total amounted to £3096. She knew because she bought supplies on a regular basis.

Where had the rest of the money gone? It had been swallowed up by salaries and corruption, she believed.[79]

She asked Duncan, if they wanted to help people permanently, why did they not buy teams of oxen to plough the fields? Until that could be done, the pack stores with the rations should be reopened, but it needed to be explained to the people that the food was free and that the slips they issued merely served as a book-keeping measure.

Duncan listened sympathetically to Emily and requested her to send him recommendations for the improvement of the repatriation scheme in writing, which she did. One of her suggestions was that ministers and church deacons be appointed to the relief committees, as they knew where the greatest need was and their involvement would win the Boers' trust.[80]

Duncan liked the ploughing-team plan, and asked her to send him cost estimations. She had already collected two thousand seven hundred pounds for this purpose; former president Paul Kruger, too, had sent fifty pounds. Emily calculated carefully what it would cost to run the ploughing plan: the wages and rations for black workers, the ploughs, feed for the animals and seed.

Her plan was to help the farmers get back on their feet for the first season or two by providing them with what they needed in order to plough and plant. Thereafter they ought to be able to sustain themselves; it was far better to teach people how to sustain themselves than to just keep doling out rations, she believed.[81]

Emily's calculation of the cost of sending ploughing teams
to the farms. It included workers' wages as well as
food for the people and feed for the animals.

Photo: Emily's scrapbook, courtesy of Jennifer Hobhouse Balme

On Sunday 6 September 1903 Emily was in Pretoria, attending the baptism of the baby daughter of Commandant A. H. Malan and his wife. Emily was the godmother of the baby, who was named after her. A few days earlier she had been intercepted by a woman who wanted to tell her that her granddaughter, too, carried the name Emily Hobhouse. 'So you see, I am multiplying,' Emily wrote to her sister-in-law Nora Hobhouse.[82]

Little Emily was a 'peace baby', one of fifty who were being baptised that day. 'We godparents were harangued and at a given point we all bowed our heads in acquiescence, I suppose, but I did not, not having had it explained. And then the mothers departed, returning from the vestry with a variety of screaming babies. Fortunately for the minister the father presented him in every case with the name written on paper, for most babies had three names.'[83] One baby was named Lemmer Gravit Spruyt after three of the Boer generals.

A week after her discussion with Duncan, he wrote to Emily to inform her of what had been done: orders had been given that rations would be resumed to those Boers who were the most destitute. This decision would be announced in the local newspapers.[84] The pack stores with food supplies would remain open until the end of March 1904.

Finally it seemed as if the colonial authorities in South Africa were taking Emily's work and her pleas seriously. Despite the suspicion cast on her as an individual and on her information over the years, she had managed to get the inflexible and unwieldy British bureaucracy moving.

The Western Transvaal was Emily's next destination. At Lichtenburg it was so dry that she crossed the Harts River without realising that it was a river. The area was in the grip of a terrible drought and the wind blew clouds of dust into the air.

At General Koos de la Rey's farm, where she stopped, only rubble indicated where the destroyed farmhouse had stood. 'We poked aside the rubbish with my parasol and found the outline of the foundations – seventy-five by forty-five feet. It feels so dreadful.'[85]

De la Rey's wife, Nonnie, could still not talk about the events. She cried constantly. He sat on the stoep of their townhouse in Lichtenburg where people would come to see him, come to talk about what they had lost.

Schweizer-Reneke seemed to Emily like a miniature Sahara. On the way to the town she and her companions travelled for about fifty-five kilometres without finding a drop of water for the mules. Only the parsonage had been rebuilt. The town consisted of tents, ruins and shanties. There were 420 destitute families, the minister told her. She wrote:

> I have seen case after case today and am sending full details up to Pretoria. These poor women in shanties – clean neat respectable people – are struggling along with several children. And Chamberlain I suppose has never given them another thought . . .
>
> Now the government is behaving like an angel towards me just to stop my mouth too, and it is amusing that they send wires down to wake the Repatriation [Board] where I go.[86]

Emily had 'the ploughing of the Transvaal' on her mind and waited anxiously for rain. Her plan started taking shape. She bought a team of oxen in the town, at sixteen pounds ten shillings a head. The people here had already decided to plough the best fields and divide the harvest among them instead of sending the oxen from farm to farm.

In Wolmaransstad she purchased more oxen. She wrote delightedly to her aunt that she had now received so much money from friends in the Cape that she would be able to get almost all the distressed districts ploughing – 'that softens their feelings [towards England] and gives them a measure of hope.'

If only it would rain.

'Famine for black and white is threatening, the young wheat is withering and full of blight, and the drought continues so the mealie crops cannot yet be put in. Everything depends on rain and that tarries . . . will it come or won't it? I am sending food to some blacks, they need it sorely.'[87]

After a brief repose in Pretoria Emily departed for Kroonstad, where she arrived at half past five in the morning on 30 September. A small crowd had already assembled at the station to meet her and tell her about their problems without delay. One of the complaints was that nothing was being done for the widows.

The distress of the black people did not escape her attention. 'The natives are perplexing me much, many of them are starving all over the country.' The missionaries, too, pleaded with her for food for their parishioners. About eleven thousand black people had flocked to Kroonstad because there was no work for them on the farms.[88]

At Ventersburg it was tragic to see how the wheat and oats that had been planted were withering. The coming Sunday had been declared a prayer day for rain by the government. Emily lost her voice from all the talking, much of it aimed at cheering up despondent people.

The seed Emily had sent to the district was of a high quality,

The inside of a church in Ventersburg destroyed by
British troops as part of the scorched-earth policy.

Photo: Anglo-Boer War Museum

a grateful Reverend Snijman told her. It had sprouted well, but
now there was nothing left because of the drought.

It was an ordeal for her to see all the burnt houses with their
'gaping mouths and staring eyes'. But she also saw the first farmhouse that had been rebuilt. It was an uplifting sight, and she got
some idea of how the people used to live on the farms and what
life had been like before the war.

Unlike previous occasions, her visit to the Fichardt home in
Bloemfontein was a sad one. Her good friend Caroline had died
while Emily was on her extensive journey through the Free State
and the Transvaal. Caroline had been one of her first friends in
the Free State and a real pillar of strength.

On 5 October she received a letter from her friend Jan Smuts in which he confirmed that nothing was being done for the widows. He did not expect anything from the government either because 'their point of view is wrong, their vision, I think, blurred by the recent past'.[89]

The more than five months of travelling on hundreds of miles of bumpy dust roads had exhausted Emily to the limit. She felt that she could not stand the sun, wind and dust a day longer. Her body could no longer endure the jolting of the 'Cape-cart'.

During the period of almost half a year that she had travelled through the country, she had spent only £112 on herself.[90] She did not buy a single item of clothing for herself – despite having lost her fur coat at the station in Pretoria.

It was time to return to the Cape, but she could look back on much that had been achieved. Her appeal in the South African News had raised more than five thousand pounds for the plough-ing plan, as well as to provide food and clothing. She had organ-ised the ploughing in most districts and supplied oxen, ploughs, seed and yokes.

More good news was that it had started raining in parts of the Transvaal and that the farmers were ploughing . . .

Within hours of alighting from the train in Paarl in the Cape, on 25 October 1903, Emily became profoundly aware of the contrast between the luxuriant, green Boland and the scorched, barren interior: 'The country behind me lay like a corpse and here one found life, growth and verdure.' Not only the landscape and climate were totally different, but also the mood of the Bolanders, who had not been affected directly by the war.

It was only when the stress of her travels and what she had experienced started diminishing that she realised how drained she actually was. 'I feel as if I lived through ten years, the work and experience have been tremendous. I like best meeting the *kerkraads* [church councils] – the very pith and backbone of the country. Fine men who got up and sung the Old Hundredth over me, and make wonderful and eloquent Dutch speeches, and nod their heads in grave acquiescence when I discourse to them about ploughs and teams.'[91]

To rest her mind and body, Emily went to stay with J. W. Sauer, a well-known Cape politician, and his wife Mary on their beautiful farm Uitkijk near Stellenbosch. She had met the couple during her first visit to South Africa two years earlier, and they had become good friends. (Mary was a daughter of Hendrik Cloete of the historic wine farm Groot Constantia.)

Sauer teased Emily about all her luggage that included packets, bags and cases, plus a sleeping bag, a fold-up camp bed, food for herself and as much food for other people as she could transport.

From Chief Justice De Villiers and his wife in Wynberg she received the good news that the 'ploughing account' now stood at seven thousand pounds thanks to her Cape friends and the *Manchester Guardian*, which had donated a thousand pounds. Other good news was that the ploughing teams were operating in areas where the drought had been broken. And the colonial government had actually bought into her plan; they had sent five ploughing teams to one district. By 17 November, thirty of Emily's ploughing teams were at work in almost as many districts. At Reitz in the Free State, where the drought had been so severe, ploughing had already been done for twenty-three families.[92]

Less good news was that Uncle Arthur was not well, and Emily sensed that her aunt wanted her to be at her side. She realised that she had to go to England, but first there were final arrangements to be made with regard to the ploughing teams. And there was also the money that been collected that could not be left to lie idle in the bank.

One day the farmers of Tulbagh witnessed something that was not only strange to them but also unprecedented. At a cattle auction, a stately English lady bid for the oxen and dairy cows that went under the hammer. Moreover, she had an eye for the best and most productive animals. When they heard who the mysterious woman was – the only one among all the men – and for whom the *geleerde diere* (trained animals) were intended, the farmers stopped bidding.

Emily bought another six oxen from Sauer and despatched them in two rail trucks to the north; a worker accompanied them, along with water and feed.[93]

She also saw to it that Patrick Duncan honoured his promises[94] and impressed on him that while more people's grants were being approved, they had not yet received them. The sum of seventy thousand pounds he had mentioned might also have been approved on paper, but little of that had reached the widows, she reminded him.

To ensure that the ploughing project did not peter out, Emily sent a letter to the ministers and church councils of the Dutch Reformed Church in every town in the Transvaal and the Free State. She informed them that she would soon return to England and could therefore do nothing more for the moment to assist those in distress. She trusted 'that the machinery is in better working order whereby relief shall be attainable for those in need of actual food . . .' She also expressed the hope that, thanks to the kind-heartedness of the Cape colonists, large-scale ploughing and planting would take place. She brought it to the attention of these community leaders that the government's pack stores with food had been reopened, and requested that they explain the provisions of the widows' scheme clearly to their communities. 'Thus no one need to be without some food.'

The church leaders should see to it that the government's paper promises were kept. 'A policy of gentle but firm insistence and persistence may bring about much improvement.'[95]

The news that Emily was due to return to England had also reached Jan Smuts. In a poignant letter to her he wrote:

My dear Miss Hobhouse, And so you are leaving us with our distress and despair and leaving behind a void which no one can fill – a void filled only by the memory of your good works and unselfish devotion.

If we could have you for ever among us, to bind the wounds which even time could scarcely heal, to be our priestess of suffering and sacrifice, how many more happy hearts there would be in this land of sorrows, how we would look up to you and give you that which is sweetest to the human heart, which no other people on earth would give you.[96]

Early in November the Dutch Reformed Church invited Emily to address their synod in the Hofmeyr Hall in Cape Town. So many distinguished people attended this event that their names would be too many to list, a newspaper reported.

'Thundering applause' greeted Emily on her arrival in the hall that was decked out in green and orange. On introducing her to the audience, the Reverend Adriaan Moorrees said that when all had been dark in the country, 'Miss Hobhouse' had appeared like a ray of light. There was no way in which she could be compensated for her work, but her name was 'deeply engraved in the heart of our nation'.

When she stood up to talk, a storm of applause erupted once more. She told the audience about the distress and poverty she had witnessed in the Free State and the Transvaal, but noted that this was being denied by the press, politicians and even governors. She spoke in detail about the repatriation problems and what the church leaders could do to ensure that the project was implemented more effectively.

She pointed out to her audience that many British people abhorred what England had done to the two former Boer republics, and these Britons had worked hard to prevent the evil in South Africa. She knew that it was now expected of the defeated burghers to forgive and to forget.

'I crave your forgiveness. No adequate reparation can we make, only we should be humbly grateful if you could accept as a token of our sorrow and our shame such small sacrifices as we have here and there made. Forget you never can. These things are laid by as sacred memories in your hearts. But I ask it of you here and now – forgive us if you can.'[97]

At the end of the proceedings the audience sang the hymn 'Laat Heer U seën op haar daal' ('Lord, may your blessing descend on her') to Emily. The atmosphere was charged with emotion as the synod took their leave.

Two days later, before sunrise, Emily, Anna Purcell and her husband William, an arachnologist and zoologist, set off to climb Table Mountain. The climb was more arduous than Emily had expected. It was very hot from early on and the rocks burned her hands, but to her it was the realisation of a dream. The beauty of the vegetation, the clear air, the blue-green sea and the view compensated abundantly for the exertion. So often had she admired this mountain and written about it in letters, even painted it, and now she had ascended it for the first time.

Just as she was about to leave for England, a letter from Smuts arrived. He, too, had bought a team of oxen, at £180, and spent £20 on seed with which a large area along the Apies River had been planted. Fortunately the area had had good rainfall.

And on the issue of the importation of Chinese labour that was a hot topic, Smuts said: 'The Chinese are almost certainly coming and their advent will be the beginning of a fresh chapter of disasters for this benighted country.'[98]

Emily agreed with Smuts, and this news reinforced her distrust of politicians. As someone who 'had been brought up to gaze with awe on all those in high places and never to question the wisdom of those in authority',[99] her experiences in the concentration camps, the lies of politicians and generals, her arrest and deportation, and the broken promises regarding the compensation of war victims had left her deeply disillusioned.

In spite of that, she again saw other possibilities that had not yet been exploited. She wrote later, 'These experiences were mainly responsible for my ardent support for the Suffragist movement. I hoped that women might bring higher and purer standards into public life, less personal ambition . . .'[100]

10

The Smuts letter blunder

'You think it is bad to be an Afrikander at this moment –
believe me it is far worse to be an English person. Your defeat
is material, ours is moral.'[1]

– Emily Hobhouse to General Jan Smuts, 1903

Wherever Emily went, the sorrows and joys of South Africa
followed her like a shadow. Or was it rather that she could not –
or would not – shake off the dust from her feet?

After a period in London, during which she got her next project
organised, she was on her way to Venice, but first travelled to
Cannes in France to visit her good friend Tibbie Steyn. From there
she took a trip to Menton on the French Riviera to visit none other
than Paul Kruger, former president of the Zuid-Afrikaansche
Republiek. He had left the country during the war and refused to
return after the conclusion of peace, partly because he did not want
to be a British subject and partly because he believed he could
achieve more abroad to help his compatriots than at home.

At the villa where he stayed, Emily stood in the passage and saw the elderly old president as he sat reading at a table. He was dressed in black. Next to him was another, smaller table on which a big Bible lay. It was a sombre picture. He was so engrossed in his reading that he failed to notice Emily. She was reluctant to disturb him, but his secretary told her to approach him.

It was the first time that the two of them had met. The conversation did not last long, as she could see that 'his mind was elsewhere and that the world ended for him'.[2] Glancing back as she walked out, she saw that he sat reading the Bible. He 'belonged so clearly to another age'.[3]

Shortly before Easter 1904 Emily sailed into Venice on a gondola. She was here to learn the art of lacemaking from Lady Layard, of whom she had heard in London.

The observant Emily had noticed four things about the Boer women and girls: that they had abundant time on their hands after the war; that they had no means of occupation in their ruined homes; that they 'had skill with the needle'; and that they 'cling to home and family life'.[4]

Even before her departure from the country she had connected all these elements and conceived another ingenious plan: home industries where the women could make items from lace. It was an art form and skill that could be a source of income for the young women in South Africa in particular. But first she had to master the craft herself. After lessons from Lady Layard, Emily travelled to Brussels, as the Belgians were famous for their lacemaking. She made notes of everything she could learn about lacemaking there.

In the course of her peregrinations Emily met Alice Stopford Green, widow of the Irish historian J. R. Green, who invited her to visit Ireland to see how the established home industries were run there. Emily needed no second invitation!

Alice showed Emily around Ireland and introduced her to many people. As a result of her visit she became convinced that spinning and weaving would be a better option than lace in the South African conditions. It was Alice who pointed out that lace items were more of a luxury that only affluent people would buy – and there were not many of them left after the war. Besides, wool was readily available in South Africa and essential for spinning and weaving.

Even before Emily's forced departure from South Africa at the end of 1901, the possible importation of Chinese to work in the gold and diamond mines had become a contentious political issue. In Britain, too, the envisaged scheme became a controversy in public debate. The Colonial Office under Chamberlain's successor Alfred Lyttelton had had legislation passed that allowed for the importation of indentured Chinese labour. From 1904 about sixty-two thousand indentured Chinese came to South Africa; the gold production more than doubled between 1903 and 1907.[5]

The Liberals in Britain were of the view that this was nothing other than slavery, as the Chinese would have to work long hours under poor conditions. As in the case of most matters that concerned South Africa or its people, Emily could not stay out of the fray. At a meeting in Westminster, Emily and others such as Leonard Courtney and Sir Charles Dilke came out strongly against the 'Chinese slavery'.

She wrote to Smuts that he might be making a mistake by not coming to England to fight the Chinese labour issue there.[6]

Smuts wrote back with much on his mind to share with her.[7] He was extremely upset because Milner had 'represented the majority of the Boers as in favour of the Chinese or, at any rate,

General Jan Smuts.

Photo: Anglo-Boer War Museum

as quite apathetic'. It was no doubt true that a large proportion of the Boers were apathetic, 'but these are the people who have lost all hope and heart,' Smuts wrote.

'For beneath this apathy there burns in the Boer mind a fierce indignation against this sacrilege of Chinese importation – this spoliation of the heritage for which generations of the people have sacrificed their all . . .' The cheap Chinese labour would deny jobs to the local people still in despair after thirty thousand of their farms were burnt down. 'I sometimes ask myself whether South Africa will ever rise again, whether English statesmen will ever dare to be liberal and generous in South Africa . . .

'We think that government must be for the greatest good of the greatest number; they think that the mining industry must be saved at all costs. And it cannot and will not be saved, for the major part of it is bogus and a sham.'[8]

If all the mines that had no chance of survival – in his opinion, about 80 per cent of them – were to be declared bankrupt, there would be quite sufficient labour in South Africa to run the other 20 per cent at a profit.

About the English statesmen he was equally outspoken: 'South Africa they regard with unconcealed contempt – a black man's country, good enough to make money or a name in it, but not good enough to be born or die in. What is there in common between such people and the Boers, the fibres of whose very soul are made of this despised soil?'[9]

And about two English leadership figures in South Africa, he wrote: 'When this reaches you Dr Jameson . . . will be Premier of Cape Colony and Lord Milner's heart will be thumping with holy joy. For he has dreamed a dream of a British South Africa – loyal with broken English and happy with a broken heart and he sees the dream is coming true . . .

'Today they are imploringly stretching forth their hands to the Boers to save them from the consequences of their evil work in the past.'[10]

These observations were certainly not meant for the eyes of Milner, Jameson and other imperialists. They were music to Emily's ears, however, and she was itching to publicise the letter more widely. She evidently had doubts about the advisability of such a course, but 'after consultation with legal and sympathetic minds we decided that with a few eliminated sentences it could do no harm, and the moment is so crucial, so intense, that immense good might be done'.[11] She sent Smuts's letter for publication to *The Times*, one of her greatest press critics.

In the meantime, Emily and Smuts continued corresponding about quite personal and emotional matters. In the above-mentioned letter to Emily, Smuts had also confessed that he no longer knew what role he could play in the country in the current circumstances. 'Hence, I prefer to sit still, to water my orange trees and to study Kant's Critical Philosophy until, in the whirligig of time, new openings for doing good offer themselves.' Emily was not impressed at all by this attitude. How dare he, a leader of stature, sit still and water trees at a time that his country needed him desperately!

'You think it is bad to be an Afrikander at this moment – believe me it is far worse to be an English person. Your defeat is material, ours is moral.'[12]

Yet she understood his feelings because she still remembered well how it had felt all those years that she had been alone in St Ive and had looked after her father; when she had dreamt about what could be and what ought to be, yet the opportunities to realise her dreams had been out of reach. So many years had passed.[13]

She tried to give Smuts insight into the role he could play: 'to be the tongue for your people'. There was no one else on the entire continent who could do this better than him. Only he, and maybe Olive Schreiner, had the ability to express the South Africans' sentiments eloquently, she encouraged him.

Smuts sent her newspaper cuttings that showed how the government was wasting money, how bad the maladministration was. If the government in Britain did not change soon, it might be too late. A big meeting was due to be held on the Witwatersrand to inform the white workers about their new Chinese competitors. Did she think that if the Liberal Party won the next election, they would scrap the decision about the Chinese labourers? 'If they don't, God alone help us.'[14] It sounded as if Smuts had sunk into the Slough of Despond: 'To scream or to make a noise, even resolutely to agitate, is not my line. South Africa is on the downward grade in every sense, and at present I see not a ray of light in the future. The whole country reminds me of that gloomy line in Keats in which he speaks of the "weariness, the fever, and the fret / Here, where men sit and hear each other groan".'[15]

Emily obtained an audience with Alfred Lyttelton, the colonial secretary. The first item on her agenda was that, a year after the conclusion of peace, most of the widows had still not received any of the promised aid. Did the government know that many of them had even been affluent before, but were now impoverished?

After having told him again about the enormous need she had found in the Free State and the Transvaal, she came to this inevitable conclusion: people did not care how much they spent on a war, but for peace and reconciliation it was hard to squeeze money out of any government.[16]

Meanwhile *The Times* had published Smuts's scathing letter about the English statesmen that had only been intended for Emily and her friends. Smuts was evidently upset about this breach of confidentiality and immediately sent a telegram in which he asked her not to publish any other letters of his. Milner was surely delighted about this because it confirmed that he, Smuts, was an irreconcilable opponent. Smuts feared that he would now have to fight for his political life.[17]

Emily was only partly sorry that Smuts regretted the publication of the letter. 'I am deeply, deeply sorry if I have really vexed or injured you . . . And yet I can't feel sorry that it is published. You really are good to write your disapproval without one word of scolding . . . Still I trust no real harm is done, and if it has made you cross the Rubicon so much the better I think.'[18]

Smuts replied somewhat melancholically that people differed so much from each other: he preferred peace and quiet – 'ever since the war I have been in this mood of ennui . . . whereas you seem to be made for battle'. If she had been an 'Afrikander' and had experienced the war in its entirety, he wondered whether she would still have had fighting power left.[19]

It was not in Emily's philosophical nature to let such a comment go by without a response.

'The consciousness of power, the sense of justice and the impossibility of composure when one knows things are going wrong, would not allow you to rest in rural peace . . . I suppose we have to accept the disadvantages of our powers as well as their advantages and amongst those disadvantages are to be reckoned, a long strife against evil in its endless forms – a hydra-headed monster – and the inability to share the rest that lesser folk enjoy until one's very last scrap of fighting power is exhausted.'[20]

During this time Emily went to stay with her Uncle Arthur and Aunt Mary, Lord and Lady Hobhouse, who had rented a house in Oxfordshire for the summer. In 1885 Lord Hobhouse had accepted the title of Baron Hobhouse of Hadspen in Somerset with a view to assisting in the judicial work of the House of Lords. He and his wife were childless, and they had been part of the lives of Emily and her siblings since their childhood. He was also a member of the Judicial Committee of the Privy Council, the highest court of appeal in the British Empire.[21]

The couple, both open-minded Liberals, had been Emily's lifeline during the war but now in its aftermath they were both elderly. Her uncle was the one with whom Emily always discussed her ideas and plans, while it was to her aunt that she poured out her heart in letters.

Mary, Lady Hobhouse (née Farrar), who was like a mother to
Emily, as well as a rock and a sounding board.

Photo: Courtesy of Jennifer Hobhouse Balme

Now they were enjoying the summer garden and the birds in
Oxfordshire. Emily sat practising her lace stitches in the garden
and wished she had taken up lacemaking at an earlier age. She
and her uncle and his little dog Meg went for long conversation-
filled walks.

The Distress Fund – with Lady Ripon, wife of the Marquess of
Ripon, as its chair – decided it was time that they demonstrated
their appreciation of Emily and her work, and they organised a
function on 11 May 1904 in honour of her on behalf of all the
subscribers and supporters of the committee.

Emily had been invited 'to have tea with friends', and money
had been forwarded to her with the instruction that she should

Arthur, Lord Hobhouse, Emily's beloved
uncle and her father's youngest brother.

Photo: Courtesy of Jennifer Hobhouse Balme

buy an article made of beautiful Venetian lace as a gift for one of
the members and bring it along to the tea party.[22]

After Emily's lease for the flat in Chelsea expired, she had moved
in with her beloved uncle and aunt in their house in Bruton Street
in Mayfair, London.[23] It was a short trip from there to the Courtneys'
home in Cheyne Walk, Chelsea. She was surprised to discover that
the event was in her honour. The Bishop of Hereford, John Percival,
and Lord Ripon were among the guests and delivered speeches in
the packed living room. Prominent Liberals such as Sir Henry
Campbell-Bannerman, Earl Spencer (great-grandfather of Diana,
Princess of Wales) and John Morley had sent messages of greeting.

The necklace given to Emily by the South African
Women and Children Distress Fund. It was created by
Charles Ashbee and is now in a private collection.
Photo: Private collection

The women presented Emily with a letter of appreciation and
admiration, a beautiful piece of Venetian lace (the very one that the
unsuspecting Emily had brought along), a small silver container,
£420 and a stunning necklace.[24] It was made by the famous designer
Charles Ashbee and consisted of very delicate gold filigree and semi-
precious stones: brown spinels, orange jacinths and green peridots.

***

One morning in March 2015 I was able to see the exceptional necklace in a private collection in Britain, along with the letter and the invitation that were sent to the subscribers of the fund.

It lies in a small, silk-lined jewellery box on which the mark of Ashbee and the words 'Guild of Handicraft – Bond Street' are imprinted. Inside is a card that describes what the necklace consists of. The box was specially made for this necklace because each part fits into its correct place. Everything has been preserved meticulously.

An accompanying note written by Lady Courtney states that Emily thanked the people with 'modest sincerity' on that day.

I took the necklace from the box with great care, held it for a while and examined the fine gold and the stones close up. How beautiful it must have looked around Emily's neck![25]

***

Emily was forty-four. She assumed that she could only work actively for about five more years. The time had come to start thinking of a place to stay in her old age. She considered buying a house somewhere, but it was not obvious to her where this house should be. 'If sickness or trouble come, here [in England] are those whom I have a right to turn to for help, while the mental and soul side of me finds no life here and turns to the country and people with whom I have been so strangely linked.'

But of one thing she was sure: 'I cannot go on living this dual life with my body in England and my mind in South Africa. I must cut myself free on one side or the other.'[26]

She asked Smuts what he thought of the idea of having a cottage built for herself in South Africa. He wondered whether it would be wise to uproot herself at this stage of her life. As one grows older, it may be better to stay where one has grown up, he replied.

Maybe she would be happier in England than in South Africa because the latter was an 'evil country'.[27] His best friends viewed it with increasing concern about the future because they believed that conflict would be part of it.

Early in October, returning from Somerset with Uncle Arthur and Aunt Mary, Emily stopped over for a day in Street at the Clarks, a Quaker family and owners of the well-known shoe company. They had asked her to address a meeting, which was where she met Margaret Clark,[28] a woman eighteen years her junior. Margaret had heard Emily speak at a meeting two years before and had been bowled over.

When she took Emily to the station, she mentioned that she would like to assist Emily in her work.

'Even in South Africa?'

'Even in South Africa,' Margaret replied.

The next day Emily wrote to her and provided more details of her plan to establish home industries in South Africa.

She also wrote to Smuts that she wanted to teach young girls in the country districts spinning and weaving. Because her money was limited, it would have to be started in only one district at first, from where it could expand. Later she could consider lacemaking too. She saw such home industries as a continuation of the ploughing teams work.

A condition was that she wanted to remain completely independent and not stay in other people's homes. She was even prepared to bring along tents in which to stay. Once a house was available and affordable, the tents could become the classrooms. Another requirement was that she had to be reasonably close to a railway line.[29]

In the meantime she sent spinning wheels she had had made in England ahead to South Africa.[30] 'I feel inspired to try and make one district "blossom like a rose" and then other people can take up other districts and do likewise.'[31]

Margaret Clark, who came with Emily to South Africa in 1905 to
establish the first weaving school. Here she is with her husband
Arthur Gillett on her wedding day in 1909.

In November the South African Women and Children Distress Fund
held its very last meeting, at the Courtneys' house. In light of the new
circumstances after the war, as well as Emily's new plans, the Distress
Fund had reached the end of the road. Its name would be changed to
support her new work: the Boer Home Industries and Aid Society,[32]
which was the start of the spinning and weaving schools in South Africa.
From now on Emily would work under this name and organisation.

There was an amount of eleven hundred pounds left in the
fund that could be used to good effect in South Africa.

Even the indomitable Emily experienced moments of doubt: 'I
wonder what will come of it all – if we shall succeed or only failure shall result.'[33]

Emily's notes about the money of the South African
Women and Children Distress Fund, which was passed
on to the new Boer Home Industries and Aid Society
after the Distress Funds dissolution in August 1904.

Photo: Free State Archives Repository

On the eve of her new project, just when Emily was most in
need of encouragement, she received a letter from the poet
William Watson that made her feel as if 'on wings I floated all
day'. He wrote: 'To you chiefly our country owes it that the most
lamentable and most tragic phase of the late war was arrested ere
its full consummation, and the English people of the future will
be as grateful to you as the Boer people of the present have reason
to be. Now that you are going among them once again, your great

influence will, I am sure, make for the reconcilement, if such a thing is possible.'[34,35]

But a heavy personal blow was also imminent. Early in December 1904 her beloved eighty-five-year-old Uncle Arthur died, and it rested on Emily's shoulders to support her aunt. 'It was hard to creep into her room that dark winter morn and break to her that the end was near, and together we stayed with him till all was over and I led her back to rest.'[36]

It was a tremendous loss for Emily and Aunt Mary. The couple had been married for fifty-six years and had rarely spent any time apart. Never before had a death affected Emily so deeply. They had been her spiritual parents since she was six years old.

Lord Hobhouse was cremated – an uncommon practice in those days – and the funeral service was held in St Margaret's Church in Westminster. Lady Hobhouse was too devastated to attend the service, but Emily represented her. At her side was her cousin Henry Hobhouse V, the Hobhouse heir and owner of the family mansion and estate Hadspen in Somerset.[37,38]

Emily found it unbearable that she would have to leave Aunt Mary on her own if she continued with her spinning-and-weaving plan. She was torn between these choices and considered staying for the time being, as her aunt was weak and frequently short of breath to boot. But Aunt Mary convinced Emily that she had come to terms with her loss and that Emily had to leave because that which she was going to do was 'good and right'.

As they said farewell, Aunt Mary opened her arms wide and they embraced closely – like a mother and daughter.[39]

'We both found it hard – physically because a lump rises in my throat which actually prevents speech . . .'[40]

'Goodbye, my darling,' were Aunt Mary's parting words. Both of them realised that this was the last time they would see each other.

11

Blossom like the rose

'All one can do in the face of need so great is to work in one little district with funds at one's command; and then I feel inspired to try and make one district "blossom like the rose" and then other people can take up other districts and do likewise.'

– Emily to Jan Smuts, 11 November 1904

Although Emily was not one who looked back once she had put her hand to the plough, this time she had misgivings about the prospects of her new project. She had only the eleven hundred pounds of the new Boer Home Industries and Aid Society at her disposal to establish the entire project and maintain herself. At least an additional one hundred pounds annually would be required. The *Manchester Guardian* had declined her offer to be their correspondent in South Africa.[1] 'Perhaps eggs and poultry would pay, or sometimes I wonder if I can succeed with sketches, but where to sell them?'

The woman who had looked after the needs of so many others became worried that she might not be cared for in her old age;

'the sense of money leakage makes me anxious'. When Emily, Margaret Clark and another helper, Adeline Darby, left for Antwerp in Belgium by train on 25 January 1905, Leonard Hobhouse and little Oliver – the apple of Emily's eye – were at the station to see them off, as well as Margaret's family and Leonard Courtney. To his words of encouragement, Courtney added a warning: expect many disappointments and failures.

In Antwerp, the three women boarded the *Kronprinz* for the voyage to South Africa. Among their fellow passengers were Tibbie Steyn and her husband, former president Marthinus Steyn, and D. F. Malan (who was returning from Utrecht where he had obtained a doctorate in divinity), as well as the sixteen-year-old Helen Botha, daughter of General Louis Botha, who had been educated in Brussels for the past four years.

While Emily was less enthusiastic about spinning and weaving than about lacemaking, she had accepted the advice that the former had a greater chance of success in the South African conditions. In the course of 1904 she had attended many spinning and weaving classes and had mastered these crafts. During the voyage she trained Margaret in her newly acquired skills.

Occasionally she read to Marthinus Steyn, passages from books such as Samuel Butler's *Utopia*, *Erewhon* and *Erewhon Revisited* and Charles Dickens's *David Copperfield* as well as poems by William Watson. In between Dr Malan gave the two women lessons in Dutch-Afrikaans.

Margaret suffered so badly from seasickness that she would stay in her cabin for up to twelve hours on end. Emily was sympathetic, but was concerned that without thorough preparation for the task ahead things could go awry from the start. Hence she followed a fixed routine every day: spinning, weaving, carding[2] and the 'Dutch' lessons.

Tibbie Steyn.

Photo: Anglo-Boer War Museum

Emily suspected that Adeline was not sufficiently trained in spinning and weaving, which could become a serious problem. Besides, she had injured her knee in a bad fall on the ship – would it not be better to leave her in Cape Town and send her back to England? In her diary, Emily weighed up her helper's pros and cons. She was undoubtedly a good teacher and Emily appreciated that she had 'fine qualities and a pure mind', but she doubted whether Adeline had much common sense.[3]

All these qualms gave Emily sleepless nights. She was a perfectionist who spent months working out her plans and then executed them punctiliously, but now all kinds of spokes were being put in her wheels.[4]

Margaret turned twenty-seven during the voyage, and Emily was the first to congratulate her. She spent more time than usual with Margaret and told her about her early life, particularly how she had been held back educationally on account of her sex and had to care for her father all those years. For Margaret, this was an 'extremely interesting but rather tragic and dreadful story. No expansion allowed and no knowledge of life possible, till her father died when she was about 35. It is difficult to picture what an experience that must have been, and how extraordinary to be flung so unprepared into the world as it is.'[5]

On 18 February the *Kronprinz* docked in Cape Town, where Jaap de Villiers was among the group of men (including Jan Smuts, Ewald Esselen and others) who had come to welcome the Steyn couple and Emily.

De Villiers was someone that she 'had so long desired to meet', Emily later wrote, without explanation. He was the former state attorney of the Orange Free State, and he was at that stage a successful advocate in Johannesburg.

'Mr de Villiers seemed to know me at once and came to sit down and talked to me. I felt full of strange interest in him. A man of whom I had heard so much that was good and noble . . .'

He immediately made a big impression on Emily as far as both his physical appearance and other qualities were concerned. 'I liked his face, very strong and rather rugged. With fine expression, dark grey eyes, full of feeling and of humour and a sweet smile shewing fine white teeth. In strong easy language he painted affairs in Johannesburg and the Transvaal. Words replete with feeling and intensity of purpose and complete grasp of the situation.'

She experienced him as 'a reliable man, strong and good'. She wrote in her diary, 'I wanted to see more of him, talk more to him, hear him tell more,' quite fascinated with this man who was eight years her junior.[6] In her account of this meeting in her diary, two lines were scratched out – perhaps because they revealed too much?

They stayed behind at the docks in the company of Smuts while the spinning and weaving equipment they had brought along was offloaded. Mary Sauer from the farm Uitkijk also arrived to welcome them.

At Customs, an official stopped the group's carriage and enquired: 'Which one of you ladies is Miss Hobhouse?'

Emily was startled, as the humiliating arrest of just over three years ago in this very port was still fresh in her mind. But her fears were unfounded.

'Because I want to shake hands with her,' the man said elatedly. 'I read her book and admire her.'

Before continuing their northward journey, Emily and Margaret stayed with Caroline Murray and her husband in Kenilworth, with Sir Henry de Villiers and his wife in Wynberg, and with Mary Sauer and her husband Jacobus at Uitkijk near Stellenbosch, where they met Mary's younger, unmarried sister Constance Cloete – or 'Tant Con', as she was called. They also paid visits to Anna Purcell and her husband Dr William Purcell in Bergvliet, Marie Koopmans de Wet and several other people.

Emily's destination was Philippolis in the Free State. In 1903, during her travels to organise the ploughing teams, she had met Tibbie's parents, the Reverend Colin Fraser and his wife Isabella, in Philippolis. They had given her a warm reception and encouraged her. Meanwhile Smuts, with whom she had been corresponding about the weaving school project, had recommended Klerksdorp as a location for the school, but when the residents of Philippolis offered her a house, her mind was made up.

On the evening of 27 February, Emily, Margaret and Adeline departed by train for the north, along with the Steyn couple who were travelling to Bloemfontein. A large group of people saw them off at the station.

Two days later the three women disembarked at Springfontein – with '17 crates and own baggage'. Three horse carts and the Frasers were waiting to take them to Philippolis. Moses,[7] a black man, had been brought along to lend a hand. He had just been released from prison, Emily was told, after he had stolen raisins and sugar from his employer's shop.

At Philippolis, a Jewish merchant, Moritz Liefmann, had put his unused house and shop at the women's disposal. They decided to live in the house and set up the spinning and weaving school in the adjoining shop.[8] After lunch that same afternoon, Emily started working.

In Emily's view, Moses, who now worked for her, was 'eccentric'. She decided that his offence – if it had actually been one – was of a minor nature. Another helper was Flora, a young black woman. Later the servant Maria, a young Basotho woman, joined their ranks.

Meanwhile Mrs Boshoff, a widow who was supposed to keep house for them, 'anxiously lurks around'. Before boiling an egg, she would first ask Emily which one she should use. Emily showed understanding of her frame of mind: 'She was in Bethulie camp, poor old thing, & lost her six youngest children there.'[9]

She decided that Moses had to clean everything both inside and outside the school; in a reversal of the customary practice, he was given a bell to ring when he needed her. Emily did not want him to walk around in the house, as his feet were too dirty. Still, he was worth his weight in gold to her, she wrote to Lady Charlotte Toler, who served on the Boer Home Industries and Aid Society committee.

Margaret wrote as follows about their first days in Philippolis: 'From the first afternoon of our arrival till the Saturday week following we toiled with scarcely a pause (save for the afternoon rest & this Miss Hob. seldom took completely) for there were 80 cases or more to unpack & sort out.'[10] According to her, this 'Cyclopean task' would probably have broken most people, and 'was a match for even Miss H.'s intrepid will and gallant spirit . . .'[11]

Though Emily's feet ached mercilessly from walking around all day, she also had to care for Margaret, who ended up in bed due to exhaustion. On top of that, the residents of Philippolis wanted Emily to visit them, but socialising was out of the question. Everything had to be made ready for the school that had to open its doors as soon as possible.

All these stresses and strains started to overwhelm Emily; she felt she might be in danger of collapsing. She sent a telegram to Constance Cloete and 'begged her to come to our rescue'.[12] Constance's immediate reply was: 'Yes.'

Around this time, Emily received a note from Aunt Mary 'welcoming me at Philippolis'. Her aunt also informed that her cough was 'getting worse'.[13]

The first spinning and weaving school in South Africa opened officially in Philippolis on Monday, 13 March 1905, less than two weeks after Emily and her companions had set foot in the town. At a time when virtually no new enterprises were being opened, the news of this unusual project had spread quickly. Six excited girls presented themselves promptly at eight o'clock that morning to start their lessons.

The first spinning and weaving school was opened in Philippolis
two weeks after Emily and Margaret Clark arrived in the town.

Photo: Free State Archives Repository

By half past five the next morning Emily was already at work
preparing the room that overlooked the courtyard for Constance.
Later that day there was great consternation when an enormous
snake found its way into the entrance hall. Emily, who had
returned to the house to check on the sick Margaret, walked in
just as she was trying to kill the creature with a rolled-up copy of
the *Manchester Guardian*. Realising the need for heavier weapon-
ry, Emily grabbed her Uncle Arthur's sturdy umbrella and
finished it off – just as she had attacked a snake with her parasol
in the Bloemfontein camp four years earlier.[14]

To everyone's joy, Constance arrived two days after the school
opened and took over the running of the household. It was such

Margaret Clark (right) and learners at work at the
Philippolis spinning and weaving school.

Photo: Courtesy of the Alfred Gillett Trust

a luxury that Emily was able to rest the next day. Adeline worked very slowly, which frustrated the dynamic Emily.

Most evenings before supper Emily and Margaret went for a walk right through the town. After supper Emily would read to the household, including Moses and Flora, from some or other book, sometimes poetry. Now that Constance was there, Emily taught Moses how to serve at table like a proper footman, apron and all.

On Saturdays or Sundays the women climbed the hill outside the town and wrote letters or entries in their diaries; picnics were a regular pastime.

Within two weeks the school's numbers had grown to thirteen girls, which was the limit of their capacity. The farmers supplied them with wool from their merino sheep and angora goats.[15] The women experimented with natural dyes from plants: broom reeds that gave the wool a pink colour, walnut shells for brown, and peach leaves for yellow. Experiments were also done with pomegranate, 'elands wortel', 'kriebos' and 'nuwejaarsbos' that first had to be boiled. They would stand for days boiling the wool in vats. To fix the indigo colour, they dipped the cloth in urine.

To the teachers' delight, the girls were quite intelligent, quick to learn and diligent, too. They took to the new skills like ducks to water.

To Emily it felt as if 'I am not living in Philippolis but in an idea'.[16] On 1 April the school held an open day for visitors, and many people came to inspect the girls' handiwork. The visitors

Colouring of threads at the spinning school, Philippolis.

Photo: Free State Archives Repository

were served tea and socialised with the weaving school's teachers and learners.

They were amazed at what had already been achieved and created. Emily was extremely talented in lacework, and her designs, which only she was making at that stage, were very popular. One was called 'Patience and Courage' and the other was a 'Wag-'n-bietjie-bos' pattern, inspired by the shrub of the same name, that would later become an institution. Emily was also a good teacher and organiser. The weavers at the school produced roughly woven, serviceable brown blankets.[17]

An example of the lace school's work. This collar was designed by Emily in what was known as the 'Wag-'n-Bietjie' pattern. It was inspired by the shrub of the same name. Emily called two of her other designs 'Môre is nog 'n dag' (Tomorrow is another day) and 'Geduld en Moed' (Patience and Courage).

Photo: Anglo-Boer War Museum

When Emily was sick at home for a few days, she started teaching Constance how to make lace – which made Margaret feel resentful. 'It makes me very jealous – poor me with that hateful knitting machine . . . they don't know in the least how much I care & so I am jealous.'[18]

One evening when Emily read to the group as usual, this time from Paracelsus (the philosopher, physician, botanist, astrologer and general occultist), eighteen-year-old Petronella (Nell) van Heerden came to listen. She was the daughter of the local magistrate, and had already paid several visits to the women.[19] Emily introduced her to several books, including John Stuart Mill's *Subjection of Women* and Aristotle's *Nicomachean Ethics*.

Another letter came from Aunt Mary; this time it was very short, and the handwriting was shaky. Emily seemed to sense that the umbilical cord linking her to the woman who was like a mother to her might soon be cut. Nor could she ignore the fact that she herself was now middle-aged.

If Aunt Mary were gone, Emily mused, 'I should have no regular correspondent, none to whom I ought to write or from whom I am sure of a letter.' But the possible loss of Aunt Mary was also about much more. 'In fact "Home" exists not for me and I begin to fear never will. The last days of my year are passing and on Sunday I shall be 45 and at that age one cannot hope or expect the once longed for joy for a real home ever will be given,' she wrote.

'One looks back on the long weary years of toil and travel and discomfort and one longs for a settlement and certainty of rest bodily and mental. Will my 46th year bring it? I dare hope no more.'[20]

A while later she remarked to Margaret that she was considering the possibility of settling permanently in South Africa. 'I can feel that hers is a hard time of life for a woman who is not married and who would have loved husband and babies as she would have done. I know she feels it was the one thing she wanted in life . . .' was Margaret's observation.

In a discussion she, Emily and Constance had had on these matters, Emily said she would rather be an 'ordinary man' than a 'distinguished woman' – whereby, Margaret wrote, she probably meant that more attention was paid to the words and deeds of 'ordinary men' than to those of distinguished women. Not only was it easier for these men to be 'heard', they also had more power and influence as a result – which went against the grain for Emily. Constance, who was also unmarried, had said she would rather be the wife of a distinguished man than a distinguished man. Margaret felt that life was hard for a woman without a husband and children.[21]

In between there were staff matters that caused headaches for Emily. The situation with regard to Adeline's inability to make the grade became untenable. Emily requested by telegram to London that the Boer Home Industries send a replacement. The conversation she had to have with Adeline was a difficult one; she felt 'much shaken' and her voice even failed her.[22] Fortunately Adeline admitted that she did not really like weaving, and agreed to leave as soon as her replacement arrived.

And Moses simply had to have a guitar; he was adamant. Eventually he got his way because, according to Margaret, Emily had a 'great weakness' for him.[23] But there was a condition: while he could play the guitar to his heart's content, it remained Emily's property. Moses had a good ear for music and learnt to play by ear. In the evenings Emily taught him to play songs such as 'Poor Old Joe', 'Nellie Gray', 'Come My Dearest' and 'Rosalie the Prairie Flower', which she would sing.

Margaret was captivated by the 'sight of her as she sang, with her sweetness, freshness and grace, and mastery all in her voice and her face and figure animated with the music'.[24]

Towards the end of April the girls at the school started weaving with cotton as well, and the dishcloths they produced were in great demand – such items had been unobtainable in the country after the war. The school's rugs, too, were very popular, and the demand for all their products kept increasing.

As a result, Emily requested more helpers and money from England as they wanted to open more schools elsewhere, particularly since Philippolis lacked sufficient water for the school's growing needs.[25]

Emily started planning a trip to Johannesburg and Pretoria to speak to Smuts and some of the other leaders about a new weaving school somewhere on the Witwatersrand. She felt that the time was ripe for such a step.

Margaret suspected that this was not the only reason for her trip. She thought Emily might be getting engaged and she knew who the man was, but she did not mention a name. 'I do believe it would be a glorious thing for her for I never knew a woman less designed for single life.'[26]

On 29 April 1905 'the Missis' left for Pretoria by train – with a bale of woven articles as samples of the school's products. The plan was that after this visit Emily would return to England during summer to spend some time with Aunt Mary. Margaret would stand in for her as the head of the school in Philippolis. They had been informed in the meantime that a Miss Picard, an expert in spinning and weaving techniques, was on her way from England.

Margaret wrote in her diary that she would miss Emily greatly: 'For more than three months I have lived so closely with Miss

Hobhouse and have done everything in such unreserve as to make parting like a widowhood and the circumstances of the going now make the parting a deeper one than I ever thought it would be.'[27]

In Pretoria, Emily stayed again with Jan and Isie Smuts. She saw numerous people, in Johannesburg too, to discuss her plans for more spinning and weaving schools. Among those she consulted was Louis Botha, the future prime minister. From the conversations and her own observations, it was clear that there was a great need for training opportunities for poverty-stricken girls and women. Slum neighbourhoods had mushroomed, and the girls in the orphanages had to find a means of livelihood. 'It was the natural outcome of the misery I had seen in 1903.'[28]

Emily did not mention a meeting with Jaap in her writings.

On 4 May, back at the Smuts home, she received a telegram that had first been sent to Philippolis. Earlier that day she had started making arrangements for her visit to her eighty-year-old aunt in England. The telegram was from her cousin, Henry Hobhouse V: 'AUNT MARY DIED PEACEFULLY YESTERDAY HENRY.'

After Emily had recovered from this shock, she explained the very special bond between her and Lady Hobhouse as follows: 'My dear old Aunt was, I think, the only relative who ever really wanted me after my father's death.'

'For me, her death left a blank nothing could fill, it was the loss of one who always understood. The full realisation of my great loss came upon me. I knew then I was absolutely alone for the remainder of my life.'[29]

Julia Farrer, a relative of Lady Hobhouse (née Mary Farrer), told Emily in a letter that her aunt's heart had been enlarged, one lung and both kidneys had been very weak, and she had suffered from severe asthma attacks. Julia gave Emily an account of her last visit to Aunt Mary: 'She said her goodbyes that day. She said in three distinct sentences, "Fond love to Emily . . . You are all very kind . . . But I am ready to go." '[30]

***

Among Emily's many letters and papers in Canada there is one packet that stands out from the rest. These letters are tied together with a piece of string, with a note pinned to the packet that reads: 'Aunt Mary's last letters to me and accounts of her death from Julia Farrar, Henry Hobhouse and Lady Iddesleigh.'

Emily had enshrined her special sorrow about her aunt in a separate packet of letters – and in a separate place in her heart.

12

Elusive happiness

'It seems to me I would give anything to make her [Emily] happy, but her nature is so confounded that I do not believe she will ever find the pure and unqualified happiness which is the only thing that could satisfy her.'

– Margaret Clark, 1906

A visit to the Reverend Abraham Kriel's expanding orphanage in Langlaagte took Emily to the dusty, windy outskirts of Johannesburg. The orphanage was only a fifty-minute walk from the station and not far from the mines, where the Chinese indentured labourers had now arrived.[1]

It was May 1905, and Emily had come to Langlaagte to establish whether she could set up another spinning and weaving school there. Kriel agreed that she could train some of the orphaned girls who were older than twelve, or other girls from the area. He offered her the use of a dilapidated house that belonged to the orphanage as accommodation, but she would have to pay for it. There was also a barn, rather rickety and with a mud floor, that she could use as a school.[2]

Emily hastened back to Philippolis to discuss this new possibility with Margaret and Constance, although she had in fact already made up her mind. Margaret and Constance supported the plan that they open a second school at Langlaagte, and they were all in agreement that they should remain as independent of Kriel's orphanage as possible.

Despite four additional spinning wheels Emily had had made, there were still too few at Philippolis. Some residents of the town were helping them to spin yarn for pay.

One evening while they were having supper, Moses announced the presence of a woman at the door. She turned out to be Miss Picard from England, whose arrival they had been expecting for the past two days.[3] Though the school was prospering and they had gained an extra staff member, Margaret observed that Emily seemed sad and quieter than usual, probably as a consequence of her aunt's death. 'It makes me bleed to know what dust and ashes the world is for her.'[4]

Emily also seemed to be withdrawing from people, at least from Margaret, who wrote that 'she manifestly turns from me & cannot do with a touch or a word from me'. Margaret and Constance felt as if they were merely like chairs and tables to Emily.[5] But Margaret yearned for Emily's recognition; she had grown to love the older woman and looked up to her.

Emily was considering the possibility of moving gradually to Johannesburg – a prospect that filled Margaret with sadness and dread. She wrote: 'I never before had work to do in which there was a person, and it has been a new world of delight to be at work with a person who stimulated and interested me, whom my whole nature could recognise as leader (in spite of some differences) and find nothing but honour in serving, whom I loved and gave every-thing I had. This indeed was worth knowing in life.'[6]

Constance accompanied Emily to Langlaagte to prepare everything for the new school. Owing to all the pigsties in the area, Langlaagte teemed with flies. Much elbow grease was required to make the house offered by Kriel habitable. Emily and Constance had to wash the floors and make curtains, as the house was empty and run down.

The only place that could be used for classes was the stable of the house in which Emily would live; there were no windows, however, and it stank badly. The girls might have to do the spin-ning on the stoep or in a tent, she thought. She had brought two spinning wheels along to start with, but hoped to have more made in Johannesburg.[7]

For the first few days Emily and Constance stayed with Jaap de Villiers until Emily's house was more or less fit for habitation and Constance could return to Philippolis.

By the beginning of July 1905 Emily could move in. It was not a permanent move, as the idea was that she would shuttle between Langlaagte and Philippolis.

Emily described the atmosphere in the house as 'rather eerie'. Apart from the usual 'strange noises in a new place', 'the rats run about overhead at night', she wrote. 'There are any amount of Chinese about as well as blacks in blankets and these as well as white loafers that infest the neighbourhood make it undesirable to walk far alone in the veld, especially at dusk.'[8]

The school was in the stable, with its earthen floor and ineradi-cable stench. The house was surrounded by stables and pigsties, and myriad flies crawled over the food, the table and the walls. Even though we kill thousands of them, Emily wrote, their numbers just keep increasing.[9]

Emily sent a girl from the Johannesburg suburb of Braamfontein, Hester Krugel, to Philippolis to be trained in spinning and weaving so that she could return to Langlaagte as one of the teachers.

The neighbourhood soon took note of Emily's activities. 'I find myself suddenly the aunt of 250 nephews and nieces who surround me in batches when I issue forth, all shouting "Auntie Hobhoos". I wish they would keep to the far prettier Dutch "tante" but they are proud of their command of English specially learnt to please me.' The children were keen to assist; some of the boys fetched water for her, while the girls helped her wash the windows and floors of the house.[10]

Emily decided to attend the Het Volk congress in Pretoria after Louis Botha had announced the formation of this new political party in January that year.[11] But she found it a depressing experience: 'It was like the burial of the dead, a pathetic scene, crowded and silent.'[12]

Alfred Lyttelton, the British colonial secretary, had announced a year earlier that Transvaal would be granted a constitution and a representative body with officials and elected members, while the executive authority would remain in the hands of British officials. The Het Volk congress, however, rejected the 'Lyttelton constitution'.

According to Emily, some at the congress eagerly looked forward to Jaap de Villiers's speech, 'which would have been the wisest and by far', but he 'remained altogether silent, feeling that his words could then be a criticism of Botha and the others'. Like Smuts, De Villiers had studied in Europe, and he was wary of the 'takhaar [ruffian] element in the party'.[13]

For most of the time Emily was the only woman at the congress, but the men were very proud of her presence and her ability to follow the discussions in Afrikaans.

Smuts and Botha made sure that all the delegates came to view the woven products of Emily's school that she exhibited there. The work of the weaving schools was also exhibited at the Rand Show, a big fair held in Johannesburg. A college in Stellenbosch ordered their sports jerseys from the weaving schools and many politicians ordered rough tweed produced by the girls for their suits, although Smuts complained that he felt like a 'female ostrich' in his.[14] Emily reckoned that he was merely unaccustomed to wearing tweed, as he looked 'extremely handsome' in the suit.[15]

On her return journey to Philippolis after the congress, Emily stayed with her friend Tibbie and former president Steyn on their farm Onze Rust outside Bloemfontein.

By this time she had made up her mind to move to Johannesburg. She did not spell out her reasons, but there were probably two deciding factors: the new weaving school in Langlaagte had to be put on a firm footing, and Jaap de Villiers lived just around the corner.

Back in Philippolis, Emily started packing up her remaining possessions. Margaret, Miss Picard, Hester Krugel and Adeline Darby would continue the work there, while Constance might join her later in Johannesburg.[16]

Maria, the young Basotho woman who had worked in the house at Philippolis, accompanied Emily to Johannesburg, but Maria had to get off the train at Springfontein as black people were not allowed to travel further on that particular train. Emily was forced to leave her in the care of the German missionary Reverend Sandrock and his family – her war-time friends – until she could take an appropriate train.[17]

The stable was now systematically converted into the new school. The building had an earthen floor and the light inside was poor, but walls were whitewashed and windows were put in, and while it was no match for the attractive school at Philippolis, it was serviceable.

The weaving school in the stable at Langlaagte on the
premises of the Abraham Kriel Children's Home. Emily
had to have windows put in to provide enough light.

Photo: Free State Archives Repository

In August Emily and her companions started training the first six
girls from the orphanage. New knitting machines were sent to premises at Vrededorp in Braamfontein, a long way from the school, so
that this work could be done there. Obtaining enough spinning
wheels was an ongoing problem. They had one made in Johannesburg,
and while it was finely made, the price was exorbitant.

During this time Emily met a Swedish woman, Mrs Augusta
Götzsche, who lived nearby with her husband, an architect. Emily
was able to order equipment from Scandinavia through her.[18] She
also asked the Boer Home Industries committee to send her some
spinning wheels, as there were now twenty-five learners at the
Philippolis school.

When Margaret and Constance visited Emily in her new environment, Margaret thought Langlaagte depressing, filthy, dry and foul smelling. She could not imagine a life there. She loved Emily, but she felt that Constance was closer to 'the Missis' and being apart from Emily was painful to her.

'It is true indeed, as the Pilgrim says, that our affection for a person is our ordeal. This sort of suffering is, I suppose, the penalty for the happiness of work which is personal. It is perhaps time I drew back into impersonal. It is very fearful to be a woman and to have to find inch by inch what that means', she wrote in her diary.[19]

On the stoep at the spinning and weaving school in Langlaagte, 1906. From the left: the two servants Black Johanna and Maria, Emily, Constance Cloete and either Hester Krugel or Hester Strauss.

Photo: Free State Archives Repository

Jaap de Villiers's residence was not far from Langlaagte, and he came to visit the women on horseback. He invited them to visit him in turn,[20] and a few days later they had a picnic on the de Villiers family farm.[21]

Meanwhile Emily had designed a rug for Jaap and had it woven at the school: it had a deep blue-green pattern against a dun-coloured background, with a border in a lighter colour on which the words '*Alles Sal Regkom*' (All will be well), a well-known motto among the Afrikaners, appeared. Each corner of the rug was adorned by an orange tree.[22]

Emily did not reveal how Jaap had reacted to the gift.

The shortage of spinning wheels still topped Emily's list of priorities. She wrote to friends in Europe and said she actually needed a shipload of these items. Countess Evelyn degli Asinelli from Geneva and Madame d'Orelli from Basel organised a collection of spinning wheels in Switzerland; some people even donated their family heirlooms. Before long Emily was informed that hundreds of spinning wheels were on their way to South Africa.[23] 'I can never forget the day when I saw the great wagons coming in procession down the road, piled high with cases containing spinning-wheels, and knew that my wish had been fulfilled.'[24]

But an unpleasant surprise awaited her when the more than hundred cases were opened. Not a single spinning wheel was still in one piece! Evidently the donors and those who had packed the cases had no idea of the type of roads and means of transport to which the spinning wheels would be subjected. After a long search, Emily and her companions tracked down a carpenter who managed to patch together a hundred and fifty spinning wheels from all the pieces.[25]

A month later Margaret was back at Langlaagte; the time had come for her to return to England. She was shocked when she saw Emily, who was very thin and seemed overworked. Yet she was cheerful, especially when she heard Margaret and the others at Philippolis were selling all their products at church bazaars.[26]

Margaret was still fascinated by what she saw as Emily's complex nature. 'I look at her in some wonder, for there are things so plain to me which she will not recognise . . . Her strength and her weaknesses both come from her being still a child; it makes her attempt what most of us have measured as impossible of attainment, but in her attempt, she achieves what we never shall . . . The greatness of her conception is not crippled by all the qualifications we are bound to make.'[27]

On Margaret's departure in December 1905, a month later than originally planned, Emily experienced 'blank pain' – particularly since she did not believe Margaret would return to South Africa. She wondered how on earth they would get by without her.

At Christmas time, everyone went off in various directions. Emily, 'Black Johanna' and their cat found themselves alone in the house in Langlaagte. Yearning for a change of scene and fresh air without flies, Emily decided to erect a tent on Jaap de Villiers's farm, with his permission, and spend Christmas there. With difficulty she managed to arrange transport for the tent and their provisions, but by the time everything finally arrived at the farm, the tent had disappeared into thin air.[28]

There was no house on the farm, only a rondavel the de Villiers family used for picnics. So she, Johanna and the cat camped under the stars in the roofless summer house. Fortunately it did not rain, and to Emily the starry skies at night were a beautiful sight.

While neither a hot summer's day nor the rice and bully beef on their menu were typical of what Emily associated with

Christmas, it was nice to have an occasional break from the traditional plum pudding and Christmas jollity, she wrote.[29] For Emily, it was a good Christmas.

Marion Rowntree, a Quaker like Margaret and a former fellow student of hers at Cambridge, arrived in South Africa on 28 December to replace Margaret at Philippolis. She first went to Johannesburg, where Emily collected her at the station, and spent a few days there to be briefed by Emily on the weaving operations and the tasks that awaited her.

In the new year Emily realised that the house in Langlaagte in which she and the other staff members lived would have to be used as accommodation for the weaving school girls who came from outside Johannesburg.

This also happened to fit in with her other plans, as Emily had long felt the need for a house of her own. She resolved to have a house built in the suburb of Bellevue. Besides, she no longer felt healthy and strong enough to devote all her energy to the weaving school on a daily basis.

She needed five hundred pounds for the project. Emily wrote to her brother Leonard, but he did not respond to her request. She scraped together enough money nonetheless, bought a stand in Bellevue and had a house built on it with the help of Jan Smuts. It was the fulfilment of an intense need, but at the same time there were signs that Emily was becoming lonely and depressive. She wrote, 'I do not want to live a day longer, but if I have to, I must have a house.'[30]

Emily undoubtedly felt alone and bereft, especially after the death of Aunt Mary. She named the house she had built at 91 Becker Street[31] 'Mara'.[32] While the site had a lovely view over the Magaliesberg mountain range, the height above sea level put a strain on her heart. Jaap de Villiers lived in the same street.

She travelled by train to Langlaagte three times a week to teach classes in design,[33] but found it hard to do some of the physically demanding work. She felt tired and weak and suffered from occasional nosebleeds. 'Indeed I felt very ill and undoubtedly was. But our family has never run quickly to doctors and it never occurred to me to seek advice. Had I done so, no doubt I should have been saved future break-down and these long years of recumbent life,' she wrote years later.[34]

During this time, one of the best spinners, Anna Muller, helped to train the orphans and Hester Krugel came back from Philippolis after she trained. Emily wanted to take Johanna along when she moved to the new house. At first Johanna's mother dug in her heels out of fear that something might happen to her daughter. The 'black Mamma' came to lecture Emily about her daughter, how she should be treated and cared for – as no white servant had ever done, in Emily's experience. The mother insisted on coming along as she wanted to inspect Johanna's new abode. It was a good thing that she did so, as she was so overwhelmed by the new house and the new neighbourhood that she spent the entire day sitting in the corner, exclaiming, 'Yah! Yah!' On seeing the basin with the hot and cold taps, Emily wrote, she 'was like the Queen of Sheba and there was no spirit left in her'.[35]

Maria, who had also accompanied Emily to the north, had left with a Zulu man to become his wife. A year later she was back, with the 'sweetest little black baby tied to her back, whose poor little head drops about as she works'. Emily wrote that she had 'never seen the Zulu, for he is afraid of the "the Great Miss" and won't come to the house if I am here'.[36]

Emily subsequently employed Zimba – a Zulu, 'calm, grave, majestic and courteous', with very strong views. They got along well, and it 'was heart-breaking' when he announced that he had to return to his village.[37]

For Emily, the devoted black people who worked for her brought 'a new and to me attractive atmosphere' into her life. She became aware of their strong sense of justice: 'This groping after justice is surely the root cause of the Native troubles while at the same time the main lever, under wise handling, for their education and general advancement.'[38]

Her opinion of the Reverend Abraham Kriel, however, was less favourable. He wanted to have the old house back in which Emily had lived, and was opposed to any further training in spinning and weaving for the girls; in his view, they did not need such skills. Emily wrote a report in which she pointed out to him that twenty-four girls had been trained at the weaving school – whereupon Kriel prohibited the children from attending classes at Emily's school in future.

True to form, Emily was undaunted by this setback. She found other premises, with more water than at Langlaagte, and situated only ten minutes on foot from her house in Bellevue. The monthly rent of fifteen pounds was less than what they paid for the house and stable at Langlaagte. Moreover, the learners would be able to stay there as well.[39]

Emily received more and more letters from towns in the country districts in which the town fathers asked that she establish weaving schools in their areas too. There was not enough money to heed these calls, and she hoped that the government would give the weaving schools a grant, which would ensure greater stability. By this time at Philippolis, the learner numbers had grown to forty.

She wrote that if she did not receive more donations soon, she would have to start scaling down some of the work. This would be a pity, as interest continued to mount and the schools were getting orders for the articles the girls produced. It would have been nice if a school of her own could be opened for each of the girls, she wrote.[40]

Back in Britain, the political tide had started turning against the Conservatives. The Conservative Prime Minister Arthur Balfour resigned in December 1905 and was succeeded by Sir Henry Campbell-Bannerman of 'methods of barbarism' fame.

In the general election in early 1906 the Liberal Party won a landslide victory by garnering 377 seats in the House of Commons – 84 more than all the other parties combined.[41] While Emily welcomed the Liberal victory, in her view the new government was still dragging its feet when it came to bringing about change in South Africa. She wrote that she was 'beginning to adopt the Boer view that no English government, be it Tory or Liberal, could be trusted.'[42]

Her brother Leonard encouraged her to write to Campbell-Bannerman, who she knew well, and explain to him why the Boers were so unhappy about the Chinese labourers – to mention just one of their grievances.[43]

Emily heard stories about the poor treatment to which the Chinese on the mines were subjected. Many of these labourers went hungry, tried to escape and ended up wandering around in the veld; some not far from her home.[44]

The chairman of the commission charged with drafting a constitution for the two new South African colonies, Sir Joseph West Ridgeway, visited Emily at her house in Bellevue. When she asked him how he would describe the war, he replied: 'The devil, just the devil. There is much in the world we can't explain without the devil. And I think he was at the bottom of that war.'[45]

With this statement Ridgeway at least acknowledged the evil of the war, but Emily was amazed that he thereby also absolved 'Chamberlain and all the others' of their responsibility.

The new Liberal government swept the proposed Lyttelton constitution – which had been rejected by Het Volk – off the table and drafted a new constitution for the two colonies in terms of which the Transvaal was granted responsible government (self-government) in December 1906 and the Orange Free State in the course of 1907.

In the Transvaal, Het Volk won the election in 1907; Louis Botha became Prime Minister, Jan Smuts the Colonial Secretary and Jaap de Villiers the Attorney General. In the Free State, Abraham Fischer became Prime Minister and General J. B. M. Hertzog the Attorney General and Minister of Education, while the Orangia Unie was the majority party.[46] Women and black people were excluded from the franchise.[47]

At Philippolis, some sixteen to seventeen girls were now spinning and weaving every day, while a total of sixty had been trained, Emily wrote to Lady Charlotte Toler of the Boer Home Industries committee. The spinners produced approximately fifty pounds (about twenty-three kilograms) of yarn per week; they had to be paid immediately, which cost between six and seven pounds per week, while the weavers were only paid when their products were sold. It was something of a battle to get them to work fixed hours, Emily said, as this was a foreign concept to the Boers.[48]

The activities of the Bellevue school were now focused on training spinning and weaving teachers. Once a girl had completed her training, she would select spinning wheels – from the Swiss spinning wheels that had been repaired – to take along to her home district. There she would train other girls and women, thereby expanding the home industries to other areas. By August 1906 some of the trained girls had already returned to Potchefstroom, Middelburg and Heidelberg, Transvaal.

The South African Women's Federation paid half of the maintenance costs for ten girls at Bellevue, and the other half was paid by the towns they hailed from.[49] More and more girls wanted to acquire spinning and weaving skills, but there was simply not enough money and equipment to take them all in. It would cost about a thousand pounds to open a new school that was assured of an adequate water supply and accommodation for the girls who came from afar.

Many people survived on the money they earned from spinning yarn for the schools in Philippolis and Bellevue. A shop at Waterkloof, a hamlet a few kilometres south of Philippolis, served as a distribution point. When Emily visited the shop in the company of Marion Rowntree, she found lots of yarn, mothers and babies. Emily drank coffee with the women and they told stories of their days in the concentration camps.

Margaret Clark, now back in England, worked closely with the Boer Home Industries committee and briefed them on how she had experienced matters in South Africa. In Emily's view, this committee did not support her as well as its war-time predecessor had done, and she asked Margaret to explain the circumstances to them. 'You see for yourself the committee does nothing and so all our work here depends upon you,' she wrote.[50] Margaret held a number of drawing-room meetings with the committee as well as public meetings at women's organisations, and particularly at meeting halls of Quakers, Friends' Houses, to solicit support.

One such meeting, held in the Quaker hall in Dundee, was 'packed floor to ceiling' with an audience of '1500 people'. Among those who attended was Alice Walsh, who reported on the proceedings to the Countess Evelyn degli Asinelli, the Swiss woman who had assisted with the collection of spinning wheels and money for Emily's cause. Walsh described the work done by Margaret and Emily, which had been news to most people, as the fruit of 'divine inspiration'. This work 'amongst our distressed sisters in South Africa must greatly help to lessen the natural feeling of bitterness and resentment they must have towards the British people', she wrote in a letter that was published.[51]

Emily was convinced that in the long run it would only be possible to maintain or expand the schools with the help of 'responsible government'. She wrote a long letter on the topic to Lord Elgin, the new British Colonial Secretary, and pointed out that the home industries not only provided an income and training in a skilled trade but also helped the women to regain their sense of self-worth and find meaning in life. Though many of the articles they produced were 'doubtless rough in the eyes of connoisseurs it is highly commendable for the first year, while some are even beautiful'.

Half of the costs related to the weaving schools were covered by contributions from the committee in England and the rest by aid from within South Africa. But the biggest contribution came from the Swiss, who had sent a few hundred pounds and spinning wheels. After the initial shipload had reached Johannesburg in a dilapidated state and the wheels had been repaired, the Swiss had undertaken to send an additional two hundred.[52] Emily asked Elgin to assist with the importation of spinning and weaving equipment and the training of more young women. The cost of training one girl and accommodating her for six months amounted to thirty-five pounds. Perhaps people in England could help to sponsor students.[53]

At the end of 1906 Marion Rowntree returned to England to get married. Constance Cloete had to return to the Cape at the beginning of 1907 after having worked at the two schools for almost two years – she had been invaluable to Emily. Fortunately R. P. Milroy, a Scotsman who was a professional weaver, arrived at the start of the new year after Emily had heard about him and offered him the position. Milroy soon started working at Philippolis, where he impressed the women with his knowledge of natural dyes.

R. P. Milroy, a professional weaver from Scotland,
dyeing yarn together with a woman at Philippolis.

Photo: Free State Archives Repository

While Emily was visiting Jan Smuts for a few days in Pretoria, he suggested that she travel to England with Louis Botha and his daughter Helen. She had been planning a brief visit in any case. Meanwhile Margaret was on her way back to South Africa for another six-month stint; she would stand in for Emily in her absence.

Emily did not relish the prospect of the voyage to England as Aunt Mary was no longer there, and 'London would seem empty'.[54] But in mid-April 1907 Emily arrived, and stayed with her brother Leonard and his wife Nora and their children in Wimbledon. Marian Ellis was now the honorary secretary of the Boer Home Industries committee. Another well-known Quaker, Ruth Fry, had also become a member of the committee; she and Emily had known each other since childhood.[55]

A meeting was held with the committee's subscribers at which both the Bothas were present. Louis Botha delivered a short speech in which he lauded Emily for the weaving project and its political and social benefits in particular: 'I wish to add that in starting this enterprise, Miss Hobhouse has done as much as any one for the cooperation of Briton and Boer, and I feel sure that as the industry grows so will the good feeling between the English and the Dutch spread throughout the whole country.'[56]

Because the Swiss had done so much to support the project – more than a thousand spinning wheels had been sent to South Africa – Emily felt obliged to thank them in person. She was warmly received in Switzerland and she presented a letter from the learners to women from, among other places, Geneva, Lucerne, Basel and Zurich.[57]

After her trip to Switzerland Emily went on a short holiday to France with her brother and his family, not only to rest but also to improve her knowledge of lacemaking. She had not yet abandoned this plan.

Shortly before her departure back to South Africa, an acquaintance persuaded Emily to visit 'a woman who read character from the hand'.

Unlike other so-called psychics who would 'read' one's palm, this woman studied the back of one's hands, which had to be placed flat on a cushion in front of her. Without looking at Emily's face, the woman talked for half an hour and gave a surprisingly accurate account of the course of Emily's life up to that point, her character and her activities. It seemed to Emily as if the woman knew her inside out. She warned: 'You will have to take care of your heart. It is going to give you trouble.'[58]

Meanwhile a new love had entered Emily's life: a St Bernard puppy. She called him Caro, which had been her pet name for John Carr Jackson, her lost American love.

At the beginning of July, Emily and Caro arrived in Cape Town aboard the *Saxon*. By this time Margaret was again well on stream in Philippolis, and the top officials of the new Transvaal government had been appointed in their posts. Emily had a discussion with the new Director of Education, J. E. Adamson. He promised assistance for the weaving project, but recommended that the school in Bellevue move to Pretoria. She and Augusta Götzsche had to get everything ready for yet another move.

Emily also had talks with Adamson's counterpart in the Free State, where there would soon be a new government, and had meetings with General J. B. M. Hertzog and Dr Hugh Gunn, the Director of Education. She was informed that the previous Conservative British government had indeed made money available for industries – a whopping five thousand five hundred pounds, but it had been given to a jam factory as bonuses![59]

Emily and her beloved dog Caro at her house in Bellevue, Johannesburg.

Photo: Courtesy of the Alfred Gillett Trust

Everywhere Emily went, the 'beautiful' Caro 'won all hearts'. Even before leaving London she had become 'possessed' by the dog. In her view, 'his intelligence was remarkable, in some things almost human'.[60]

When Emily went shopping, he would carry her basket or parasol. Strangers often stopped in the street and inquired what price she wanted for him. One man even offered her a thousand pounds. But selling him was out of the question, albeit that she could have purchased quite a few spinning wheels with such an amount. As Caro grew, he became so strong that when they were out walking he would drag her around by his chain. After someone gave her 'a few simple rules on discipline for big dogs', Caro was soon cured of this habit.

Another habit he developed was that of welcoming people at the door, Emily included, 'by standing on his hind legs and throwing his arms around your neck'. This was 'alarming to strangers and disastrous to clean summer muslins', but 'a couple of lessons sufficed' to rid him of this behaviour too.[61]

The girls at the school loved 'to play at hide and seek with him around the looms'; sometimes the game became so boisterous that Emily had to call a halt to it. She taught Caro to swim in the stream behind the school – 'which he was loath to do, suspecting it might be another bath, which he disliked intensely'. She took him to a deeper pool where she taught him to fetch a huge doll she would throw into the water. Emily felt confident that he could have saved a drowning child with ease.[62]

While she was relieved that the government had finally become involved in her schools, she also knew that the project required loving care from someone who was familiar with the process and the people. Smuts shared her concern; he thought that an industry board should be established to control the schools and that Emily should remain the adviser, with Augusta as the principal.

The school moved to a new home: Die Weverij in President Street, Pretoria, also known as the Central School. Thanks to the government, Emily found a small house in the area in which she could live temporarily, at 305 Wessels Street[63] (near the present-day Pretoria Art Museum). She rented out the house in Bellevue in Johannesburg.

They received many visitors at the school, especially mothers with daughters. One of these children, a sweet little four-year-old with big blue eyes, stayed in Emily's memory – her mother had been in the camp at Norvalspont.[64] Little Emily had come to the school 'to see the wheels go wound'.

Emily and Margaret did not see much of each other any more, partly because Emily was slowly detaching herself from the schools so that they could operate independently of her in future. Like the ploughing teams, they, too, had to become self-reliant. This time Margaret was only in South Africa for six months to help out before she was due to return to England.

When Emily explained to the Boers that the girls had to become independent and create small home industries, the fathers were sceptical. It won't work, they said; their daughters knew nothing about business. But Emily shrugged off their pessimism; she taught the girls the basic principles of a business enterprise, and the results were promising.[65]

When Emily paid another visit to Olive Schreiner in De Aar at the end of the year, they again enjoyed each other's company. Olive's 'pet meer-cats' were a source of pleasure to Emily, and the two women played with these animals, roamed in the veld all day and talked. Olive would do most of the talking, while Emily listened receptively. She was used to being silent for long periods; she had sometimes spent whole weekends alone in her houses in Langlaagte or Bellevue.[66]

The 'craving for the relief of speech' that she discerned in Olive during this visit was something she herself often experienced in later years, Emily wrote. 'It is common to most spinster women who, debarred from the contacts arising from work or pleasure owing to ill health and small means, pass their days in a silence which becomes oppressive.' She added, however, that she would 'be the last to disparage solitude'.

'I was fond of it from a child, and at last, though not without painful initiation, have accepted it as the most abiding factor in my life. I could not, now, exist without long spells of it.' She believed that there was much truth in the French saying *Tout notre mal vient de ne pouvoir être seuls.* (All our unhappiness comes from our inability to be alone.)

'Still, everything in reason, and there are periods in life and certain conditions of health that demand sympathetic companionship.'[67] Perhaps Emily was also alluding here to her 'relationship' with Jaap de Villiers; that she, too, would have liked to be married and to love someone.

In a letter to Isie Smuts she put it as follows: 'Chinese labour and the rise and fall of governments and [political] parties and the well-being of colonies and suchlike – to fill the blank caused by the absence of a home and children . . . I deem the rearing of one baby far more important than all those things piled together.'[68]

Alas, whatever had existed between her and Jaap – if anything – had evaporated by this time.[69] Jaap married a woman who was much younger than him – the twenty-year-old Mietjie Meintjies – a 'ninny', according to Olive; someone who was in the habit of putting her foot in it, certainly not Jaap's equal.[70]

At that very time Caro fell ill with biliary fever. Emily immediately took him to a vet, who warned her that 'he must be nursed like a human being. He was. I spared no pains or strength.' She sat up with Caro night after night, and every two hours she gave him beef tea, eggs or some brandy. This stimulant had always been her standby for reviving sick people, and now a sick dog.[71]

During the fifth night she suddenly woke with a start after she had fallen asleep next to Caro's bed. Something was wrong. She was late with the beef tea. Caro raised his head, but 'the effort was too great'. Before she could stand up and reach him, he died.

Nothing or no one could fill Caro's place in Emily's life. 'I missed his welcome, and having someone to speak to; it was the blank left by an intelligent and devoted companionship.' She never got another dog. Caro's collar and chain and the whistle he responded to so faithfully she preserved, unused, for the rest of her life.

For years afterwards, whenever Emily came across a St Bernard, she would stop for a chat with the owner and the dog. But she never saw one as intelligent as Caro, and with such beautiful eyes. He had been her 'one friend and close companion', she wrote to Ruth Fry.[72]

***

Margaret Clark wrote in her diary of 1905 of photos she had taken occasionally in South Africa with her Kodak camera. But what had happened to them?

The renowned footwear company Clarks, which was founded in Street in Somerset, England, and still has its headquarters there, has a shoe museum that tells the story of the company from 1825, but there are also Clark family archives, under the banner of the Alfred Gillett Trust, that go back more than four hundred years.

The archivist, Dr Charlotte Berry, said she did not think that were any photos of Emily in Margaret's collection, but I could fill in the forms and go through the material. On a very cold morning in March 2015 I was there when the archives building opened its doors at ten o'clock.

There were three boxes of photos pertaining to Margaret – she evidently loved taking photos, as there were heaps of them. The first box was a fairly big one with photos of Margaret as a little girl, on her wedding day and so on. The other two were as deep as banana boxes, with rows and rows of envelopes crammed full of photos.

By this time I would recognise Emily at any hour, day or night. The prominent nose, the somewhat sad eyes, the slightly wavy hair, always combed away from the forehead.

It was three o'clock. The last box. There were many photos of children. Then a Kodak envelope marked: 'S.A.' and faintly in pencil: 'Uitkijk'. The Sauers' farm near Stellenbosch.

On one photo, Constance Cloete and her sister Mary sitting on a bench on the farm. Another showed the farmstead. Then another one, faint, of Margaret and two girls at the weaving school in Philippolis.

And, then, there stood Emily! Smiling, as one rarely sees her on photos. In front of her, Caro with her parasol in his mouth.

It was a beautiful, totally unknown photo. Which had lain buried here among Margaret's other snapshots for many years.

***

Towards the end of April 1908 some of the weaving schools' products were on sale at the three-day Cape Town Exhibition, which was opened by the Premier of the Cape Colony, John X. Merriman. Emily had worked hard at showcasing the best products from the schools. Various tweeds were being exhibited and the retail group Hepworths wanted to buy all of it immediately at £170, but she could not let it all go at the start – the visitors first had to see their wares.

In the end, all the rolls of tweeds were sold. The items the girls had made included coats, curtains, shawls, blankets, dishcloths and rugs. Almost everything went, and the schools were inundated with orders.[73]

Shortly after this exhibition Emily met the painter Hugo Naudé and helped him to organise a small exhibition of his work in Pretoria. For this occasion, he also made a painting of Emily. While she thought that 'one cannot judge oneself', she was nonetheless not very impressed with it. It certainly looked like her; it was dignified and a good picture, 'but I fancy it lacks force. It is my most dreamy, miserable and forlorn self'.[74]

One of the first blankets woven by learners, c. 1905.

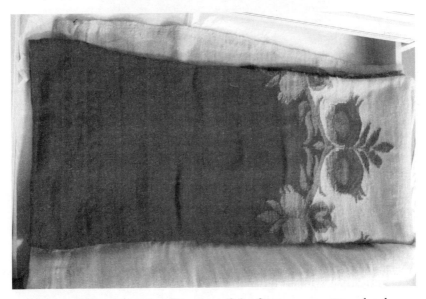

Some of the curtains made at one of the first two weaving schools.

The portrait of Emily that Hugo Naudé painted
in 1908. She did not like it very much, and left it
behind in South Africa on her departure.

Painting: Ditsong National Museum of Cultural History/Annemarie Carelsen

She left the painting in the care of Jan Smuts and bequeathed it to the 'Women of South Africa'.[75] (It is not clear whether Emily had posed for the painter or whether he had used a photograph. Although she did not want the painting to be reproduced, a reproduction of it appeared on a South African postage stamp in 1976, fifty years after her death.)

Meanwhile, spinning and weaving schools – no fewer than twenty-six – had been established in towns across the country. They produced linen and cotton textiles, as well as baskets and leather items. By October 1907 there were weaving schools in Philippolis, Bloemfontein, Winburg, Ficksburg, Bethlehem and Smithfield, and spinning schools in Boshof, Brandfort, Heilbron and Bultfontein, Emily wrote in her last report to the committee. In the Transvaal, besides the big spinning and weaving school in Pretoria, there were weaving schools in Ermelo, Schweizer-Reneke, Belfast and Lichtenburg, and spinning schools in Vrededorp, Roseville, Irene, Heidelberg, Roodepoort, Lydenburg and Rustenburg as well as on the farms Bloemhof, Standerton and Horingnestkranz.

The people of the Transvaal and the Free State had established their own boards to administer the schools, and although Emily was an adviser to these boards, she was now rarely approached for advice. In the end Emily resigned from this capacity because she and the boards, especially the one in the Transvaal, disagreed on how her 'only child that must still be led by the hand of an experienced nurse' should be handled. It was good news, however, that the government had decided to allocate between four and five thousand pounds to the schools.[76]

Smuts realised that this heralded the end of Emily's work in South Africa, and thanked her in a moving letter for having devoted eight years to working for the people of the country, particularly the women and children. 'You did your best to mitigate the miseries of war and thereafter you did your best to repair its ravages.'[77]

In October 1908 Emily left for England from Delagoa Bay (the present-day Maputo). At her side was the 19-year-old Johanna Rood, who had been born on the farm Goedehoop outside Ermelo[78] – a Boer girl with great potential, in Emily's view. She had known Johanna and her family from earlier times and must have contacted her again, because she now accompanied Emily to

Italy. Johanna's father was affluent; she had studied in Dresden, Germany, and could speak English, German and French.[79] Emily had still not abandoned her lacemaking dream, and this was where Johanna fitted into her plans.[80]

Apart from this, however, her imagination had already been gripped by a new cause.

13

A living flame

'Is not the true way to recognise that the Spirit of Freedom in women so long smouldering has burst at length into a living flame which no earthly power can quench? It can only be met by the Spirit of true Sympathetic Justice from those in power.'[1]

– Emily to British Home Secretary
Herbert Gladstone, 4 November 1909

Her exposure to the fate of women in South Africa – especially during the Anglo-Boer War – brought home to Emily three things in particular: that women had little control over their own lives; and that they were often the victims of decisions and actions of men who had no intention of relinquishing their position of power; but also that women had the will and the strength to change their circumstances themselves.

In Britain, the situation of women – if one left the war out of account – did not differ much from that of their counterparts in South Africa. The vocational training they received was inferior to that of men, and their career prospects were limited, and without the vote they had few political means at their disposal to improve their status.

It was almost predictable, therefore, that in England Emily would throw in her weight with movements that campaigned for women's rights.

On 17 December 1908 she attended a women's suffrage meeting, organised by the Women's Liberal Federation, in the Queen's Hall in London.[2] It was attended by three thousand women who, according to her, 'pleaded their cause with dignity and force'.[3] The next day saw an even bigger suffrage meeting where eleven thousand men and women congregated in and outside the Albert Hall, with David Lloyd George, leader of the Liberal Party, as the main speaker. Emily was invited to sit with him on the podium.

The women's suffrage movement immediately appealed to Emily, who considered it a 'glorious [movement] and the only one with real vitality in it'.[4]

But the campaigners for women's suffrage were divided. There was no love lost between Emmeline Pankhurst's Women's Social and Political Union (WSPU) and the other women's groups. Their members kept heckling Lloyd George as he tried to deliver his speech.[5]

The women who belonged to the WSPU, which had no male members, engaged in radical and violent actions such as stone throwing during public protests, arson and chaining themselves to the railings of government buildings. When they were arrested, many of them went on hunger strikes, which led to their being force-fed by the authorities. They were opposed to talks with the government.

At the time, the term 'suffragette' referred more specifically to these militant women while 'suffragist' referred to a supporter of the suffrage movement and implied a non-militant and law-abiding approach. Millicent Fawcett, Emily's old adversary from the concentration camp days, was a more moderate suffragist and leader of the National Union of Women's Suffrage Societies (NUWSS).[6] In her view, there was no connection between feminism and anti-militarism, and she was not opposed to war.[7]

Emily firmly believed that reform of the political system and radical, liberal and ethical social reforms would bring about a renewal that would promote moral progress.[8]

She confessed to her 'dear Oom Jannie' (she used 'Uncle' to General Jan Smuts as a term of endearment, although he was younger than her) that reading *Justice and Liberty* by Goldsworthy Lowes Dickinson had made her 'a complete socialist', as it had removed her last remaining doubts.[9]

She also made use of this chance to try to bring Smuts around to her way of thinking, because as part of the new Transvaal government he could play a major role in establishing a new order: 'How much easier it would be for all if only you would seize this golden opportunity to sweep away the leavings of bad systems and governments and boldly adopt the only equitable system of Socialism, living for "public service" as opposed to "private good".'[10]

The following year, 1909, Emily was invited, along with her brother Leonard and the philosopher and writer Bertrand Russell, among others, to help found the People's Suffrage Federation (PSF), which the Women's Labour League and the Women's Railway Guild joined. Emily was the chair of the executive committee, while Margaret Llewellyn Davies and Mary R. MacArthur served as joint secretaries.[11]

Emily was becoming increasingly estranged from the Liberal Party that she and her family had supported for many years. She had become more of a socialist than a liberal, and she regarded the Liberals' political and social reforms as totally inadequate.[12]

Leonard put it as follows: 'There is a real and deep division between the men who are for developing and expanding the radical tradition and those who regard Liberalism as the more enlightened method of maintaining the existing social order.'[13]

The PSF had both male and female members and advocated universal adult suffrage. Their motto was: 'No sex discrimination. No Marriage Disqualification. No Property Disqualification, but one man one vote, one woman one vote.'[14]

At that stage, a system of qualified franchise applied to men (those who were qualified to vote were mostly the wealthy above the age of twenty-one), while women were excluded from the franchise. Only 7.5 million of the 24.5 million British adults were eligible to vote.[15]

Most of the other organisations that campaigned for the extension of the franchise believed the right to vote should initially only be granted to women above the age of thirty who owned property and/or were married. Emily wrote a letter to the press in which she pleaded that, in the interest of the country as whole but more particularly that of women and the poor, there had to be 'true' political representation. Society could not be free as long as women were not free, she argued.[16]

Emily was now spending long periods in Italy, mostly in Rome, as the milder climate was better for her health. At the end of 1909 she returned to London for a month, where she stayed in Cowley Street, Westminster. 'Now all my soul is in the adult Suffrage,' she wrote after a meeting of the PSF committee that had lasted for more than three hours, followed by three public meetings.[17]

She firmly believed that England was facing a decisive moment. If legislation extending women's suffrage were not passed, 'England is done for; one cannot contemplate what it means – to be thrust back "into the night, into the night",' she wrote to Smuts.[18]

On 3 November 1909 Emily headed a delegation of PSF leaders who went to see the Home Secretary Herbert Gladstone (who was appointed the first Governor General of the new Union of South Africa soon afterwards). She informed him that those in power were ignoring what was at the heart of the struggle between the women and the government: 'Namely you are fighting a spirit. Can the material conquer the spiritual?'[19] she asked him, and pointed out the women's solidarity and fighting spirit.

'Spirit crushed in one spot only springs up the stronger in a thousand places,' was her warning to Gladstone.[20]

The next day she followed it up with a letter in which she asked whether 'the true way' was not rather 'to recognise that the Spirit of Freedom in women so long smouldering has burst at length into a living flame which no earthly power can quench?'[21] She added that it was high time women had an influence on national questions, as the way affairs of state were handled would, she believed, continue to 'be very inadequate till women's brains are also brought to bear on them'.

Emily's dramatic plea left Gladstone cold, and a few days later he replied in a letter that passing a new law to extend the franchise to all adult men and women was absolutely out of the question.[22]

Emily had not abandoned her dream of a lace school in South Africa. In early 1909 she left for Italy with Johanna Rood and Ruth Fry to research the lacemaking industry. They visited Rome, Bologna and Venice.

Johanna not only learnt lacemaking but also how to run such an enterprise as a business. The training was part of the Aemilia Ars Society in Bologna, which had been founded by a group of aristocrats in 1898. In Venice she learnt the delicate art of Burano and Reticella needlepoint lace.[23]

Johanna Osborne (née Rood), who started the first lace school
at Koppies in the Free State in 1909. She remained at the
school until 1931 and lived to the age of eighty-nine years.

Photo: Anglo-Boer War Museum

In Venice Emily stayed at home of the Marchesa Harriette De
Viti de Marco, wife of the economist Marchese Antonio De Viti
de Marco, where she met the young Lucia Starace, a relative of the
Marchesa. Lucia agreed to accompany Johanna to South Africa to
open Emily's first lace school at Koppies (then known as Kopjes)
in the northern Free State, about 140 kilometres south of
Johannesburg.

In the preceding months, Emily had written more than one
letter to J. B. M. Hertzog, Minister of Education in the Free State,

Lucia Starace, from Italy, who taught at Emily's first lace school at
Koppies and the black cat that accompanied them to the settlement
when the school was opened there. This photo was taken there.

Photo: Courtesy of Ferdinando and Hilda Coppola

explaining the necessity of a lace school and what was needed for
such a project.

Lucia, Constance Cloete, Johanna and a black cat arrived in
October 1909 at the poverty-stricken settlement on the banks of the
Renoster River.[24] The three women had to set up a school in old
military barracks. They decided to divide the corrugated-iron building into two sections: one for the lace school and the other for the
teachers' accommodation. Everything was very basic and modest.
Johanna and Lucia's first task was to recruit learners. They rode

through the district on horseback and spread the news of the project to people they encountered.[25]

Emily was not happy at all when she heard that there was no proper building for the lace school. She had also explained that the school should be close to a big settlement of impoverished people from which girls could come to be trained.[26] The school should have been constructed by this time. She took up her pen at once and wrote another letter to Hertzog.

It was an uphill battle to get the school going. The girls who wanted to learn lacemaking had to travel long distances. The women came up with a plan and founded 'home schools' that took the training to the girls: the teachers would travel from farmhouse to farmhouse, training a few learners at a time.

According to a letter written by Emily, the girls loved making the coarser Reticella lace (needlepoint) by working every stitch by hand, instead of the bobbin lace that was made by braiding and twisting lengths of thread that were wound on bobbins. Ordinary flaxen or linen yarn was used for that, not cotton.[27] According to her son, Johanna had taught the girls more than just lacemaking. His mother had introduced the girls to Afrikaans poetry and literature besides teaching them geography and history, Stephan Osborne told the *Volksblad* years later.[28]

Emily depended on Johanna to get the lace school off the ground. She herself never got to the school, mainly because of her deteriorating health. She wrote regularly to inspire Johanna with courage, and prescribed the pillars on which she had to build the work: 'Time (Rome was not built in one day). Patience (Mistakes will be made . . .). Prudence (Look before you leap). Pluck (Never be discouraged). Economy (Take care of the pence).'[29]

For some time now Emily had been living in Rome, where life was considerably cheaper than in London and the climate more pleasant. She was forty-nine years old, and suffered from angina and rheumatoid arthritis. She spent most of her time lying on her sofa in her flat, barely able to walk.[30]

The flat she rented in Rome was next to the Palazzo Orsini in the Monte Savello area and overlooked the Roman Forum – a beautiful view. But Emily was blind to her own limitations; there were close to a hundred steps leading from the ground level to her flat, but her ill health prevented her from climbing stairs. Whenever she wanted to go out she had to be carried up and down, which cost money.

At times she would spend long periods in the flat without going out, but she had a personal attendant who looked after her.[31] And at least her nephew Oliver Hobhouse, Leonard's son, visited her, as did Eleanor and Maud, the daughters of her cousin Henry Hobhouse V, and her sister Maud.

On a visit to London, towards the end of 1909, Emily saw a doctor after she had been forced to cancel several 'suffrage' appointments for speeches under the banner of the PSF. The doctor's diagnosis was that her heart did not function properly, and that she suffered from rheumatoid arthritis (which she knew already). Moreover, she felt 'horribly fat and bloated', while she had never been overweight in her life.[32]

Alice Greene, an old friend from South Africa, visited her in London and was shocked to see how weak Emily was. 'She is just very ill and very lonely and no wonder. She has broken down her health for the sake of others and I doubt whether there is one person both able and willing to help . . .'[33]

Regarding her 'poor heart', Emily remarked to Smuts: 'I think South Africa would be found stamped on it for South Africa wore it out. Nevertheless one often loves the very thing that kills.'[34]

Emily returned to Italy with great reluctance as she yearned to participate in the British women's fight for political rights. A year later, in November 1910, Emily was also absent when Prime Minister Herbert Asquith received a delegation from the PSF. It was a decisive event; shortly afterwards, Asquith announced that the franchise would be extended to all men while it was also being contemplated for women, as proposed in the Conciliation Bill of 1910.[35]

Earlier that same year, on 31 May, South Africa had officially become a Union, a self-governing dominion of the British Empire. Louis Botha became the Prime Minister and Minister of Agriculture; Jacobus Sauer of Uitkijk the Minister of Railways and Harbours; Jan Smuts the Minister of Interior Affairs, Mines and Industry, and Defence, and J. B. M. Hertzog the Minister of Justice – all people whom Emily knew. Jaap de Villiers was appointed Judge President of the Transvaal division of the Supreme Court. As a result of the death of King Edward VII on 6 May, however, festivities had been muted.[36]

From her sofa, Emily wrote to Smuts in pencil to congratulate him on the fact that the 'first act of your Union Cabinet was one of justice towards Dinizulu'.

Dinuzulu, a son of Zulu King Cetshwayo, had been captured by the English in 1890 and exiled to the island of St Helena for seven years on account of an armed rebellion against the British annexation of a part of Zululand. Nearly a decade later, Dinuzulu was charged with fomenting the Bambatha Rebellion of 1906. He was found guilty of high treason and sentenced to four years' imprisonment. After Botha became prime minister of the Union, he ordered that Dinuzulu be released and allowed to live on his farm Uitkyk in the Transvaal.

Emily also seized the opportunity to convey a pacifist message to the new Minister of Defence. 'Well, dear Oom Jannie, mark my words – you will defend your country best by not defending it.'[37] She warned him against having a standing defence force, as it was an evil.

Always attuned to health and a frugal lifestyle, and old-fashioned in some respects, she urged Smuts not to use his new official motor car but to rather stick to his horse. Horse riding kept a man healthy. He should get the children ponies to ride on. In crowded Europe, motors had become 'a pest of noise, dirt, danger and smell'.[38]

He should also listen to Parliament, which was the voice of the people through its representatives, and guard against becoming an autocrat or 'a Czar'. She reminded him that 'we, the people, we democrats, want to have a say in matters concerning ourselves . . .'

She was beginning to wish, she wrote, that not merely kings but also ministers could be done away with, as it seemed to her that cabinets were 'hotbeds of mischief manured by ambition'. She held cabinets responsible for 'endless evil and little good, and I believe the secrecy appertaining to their counsels is the root of the evil'.[39]

A letter from Smuts in which he had referred to politics as 'worldly' and a 'sorry business' upset her so much that Emily reprimanded him angrily. Politics was in such a sorry state 'because you men let it be and because you won't or don't lift it out of the rut'.

'That has been from the beginning of history the fault with men's management of politics and public affairs – and I look above all to the entrance of women into politics to purify them and lift them to a higher level. Secrecy is one of the first things to get rid of . . . Oh! It makes me mad to think what great issues lie in the hands of a few stupid and obstinate men!'[40]

She expressed the hope to Smuts that they in South Africa 'will be wise and firm and keep yourselves to yourselves and not have any standing army or any battleships[41] – for these things are the beginning of all Evil'. 'The next thing is you want an opportunity to use them . . .'[42]

In the autumn of 1911 Emily was in Florence, Italy, where she hoped to find a cure for her health condition. But, as one could expect from an art lover, she first visited the museums, including the Palazzo Piti where, ironically, she was overwhelmed by Sandro Botticelli's painting of Minerva – the goddess of wisdom, but who was usually depicted holding the weapons of war with which she had come into life.

In Botticelli's painting the barefooted Minerva stands one step higher than the centaur next to her, whose long hair she has in a firm grip. He looks sad and submissive. A wreath of entwined olive branches on her head resembles a halo, while a mesh of olive shoots encircles parts of her upper body and her partially revealed breasts; in her other hand she holds a halberd, her ginger-brown hair falling in loose waves over her shoulders.

'I think it the most beautiful female figure in the world,' an enraptured Emily wrote to her nephew Oliver, now a student at Oxford.

In Florence, Emily went to see a Doctor Carloni who had apparently developed a special treatment for people with heart disease; she had heard it had been wonderfully successful in some cases.[43] After the first examination he found that she had over-exerted herself mentally and physically, and that her heart was enlarged. She had to learn to sit still 'and possess my soul in patience'.[44]

Carloni used electric pumps, breathing apparatus, diets and other methods to treat his patients. Among others, they had to breathe in iodine through a device he had built.[45] Emily also had to lie in a bath of carbolic acid, which worked 'wonders' for her.[46]

Within two months she felt like a new person; her cheeks were 'as rosy as a Dutch doll's', and she had regained her slim figure. She was especially pleased about this, as she set great store by her appearance.[47]

After five months in Florence she decided to return to Rome. She had been in the Valley of the Shadow of Death but life had suddenly broken through again within her, she wrote to Tibbie Steyn.[48] For the rest of her life she would keep to the advice she had been given in Florence by the Italian doctor – small portions of food, a diet of eggs, cheese, lots of vegetables and fruit, as well as bread and other starchy food. She almost never ate meat or fish again, except for occasional pieces of biltong from South Africa.

But the doctor had to be paid, and Emily was struggling to make ends meet; she lived mainly on the proceeds from her small investment, the money she had left of her inheritance, and the rental of her house in Bellevue. The only person she felt she knew well enough to approach in this regard was Smuts. It could not have been easy for the proud Emily, but nonetheless she requested a loan of fifty pounds, which she would repay at six per cent interest.[49]

Smuts sent her one hundred pounds – along with the remark that he considered Carloni a quack.

'Dear, dear Oom Jannie, What am I to say? What am I to do? Your generosity is so overwhelming . . .'[50] But she stood by her doctor, saying she had personally seen him cure asthma sufferers 'like magic'.

In November 1912 Emily was back in Rome, where she saw Tibbie and her husband former president M. T. Steyn from time to time. Six years earlier Steyn had already conceived the idea of erecting a memorial of some kind for the women and children who had died in the Anglo-Boer War. A monument committee was established and various cultural organisations, churches and political parties were mobilised to raise funds and create enthusiasm for the cause. Hundreds of collection lists were distributed throughout South Africa for this purpose. Emily donated a small amount Tibbie had sent to her for her medical costs to the committee that raised funds for the envisaged monument.[51]

Prime Minister Louis Botha, however, disapproved of Steyn's monument proposal as he had adopted a policy of post-war reconciliation between the former adversaries, and wanted them to erect a memorial to Voortrekker leader Piet Retief instead, who was murdered by Zulu king Digane in 1838 during the conflict over Natal. But Steyn was opposed to this, as it would again draw attention to black people as the 'enemy'.

In the end the committee decided to erect the monument in honour of the women and children at Bloemfontein, and the city council donated twenty *morgen* (about two acres) of land for this purpose. The fundraising campaign had yielded more than ten thousand pounds. It was also decided to commission the sculptor Anton van Wouw to create a central group of bronze figures to stand at the base of a high obelisk.[52]

He would do the work in Rome, where Emily would advise him and the figures would be cast. The inspiration for the group of figures was the heart-rending scene Emily had witnessed at the Springfontein station where six hundred people had been left to their fate without food or shelter for days, and where some of the women had clung to Emily.

This was where the woman had sat with her dying child on her knees, as Emily had put it so movingly at the time: '. . . deathly white, she sat there motionless looking not at the child but far, far away into depths of grief beyond all tears'.[53]

It was this emotion that van Wouw was supposed to convey in his representation of two sorrowing women and a dying child, but his first attempt fell far short, in Emily's estimation.

He had failed to capture the pain of a mother whose grief was beyond tears. The depiction of the mother's face was 'soulless and expresses nothing', and as far as Emily was concerned, 'the group in its present stage is meaningless'.[54]

Also, the figure of the child looked as if it were sleeping peacefully. Capture death, she instructed van Wouw, and if he did not know what a dead child looked like, he should visit a hospital and see for himself. Or he should look at Michelangelo's Pietà of Mary with the dead body of Jesus draped across her lap.[55]

Van Wouw took Emily's criticism to heart and redid the sculptures. While Emily was more satisfied with his second attempt, she felt that van Wouw was no genius.[56] 'Oh! Why oh why did they not put the thing into the hands of Rodin & some really great sculptor?' she wrote to Isie Smuts.[57]

In February 1913 Emily received an official invitation from Tibbie Steyn to unveil the Women's Monument outside Bloemfontein later that year – the first monument in the world dedicated to women and children.

Emily was honoured by the invitation, but doubted whether her health would stand up to the long and exhausting journey. 'I cannot suffer any vibration, the walls of my heart may give way.'[58] In Italian her condition was called 'angoscia', a kind of 'heart nightmare'.

There was something else that bothered her, she wrote to Tibbie. She often thought about the black people; many had died in a war that had not been theirs. She wanted to know from Smuts 'if this really is a national monument,[59] provided by a national movement', or had it become 'only a Free State affair'. 'Personally,' she wrote, 'I cannot think it either should or could arouse racial animosity . . .'[60]

The Afrikaners were probably unaware of these sentiments of Emily's, but in important respects they and their heroine had already moved in different political directions. She was an internationalist who espoused universally accepted democratic values, while they had developed into ardent nationalists.

But the Afrikaners were stubborn, like her, and by nature not inclined to unanimity. Eleven years earlier they had united against the English and signed a peace treaty together, but now there was division about a war monument. Louis Botha was apparently aggrieved because Steyn had not involved him to a greater degree in the plans for the monument. He was also of the opinion that the monument would fan further hate and bitterness.[61]

There was no room for bitterness, Emily wrote. She would be very disappointed if she arrived in Bloemfontein and 'found this function not national in character'.[62]

Beneath the surface, South African politics was changing radically during this period. Under the leadership of the lawyer Pixley ka Isaka Seme and others, the South African Native National Congress (the precursor of the African National Congress) was founded in Bloemfontein in 1912. Two years later, also in Bloemfontein, Afrikaner nationalists founded the National Party that would come to power in 1948 and govern the country for forty-six years. In 1910 Mahatma Gandhi, the later world-renowned human rights activist and pacifist who spent twenty-one years of his life in South Africa, established the community of Tolstoy Farm outside Johannesburg where he preached and practised his philosophy of passive resistance.[63]

Emily had kept pace with political developments in South Africa. She had 'an entire nation' in mind when she decided to unveil the Women's Monument after all. When she reflected on her past actions, Emily wrote to Caroline Murray, she realised that she had been impelled by three motives.

Firstly: 'A sense of justice towards the innocent victims of a great injustice.' Secondly: 'An overwhelming pity for suffering childhood which could not understand but must suffer.' Thirdly: 'A determination to uphold those higher standards of human feeling and action which England holds in sane and sober moments.'[64]

Above all, it was her sense of duty that had settled the matter. 'I feel it so and it is a Sacred Duty with a big D to respond to their feelings by accepting, be it in my power to do so. It seems to me it would be a seal upon the Past.'

After a twenty-one-day voyage on the *Galway Castle* Emily arrived in Cape Town in mid-September 1913.[65] Here she stayed with her friends Anna and Dr William Purcell at Bergvliet.

By now Emily could climb one flight of stairs, walk for half an hour with her fold-up chair under her arm, and sit upright while eating. She was in a much better condition than she had been before the treatment in Florence.[66] 'My looks are the best part of me now,' she remarked jokingly to Smuts.[67]

Because the high altitude in the interior placed a strain on her heart, she waited until 24 November before leaving by train for Bloemfontein, where the unveiling of the monument would take place on 16 December.[68] Tibbie had arranged for a luxurious saloon car that could switch between trains so that Emily could acclimatise slowly. In Bloemfontein, everything had been organised to make things as convenient as possible for her: a special chair in which she would be carried around, a motor car that would transport her to the Women's Monument on the day of the unveiling . . .[69]

But all of this was in vain. On 29 November Emily had to be hastily helped from the train at Beaufort West after her heart had almost stopped. Her pulse rate was so fast that the doctor instructed her to turn back to Cape Town at once. The heat of the Karoo also aggravated her condition.

Emily, now fifty-three years old, did not give up hope. From the parsonage of the Reverend J. G. Steytler, where she was staying, she sent a telegram to Bloemfontein to inform them that she would remain at Beaufort West for a week and then resume her journey. 'Believe me, if my body will do it, I shall come . . .'[70]

She had no illusions about the poor state of her health, however. A few days later she wrote to Tibbie: 'Alone, exiled and invalided as I am I always feel [there] need be "no sadness of farewell when I have crossed the bar" and I am ready, almost anxious to go. Still, I shall try my very best to get to you that day.'[71]

All this uncertainty put the Monument Committee in a dilemma that they had to convey to Emily. Gordon Fraser, Tibbie's younger brother, drafted the carefully worded telegram they sent her: The committee 'wish to express their deep sense of gratitude for your willingness to sacrifice yourself for the unveiling of the national monument but . . . they and the people on no account desire you to take any risks which may have serious consequences . . .'[72]

A few days later she wrote to Smuts: 'Why, oh why, did you urge such a derelict, such a broken-up wreck to come so far? Here I am, held up, by that incapable organ, my heart.' She would wait two or three days longer to see whether her condition would improve under the doctor's watchful eye.[73]

The ever-practical Emily did not exclude the worst, and informed Smuts that she had left her will with her brother in England. There was money in her Standard Bank account in Pretoria; would Smuts please see to compensation for the Purcells who had accommodated her? And there was money available for a funeral.[74]

After a few more days with no improvement in her condition, Emily was forced to accept the inevitable: she was too weak to continue her journey to Bloemfontein.

'Not even all the luxuries or comfort so generously afforded me could carry me through,' she lamented. 'The old horse fell exhausted (though I think I may say in harness) at the last stage of the journey, and I write to tell you how sorry and in a way how humiliated I feel.'[75]

Smuts expressed his sincere regret because he knew his 'dearest little Auntie' had an 'iron constitution'. He assured her that 'I shall miss that face and figure which represent the noblest message of the Englishwoman to the Boer woman . . .'[76]

On 6 December, back at the Purcells in Cape Town and free from the heat and thin air of the interior, Emily arranged urgently with the journalist Sanni Metelerkamp for her Monument speech to be translated[77] – 'which I hope will be more Afrikander than High Dutch'.[78] She also insisted on checking the proofs herself, even if she had to do it while lying in bed.

Emily arranged, and paid, for four thousand English copies of the speech to be printed and the same number of the 'Afrikander' version. Sanni herself took the printed copies along to Bloemfontein to distribute them among the people there.[79] Emily asked John X. Merriman (who had been prime minister of the Cape Colony up to 1910 and was now a member of the Union Parliament) to read out her speech in Bloemfontein, but he had already committed himself to another appointment on 16 December.

Meanwhile the Monument Committee had decided that Charles Fichardt would read out Emily's speech, while Tibbie would perform the unveiling.

14

A prophetic warning

'We in England are ourselves still dunces in the great world-school, our leaders still struggling with the unlearnt lesson, that liberty is the equal right and heritage of every child of man, without distinction of race, colour or sex. A community that lacks the courage to found its citizenship on this broad base, becomes "a city divided against itself, which cannot stand".'

– Emily, 16 December 1913

The prominent hill south of Bloemfontein was dotted with black and white specks. The scene was almost reminiscent of the white tents that had stood here on the Free State plains and elsewhere in the country more than ten years earlier: symbols of humiliation and revilement, disease and death.

But on this day each of the more than twenty thousand specks on this terrain was a human being, intensely aware of life. Because the crowd dressed in solemn black and white had assembled here to honour their dead, the approximately twenty-eight thousand

The Women's Monument in Bloemfontein.

Photo: Anglo-Boer War Museum

Afrikaner women, children and men who had perished in the concentration camps of the Anglo-Boer War. The tall sandstone obelisk reaching heavenward here at the foot of the hill would keep their memory alive in the minds of those present and their descendants.

It was suffocatingly hot, as could be expected on a midsummer day in this unforgiving landscape, but no one in the crowd shed any of their Sunday clothes. Members of the Kimberley Volunteer Regiment played the funeral marches of Chopin and Beethoven. A devotional silence hung over the proceedings.

About sixteen hundred men on horseback had led a solemn procession from the Tweetoring Church in the city centre to the site of monument. Behind them had followed dozens of ox-wagons draped in purple cloth. And then four hundred girls, dressed in white, each carrying a small white wreath.[1]

All along the route hundreds of people had stood watching the procession, with someone here and there waving at them – in search of some form of contact with the past. The Union Jack, to many still a symbol of the British Empire's oppression, was flying at half mast nonetheless.

Tibbie Steyn, the wife of the former Free State president M. T. Steyn, came forward to unveil the monument. After a brief message from her, the cloth that covered the monument's group of figures fell away.

A rustle of recognition ran through the crowd because the expressions, clothing and body language of the statue group – especially the moving figure of a mother with her dead child – was in some way familiar to all, whether from their personal experience of the camps or from photos that had been etched into the Afrikaner nation's visual memory.

When a flock of doves was released, the birds, as if they were orienting themselves, circled once high above the monument and then set course for home through the blue sky.

One person's absence was palpable: Emily Hobhouse, whose name and deeds were to the crowd a piece of the war's jigsaw puzzle, part of the good news about an evil war – that a foreign woman from the country of the enemy had taken pity on them, had even saved the lives of many.

Her poor health prevented her from attending the ceremony, so she sent her speech with this covering message:

The central sculpture group of the Women's Monument: the
grief-numbed woman with her dead child on her lap and
another woman standing behind her. It was the scene Emily had
witnessed at the Springfontein station. Anton van Wouw was the
sculptor whose first attempt, Emily felt, failed to do justice to
the emotion she had wanted him to depict.

Photo: Anglo-Boer War Museum

In great weakness I struggled 7000 miles to unveil your monument. At the last stage my body failed. Only in heart and spirit
may I be with you today. We can never meet again. The words I
hoped to speak must go to you in print. Accept them from me.

In bidding you farewell, I leave you in lofty companionship
– that of the spirits of the simple but heroic dead. None more

deeply than I, share with you today, in according all honour to
the dead.[2]

Charles Fichardt – the son of Emily's deceased friend Caroline –
stepped forward and, with much feeling, read out the speech that
Emily had intended to deliver here herself, in both Afrikaans and
English.[34]

It started off with a quotation from a drama by Euripides from
The Trojan Women: 'Would ye be wise, ye cities, fly from war! Yet
if war come, there is a crown in death for her that striveth well
and perisheth unstained.'

Then Emily's insightful and prophetic message followed:

Friends,

From far and near we are gathered to-day to commemorate
those who suffered bravely and died nobly in the past.[5]

Of old a great man[6] said: 'Acts deserve acts, and not words in
their honour,' and this is true. Yet having come so far at your
request to share in this solemn dedication, and having been
most closely bound with the last hours of their lives, I feel
constrained to offer my tribute to the memory of those women
and those little children who perished in the Concentration
Camps.

Many of them it was my privilege to know. How strange a
thought that from their memory to-day flows a more vital
influence for good than can be found amongst those who have
lived and prospered. In this way, perhaps, is the prophetic
vision fulfilled: 'Refrain thy voice from weeping and thine eyes
from tears; they shall come again from the land of the enemy;
thy children shall come again to their own border.'[7]

Do we not in a very real sense meet them again this day?

Yet another thought urges me to offer this tribute of words.

From ancient times men have pronounced eulogies over the graves of their fellow-men who had fallen for their country. To-day, I think for the first time, a woman is chosen to make the Commemorative Speech over the National Dead – not soldiers – but women – who gave their lives for their country.

My Friends, – This day, this *Vrouwen-Dag* [Women's Day] is good. Like the Sabbath in the week, it breaks into the hurrying years, and in the pause, the past can calmly be recalled, its inspiration breathed afresh, its lessons conned once more.

Let us take this moment to consider where we now stand and what these lessons are.

You are gathered here from all parts to consecrate this spot to women and children who were stripped of all – I say it advisedly – of all. Husbands and sons, houses and lands, flocks and herds, household goods and even clothing. Denuded, it was good to watch how yet they 'possessed their souls'. 'It is tragic,' says a writer,[8] 'how few people ever possess their souls before they die.' That these did I know, because I saw. I bridge in mind the years, the thirteen years, and move once more amid the tents that whitened the hillside. Torn from familiar simple life, plunged into sickness and destitution, surrounded by strangers, were those poor souls – stripped bare. The sight was one to call forth pity, yet pity did not predominate. Quite other feelings swallowed that. Even throughout the deepest misery the greater pity was needed elsewhere. 'Christ', I have read, 'had pity for the poor, the lowly, the imprisoned, the suffering, and so have we, but remember that He had far more pity for the rich, the hard, those who are slaves to their gods, who wear soft raiment, and live in kings' houses. To Him riches and pleasures seemed greater tragedies than poverty and sorrow.'

So, as we turn our minds back thirteen years to dwell on the stormy past, pity enters in, but whom is it that we pity? Surely, had you watched the inward and spiritual graces that shone forth from that outward and visible squalor you yourselves might have felt that it was not the captives in those foul camps that were most in need of pity. The rich and highly-placed, the financiers, who wanted war, the incompetent statesmen who were their tools, the men who sat in the seats of the mighty, the blundering politicians of that dark story – all the miserable authorities incapable of dealing with the terrible conditions they themselves had brought about – these needed and still need our deeper pity. That vast tragedy as it rolled through your land its bloody way, came at length face to face with the great array of the women and children – the weak and the young. Wholly innocent of the war, yet called upon to bear its brunt, nobly they rose to meet the trial that awaited them. Sympathy indeed they craved and did receive, but they towered above our pity.

And so today. What gave the impetus to this movement? What stirred you to gather pence for this monument? What brought you here from far and wide? It was not pity, it was Honour.

Yet if you have pity to spare, give it even now to those, who still alive, must ever carry in their hearts the heavy memories of the blundering wrong by which they wrought that war. You and I are here to-day filled only with honour for those heroic and innocent victims who passed through the fire.

For this monument is a symbol.

Far away in Rome, I have been privileged to watch its creation. I noted its conception in the Sculptor's thought, I saw it first issue in the common clay: moulded by his hand it passed into the pure white plaster; at length chastened to his mind and meet for the supreme ordeal it was cast into the pit of burning metal whence issued the perfect work.

Even so did Destiny, the mighty Sculptor – like clay in his hands – take those simple women and children from their quiet homes, mould and chasten them through the successive stages of their suffering, till at length purified and perfected to the Master-mind by the fierce fire of their trial, they passed from human sight to live forever a sacred memory in your land.

Their spirit which we feel so near to us today warns ever: – 'Beware lest you forget what caused that struggle in the past. We died without a murmur to bear our part in saving our country from those who loved her not but only desired her riches. Do not confuse the issues and join hands with those who look on her with eyes of greed and not with eyes of love.'

Is it not the glory of those weak sufferers to have laid down this principle: In this South Africa of ours, true patriotism lies in the unity of those who live in her and love her as opposed to those who live on her but out of her. The Patriots and the Parasites.

This issue though fought out of old is ever with you, it is alive to-day; voices of the dead call to you, their spirits lay a restraining hold upon you as they plead: 'Here is the true division beside which all other cleavages are meaningless. There can be no permanent separation betwixt those who love our country, live in her and are bound up with her. At bottom such are one.'

Alongside the honour we pay the Sainted Dead, forgiveness must find a place. I have read that when Christ said, 'Forgive your enemies,'[9] it is not only for the sake of the enemy. He says so, but for one's own sake, 'because love is more beautiful than hate'. Surely your dead with the wisdom that now is theirs, know this. To harbour hate is fatal to your own self-development, it makes a flaw, for hatred, like rust, eats into the soul of a nation as of an individual.

As your tribute to the dead, bury unforgiveness and bitterness at the foot of the monument forever. Instead, forgive for you can afford it, the rich who were greedy of more riches, the statesmen who could not guide affairs, the bad generalship that warred on weaklings and babes – forgive – because so only can you rise to full nobility of character and a broad and noble national life.

For what really matters is character. History clearly teaches this.

In the present day, minds are strangely confused, eyes are blinded, and it is the almost universal idea that the all-important thing for the country is Material Prosperity. It is false.

Noble Character forms a great nation. Statesmen who aim at material prosperity as if it were an end in itself, forget or have not recognised, that too often great national prosperity is accompanied by deterioration of national character and the highest well-being of the people.

For it is not the rich and prosperous, who matter most, but you who live the simplest lives, and upon whom in the last resort, if trial comes, falls the test of the national character.

This thought ennobles the humblest life. The dead we now honour met that test and did not shrink. They died for freedom; they clung to it with unfaltering trust that God would make it the heritage of their children. The years have brought changes they little dreamed, but South Africa is one and it is free. Its freedom is based on all they did; they suffered; they died; they could do no more. The supreme offering was made, the supreme price paid. Their sacrifice still bears fruit. Even could the graves open and give up their dead, we would not wish those women back, nor have them relinquish the great position they have won. Not even the children would we recall, the children, who – counting the vanished years – would stand before us now, some 20,000 youths and maidens, fair and comely – a noble array – peopling the too solitary veld. For who does not feel their spirit move amongst us here to-day? Who fails to recognise the noble example by which they still live?

In this vast throng can there be found one unresponsive soul? One heart that will not go hence filled with resolve to live more worthy of the dead?

My Friends, memories and emotions throng. Thirteen years have passed since under the burning January sun I trudged daily forth from your wire-girt [wire-held] town[10] to the kopje [hill] of many tears. Daily in that camp, as later in others, I moved from tent to tent, witness of untold sufferings, yet marvelling ever at the lofty spirit which animated the childhood as well as the motherhood of your land. So quickly does suffering educate, that even children of quite tender years shared, the spirit of the struggle, and sick, hungry, naked or dying prayed ever for 'no surrender'.

Think what it meant for an Englishwoman to watch such things.

Did you ever ask yourselves why I came to your aid in those dark days of strife? I had never seen your country nor even known anyone of you. Hence it was no personal link that brought me hither. Neither did political sympathy of any kind prompt my journey.

I came – quite simply – in obedience to the solidarity of our womanhood and to those nobler traditions of English life in which I was nurtured, and which by long inheritance are mine.

For when Society is shaken to its foundations, then deep calleth unto deep,[11] the underlying oneness of our nature appears, we learn that 'all the world is kin'.[12]

And surely, the honour of a country is not determined by the blundering acts of some passing administration, or weak generalship, but lies in the sum-total of her best traditions which the people at large will rise up to maintain.

Even as the noblest men are ever ready to admit and remedy an error, so, England as soon as she was convinced of the wrong being done in her name to the weak and defenceless confessed it in very deed, and by thorough reformation of those camps, rendered them fit for human habitation.

Thus she atoned.

I stand here as an Englishwoman, and I am confident that all that is best and most humane in England is with you also in heart to-day. Reverent sympathy is felt with you in this Commemoration and in your desire to accord full honour to your Dead.

You and I were linked together by the strange decrees of fate at that dark hour; we stand now face to face for the last time.

One thing I would ask of you.

When you remember the ill done, remember also the atonement made.

Dwell also upon all you have gained through this great episode, in the legacy left you by the Dead.

Let me explain. It is not mainly sorrow that fills your heart to-day; time has already softened personal grief. Therefore many may and do say it is useless to perpetuate as we do to-day memories so drear. But these very memories are needful because they embody that precious legacy from the past. My own face is now turned towards the West,[13] and soon each one of us who witnessed the sufferings of the Concentration Camps will have passed to our own rest; but so long as we who saw those things still live, they will live within us not as memories of sorrow, but of heroic inspiration. For what never dies and never should die is a great example. True it is of your dead that which Pericles said of his countrymen: – 'The grandest of all sepulchres they have, not that in which mortal bones are laid, but a home in the minds of men; their story lives on far away, without visible symbol, woven into the stuff of other men's lives.'

Your visible monument will serve to this great end – becoming an inspiration to all South Africans and to the women in particular. Generation after generation it will stand here pressing home in silent eloquence these great thoughts: – In your hands and those of your children lie the power and freedom won; you must not merely maintain but increase the sacred gift. Be merciful towards the weak, the down-trodden, the stranger. Do not open your gates to those worst foes of freedom – tyranny and selfishness. Are not these the with-holding from others in your control, the very liberties and rights which you have valued and won for yourselves? So will the monument speak to you.

Many nations have foundered on this rock. We in England are ourselves still but dunces in the great world-school, our leaders still struggling with the unlearnt lesson, that liberty is the equal right and heritage of every child of man, without distinction of race, colour or sex. A community that lacks the courage to found its citizenship on this broad base, becomes 'a city divided against itself, which cannot stand'.[14]

Lay hold of and cherish this deal of liberty then – should your statesmen be hostile, or coldly neutral, should your rich men be corrupt, should your press which ought to instruct and defend the liberties of all sections of the people, only betray – never mind – they do not constitute the nation. 'The nation,' said John Bright, 'is in the cottage.'[15]

You are the nation, you whom I see here to-day, you, most of whom live in remote villages and silent farms leading simple hard-working lives. You are your nation's very soul and on you lies the responsibility of maintaining her ideals by the perfecting of your own character.

The old, old watchword Liberty, Fraternity, Equality cries from the tomb; what these women, so simple that they did not know that they were heroines, valued and died for all other human beings desire with equal fervour. Should not the justice and liberties you love so well, extend to all within your borders? The old Greeks taught that not until power was given to men could it be known what was in them.

This testing time now has come to you.

For ponder a moment.

We meet on Dingaan's Day [from 16 December 1838, when the Battle of Blood River was fought in Natal during the Great Trek between the Boers and the Zulus], your memorial of victory over a barbarous race. We too, the great civilised nations of the world, are still but barbarians in our degree, so long as we continue to spend vast sums in killing or planning to kill each other for greed of land and gold. Does not justice bid us remember today how many thousands of the dark race perished also in Concentration Camps in a quarrel that was not theirs? Did they not thus redeem the past? Was it not an instance of that community of interest, which binding all in one, roots out racial animosity? And may it not come about that the associations linked with this day will change merging into nobler thoughts as year by year you celebrate the more inspiring 'Vrouwen-Dag' we now inaugurate. The plea of Abraham Lincoln for the black comes echoing back to me: 'They will probably help you in some trying time to come to keep the jewel of liberty in the family of freedom.'

Still more intimately will this Monument speak to the womanhood of South Africa and beyond to a yet wider range.

To you, women, it should cry ever: 'Go back, go back, to simpler lives to nobler principles; from these martyrs learn the grandeur of character that chooses rather to suffer to the uttermost than to win life by weakness.' Women, high or low, rich or poor, who have met in your thousands to-day; do not go empty away. You cannot be as if these Dead had not died. Your country demands your lives and your powers in another way. As the national life broadens, difficulties appear, little dreamed of in a simpler state. Complicated problems arise which seriously affect the well-being of your sons and daughters. It is for you to think out these problems in your homes, for you to be the purifying element in the body politic, for you to help guide the helm of the state.

The Dead have won for you a lofty place in the life of your nation, and the right to a voice in her counsels. From this sacred duty you surely dare not flinch. No one is too humble or unknown; each one counts.

For remember, these dead women were not great as the world counts greatness; some of them were quite poor women who had laboured much. Yet they have become a moral force in your land. They will enrich your history. As the diamonds and the gold glitter in the bedrock of your soil, so their stories written or handed down, will shine like jewels in the dark annals of that time.

And their influence will travel further. They have shown the world that never again can it be said that a woman deserves no rights as Citizen because she takes no part in war. This statue stands as a denial of that assertion. Women in equal numbers to the men earned the right to such words as the famous Athenian[16] uttered at the grave of his soldiers: 'They gave their bodies to the commonwealth receiving each for her own memory, praise that will never die.'

Nay, more – for they gave themselves, not borne on by the excitement and joy of active battle, as men do; but passively, with open eyes, in the long-drawn agony of painful months and days.

My Friends: Throughout the world the Women's Day approaches; her era dawns. Proudly I unveil this Monument to the brave South African Women, who sharing the danger that beset their land and dying for it, affirmed for all times and for all peoples the power of Woman to sacrifice life and more than life for the common weal.

This is your South African Monument; but it is more; for 'their story is not graven only on stone, over their native earth'.

We claim it as a WORLD-MONUMENT, of which all the World's Women should be proud; for your dead by their brave simplicity have spoken to Universal Womanhood, and, henceforth they are 'woven into the stuff'[17] of every woman's life.

The day after the inauguration, the Monument Committee sent a long telegram to Emily in Cape Town to inform her of the day's events:

Unveiling ceremony a thrilling success. Your message impressively read by Charles Fichardt in both languages. It was received with every mark of deep respect and affection by the twenty thousand people present, many of whom were moved to tears by its pathos and beauty. The great heart of the teeming multitude went out to you in a mighty sob of sincere gratitude and loving sympathy. The hearts of thousands who owe their lives to you responded reverentially to the prayer. May God bless you and give you in His good time the rewards befitting your noble self-sacrifice.[18]

Another sign of the Afrikaners' appreciation of Emily was the numerous Christmas gifts sent to her hosts in the Cape. One that stood out was a beautiful karos of silver jackal fur and ostrich feathers that the writer C. J. Langenhoven had sent all the way from Oudtshoorn.

It cheered Emily up: 'I felt all the charm and excitement that comes with the unexpected, the unknown and the beautiful.'[19]

15

Gandhi, Emily and the leaders

'To be with her is a spiritual uplifting for me.'
– Mahatma Gandhi about Emily, 1914

Tension between the Government and the Indian population had already been mounting for some time when Emily warned the Afrikaners at the inauguration of the Women's Monument against 'withholding from others in your control, the very liberties and rights you have valued and won for yourselves'.

Natal's Indian population had arrived for the most part as indentured labourers destined for the sugar plantations in a succession of shiploads since 1860. They were mainly low-caste Hindus from Madras, and more than a third of those who arrived were women.[1] The Transvaal Asiatic Law Amendment Act, which was passed in 1906, subjected all Indians and Chinese residing in the Transvaal to compulsory registration and identification by means of fingerprints. Registration certificates had to be carried at all times, and without such a certificate members of these two groups were unable to trade and could be imprisoned or even summarily deported.

Mahatma Gandhi, who had been part of the Natal Indian Ambulance Corps, carrying injured British soldiers during the Anglo Boer War, was particularly irked by this as he believed only criminals' fingerprints should be taken.

In terms of other legislation, all indentured Indians, regardless of age, who had come to South Africa between 1860 and 1911 and whose indenture had expired had to pay an annual tax of three pounds to be able to stay in the country.[2] At that stage, Indian labourers earned about one pound ten shillings per week.

Gandhi doing service as a Red Cross carrier during the Anglo-Boer War.

Photo: Anglo-Boer War Museum

In Cape Town, the Supreme Court had recently decided that traditional Indian Hindu and Muslim marriages would no longer be recognised. Children from such marriages would be deemed illegitimate.[3] Henceforth only 'Christian marriages' that were registered with the government would be legally recognised.

South Africa's Indian population was deeply aggrieved by these measures and laws, and others to which they were subjected.

In 1912 the leader of the Indian National Congress, Gopal Krishan Gokhale, visited South Africa to discuss the Indians' grievances with the government, but nothing came of it.[4] Gokhale was a friend of Gandhi, who mobilised mineworkers in Natal in October 1913 and led a protest march to the Transvaal.

When the marchers crossed the border on 6 November, Gandhi was arrested. On the sugar plantations and in factories in Natal, thousands of indentured labourers went on strike.

Pressure from England and at home compelled Smuts, the responsible minister, to institute a commission of inquiry into the causes of the strike. Gandhi and other leaders who had been arrested were released unconditionally.[5] By the end of November about twenty thousand striking Indian workers had returned to their workplaces.

Emily's friend Betty Molteno was in Natal from the end of November to late December 1913 and also visited Phoenix where Gandhi lived, where she experienced the 'Indian cause' at grass-roots level.[6] Thanks to the contact Emily had in the Cape with Alice Greene, Molteno's life partner, she obtained first-hand information about the events and the Indians' frustrations. Molteno wrote to Greene almost daily.

After attending the inauguration of the Women's Monument in Bloemfontein, Molteno returned home to Cape Town for Christmas. There were many aspects of the current political situation to discuss with Emily, who had long been aware of the unhappiness in the Indian community, referring to it in earlier letters.

As usual, Emily took up what was arguably her best weapon: the pen. Two days after Christmas she composed a telegram to Gandhi, with an Indian shawl draped around her shoulders.[7]

She had taken note of his intention to lead another big protest march to Pretoria on New Year's Day 1914, and while she had sympathy with the Indians' grievances, she beseeched him to postpone the march until the opening of Parliament. A big public march on 1 January might only arouse antipathy. She assured him of her appreciation of the Indian cause, as the women of England, too, still had few political liberties.[8]

There was 'excitement about Miss Hobhouse's telegram and a long reply telegram to her was read to me,' Betty wrote to Alice.[9] Gandhi had consulted his colleagues at Phoenix 'and agreed because of his esteem for her'.

Emily, the bridge-builder, appealed to her old friend Jan Smuts who was at the centre of the events. He would probably think an invalid like herself 'who has hardly come back from the brink of the grave' should rest and 'not mix in public affairs', but once one had developed a public conscience, it could not be silenced, she wrote. 'And we women, you know, are developing public consciences at a surprising pace.'[10]

The reason why Emily was writing to him was that Smuts was a minister and that Gandhi[11] had requested her to do so. She told him in no uncertain terms that political influence had multiple origins and was to be found on many levels. 'How many little things done by little people go to make up the turning points in history. It is not only what you big people do in your powerful offices.'

If Smuts had ever wondered where her sympathy lay in the conflict between the government and the Indians, this letter would have removed all doubt: 'I range myself more or less with the Indians. I have many personal friends Indians – people of vastly superior abilities to myself . . . Then too, being an unenfranchised woman I feel the solidarity that unites all who lack representation.'

She had no doubt that he wanted to change the marriage law in respect of Indians, and do away with 'that stupid £3 tax'. And her last blow: the indenture system was an evil that should never have been on the statute book.

The Indians' 'grievance is really moral not material', and 'governmental physical force' would never prevail against moral and spiritual convictions. 'Wasted time and wasted energy, dear Oom Jannie.' She appealed to him to rather promise the Indians 'recognition as befits a civilised section of the community' and consult them about matters affecting their interests.

She thought she could be useful in the current conflict, 'so use me or refuse me or abuse me just as pleases you dear Oom'. Gandhi had asked her to do what she could, and often in her life she had 'been able to effect reconciliations and agreements, when it was awkward for the principals concerned to lower their dignity without a human bridge to help facilitate'.[12]

Emily's pleas evidently did not fall on deaf ears, though she would certainly not have been the only person of whose opinion Smuts took note. On 21 January he and Gandhi came to an agreement about the Indians' grievances in Pretoria. Their marriages would in future be recognised along with those of other religious groups that allowed polygamy, and the three pound tax would be lifted.[13]

Shortly afterwards, Gandhi wrote to her: 'It was during the Boer war that I came to admire your selfless devotion to Truth, and I have often felt how nice it would be if the Indian cause could plead before you for admission . . .'[14] He was sorry to hear about her illness, and invited her to visit Phoenix where there would be 'loving hands to administer to your wants'. 'I hope that God will restore you to health and spare you for many a long year to continue your noble and unassuming work in the cause of Humanity.'[15]

Towards the end of January Emily went to stay at Groote Schuur, Prime Minister Louis Botha's official residence in Cape Town. It was here that Gandhi and his wife, Kasturba, met Emily for the first time a few weeks later. Gandhi told her that he had written several times in the past to request a meeting with the prime minister, but his approaches had been rebuffed.

Emily invited Gandhi again to Groote Schuur, this time for a meeting at which Botha and his wife were also present.[16] Gandhi later described it (as part of a compliment to Emily) as 'a perfect pilgrimage'.[17]

Later he thanked Betty Molteno 'for having brought me in contact with that noble soul. To be with her is a spiritual uplifting for me.'[18] On two occasions they had long private conversations, Emily wrote.[19]

During this period Emily felt that she was increasingly becoming politically estranged from Louis Botha and Jan Smuts, not to mention J. B. M. Hertzog. Hertzog had not even responded to her letters about Koppies and the lacemaking project.

Governing South Africa could be compared to governing four countries along with three racial groups – here she is referring to white, black and coloured people (including Indian) – with divergent ideals, as was apparent from the local Europeans who still talked of Europe as 'home', she wrote to Lady Courtney.

Yet they all wanted to have things done in their own way. 'A country unified but not united, just as I always felt it would be.'[20]

Smuts and Emily attended the opening of Parliament together. He was friendly, as usual, but she perceived a growing gulf between them about the government's racial policies that was unbridgeable. 'Well, well, I think they will live to see the trouble put down will crop up again and again and be a fretting sore . . .'[21]

When Emily departed for England in March 1914, Gandhi was on the quay in Table Bay to see her off. It was to be her last visit to the country that was so close to her heart but also had caused her so much heartache.

16

Into another battle

'We believe, not in narrow nationalism, but in internationalism, the brotherhood of man and we recognise no enemies; all humanity are our friends and our interests everywhere are one and the same. Preach this and you will be a great Statesman.

– Emily to Jan Smuts, 1914

Nationalism was one of the biggest causes of the First World War, which broke out on 28 July 1914 – barely four months after Emily's departure from South Africa.

Nowhere was nationalism a more compelling issue than in the Austro-Hungarian Empire that had been ruled by Emperor Franz Joseph since 1848. This empire, which had acquired that name in 1867, was essentially a patchwork of different ethnic minorities, with its stability constantly threatened by Slavic nationalism.[1]

The solution proposed by Archduke Franz Ferdinand, the heir to the throne, was to make the dual monarchy a triune monarchy in which the empire's Slavic peoples would have an equal voice. He called this policy 'Trialism'.

Germany, one of the strongest military powers in Europe, was the major ally of the Austro-Hungarian Empire and had by now got back to its feet after the Franco-German War of 1870–71. This made the French feel isolated, with the result that they entered into a new alliance with Russia against Germany in 1894.[2] France and Britain had a diplomatic understanding as a result of the Entente Cordiale they signed in 1904, which had resolved long-standing colonial disputes between the two countries.

Serbian nationalists who were members of a secret society known as the Black Hand, which sought to prevent the implementation of Franz Ferdinand's Trialism, assassinated him and his wife Sophie on 28 June 1914 in Sarajevo, Bosnia, while the couple were driving in an open car. This was the spark that ignited the powder keg in Europe.

Different countries became involved in the war at different stages, but by 10 August it was in full swing. On one side were the so-called Central Powers: Germany, Austria-Hungary, the Ottoman Empire (which included present-day Turkey, Syria, Lebanon, Iraq, Israel, Jordania and a part of Saudi Arabia) and Bulgaria, and on the other, the Allied Powers: Britain, France, Russia and Italy.[3] (After a period of neutrality, the United States entered the war on the side of the Allies in 1917.)

Not only was Emily a pacifist, she was at heart opposed to 'narrow nationalism', which she believed to be responsible for much of the conflict in the world. A few days after the outbreak of the First World War she wrote to the young Arthur Hobhouse, her cousin's son: 'Tragic days have dawned and I will not write of them. But events like these pierce into all our lives, however simple . . . and modify plans.'[4]

In a letter to Emily, Leonard wrote: 'My view now is that we can say nothing about neutrality or make no criticism of policy until the country is out of danger, which will not be till we have command of the sea.'[5] Any talk of mediation between the warring countries was futile, Leonard believed. 'You might as well ask a number of mad dogs to come and be petted . . . All our hopes for political and social progress are shattered once and for all.'[6] That same day a dejected but still resolute Emily wrote to Smuts: 'The Crash has come and Europe is armed to the teeth – Armageddon. Indeed. Our wretched Imperialists have, first by their secret

General Jan Smuts and Emily corresponded regularly for years. Most of their debates were about the topic of war.

Photo: Property of Elsabé Brits

diplomacy and lastly by their hasty actions drawn us into war which will ruin England also. Physical force has once more triumphed and all we have laboured to build up and do and teach for the last two generations and more is shattered.'[7]

She pleaded with Smuts not to let South Africa become involved in the war. What she would like to do was to put the British Foreign Secretary Sir Edward Grey in a battleship and Germany's Kaiser Wilhelm II in another, 'and let those two sink each other if they are so anxious to'.[8]

Emily firmly believed in mediation as a way of ending the conflict. Leonard did not agree, and believed Britain had to protect France and Belgium against the Germans.[9]

With the outbreak of the First World War, none other than Lord Kitchener, Emily's former opponent, was appointed as the British Secretary of State for War. He became the face of the war, with his image on thousands of recruiting posters: 'Britons, Kitchener wants you – join your country's army!' Another showed the Butcher of Khartoum with a commanding forefinger pointed at the viewer: 'Your Country Needs You'.[10] The life expectancy of the British soldiers who landed in France was about three weeks – they were simply decimated.[11]

In October 1914 Emily's old friends – the Courtneys, Bertrand Russell, Ramsay MacDonald, Arthur Ponsonby, Patrick Lawrence, Charles Trevelyan and others – established a left-wing pressure group, the Union of Democratic Control (UDC). The aim was not to call for an immediate end to the war, but 'to win the war at home' by tempering the hysteria with reason. They were especially opposed to the government's foreign policy and 'secret diplomacy', and advocated an open, democratic and negotiated peace settlement.[12]

Emily supported this group and wrote for their publication. She wrote an open letter to the women of Europe in which she said that as far as she was concerned, there was no difference between the people of Germany and those of Britain. To her, people were just people.[13]

> The war is crushing helpless millions. These are mostly women and children . . . If the war continues, die they must.
>
> A hundred years ago men proclaimed they fought, as each country asserts it is fighting to-day, to secure the rights, the freedoms and the independence of all nations. War failed to secure those objects then, can we reasonably suppose it will do so now?
>
> For militarism cannot kill militarism, nor war end war.[14]

Shortly after Britain entered the war in 1914 on the side of the Allied Powers, it requested South Africa to invade German South-West Africa in order to curb Germany. As a British dominion, South Africa was automatically involved in any British armed conflict, but had a say with regard to the nature of its support.

The South African government, with Smuts as Minister of Defence, acceded to Britain's request – which led directly to the rebellion of 1914 when Generals Christiaan de Wet, C. F. Beyers and Jan Kemp and about 11,470 men revolted against this decision. Only twelve years had passed since the Anglo-Boer War, and for many Afrikaners it was unthinkable to take up arms on the side of the former British foe, especially against Germany, with which many South Africans had a great affinity.[15]

Emily wrote to Smuts that he was leading his people on the 'imperialist path', which was precisely what 'we radicals' were opposed to. She could not bear the idea that the Boer generals – 'good, brave men' – might be sentenced to death for their rebellion, and pleaded with him not to have them executed.[16]

The rebellion failed, and in the end only Jopie Fourie was executed by firing squad after D. F. Malan had persuaded Smuts to show clemency to the others. Kemp and de Wet received the longest prison sentences and the heaviest fines, while Beyers drowned when he tried to escape.[17] All the rebels were released before the end of 1916.

The whole world, Emily wrote, was committing the greatest crime of all time. It would be an interminable war of attrition, and no one knew where it would end – perhaps in disease and famine. 'Oh! That Defence Force of yours, how often I wrote to you that it would lead to trouble and that if you had it you would not stop at defence, but begin to invade, and so it is.'[18]

'Till women have an equal voice in the guidance of world affairs men will go on with this mad destruction of all that makes life precious . . . But what thousands of widows and orphans all the nations are making for each other,' Emily wrote to Johanna Rood (now Osborne) at the lace school in Koppies. She also mentioned that the letters she received were being censored. No doubt the same applied to those she sent.[19]

Emily, who was now in Rome, believed that peace was in the hands of women; hence she wrote an 'Open Christmas Letter' to the women of Germany and Austria, which appeared under her name in the feminist monthly *Jus Suffragii* (The Right of Suffrage), the mouthpiece of the International Women's Suffrage Alliance. More than a hundred of the most prominent pacifists, all women and leading thinkers of their day, had added their signatures to the letter.

Emily's voice rang out clearly in the letter:

The Christmas message sounds like mockery to a world at war, but those of us who wished and still wish for peace may surely offer a solemn greeting to such of you who feel as we do. Do not forget that our very anguish unites us, that we are passing through the same experiences of pain and grief. Caught in the grip of terrible circumstance, what can we do? Tossed on this turbulent sea of human conflict, we can but moor ourselves to those calm shores whereon stand like rocks, the eternal verities – Love, Peace, Brotherhood . . .'[20]

Is it not our mission to preserve life? Do not humanity and commonsense alike prompt us to join hands with the women of neutral countries and urge our rulers to stay further bloodshed? Can we sit still and let the helpless die in their thousands, as die they must – unless we rouse ourselves in the name of humanity to save them? There is but one way to do this. We must all urge that peace be made with appeal to wisdom and reason.[21]

The large group German Socialist Women endorsed these sentiments, publishing a letter in *Jus Suffragii*, signing it with their names. They thanked Emily and her co-signatories for this initiative.

Emily also wrote to Smuts and told him about the International Women's Congress for Peace and Freedom (IWCPF) that would take place in April and May 1915 in The Hague, an event that British Prime Minister Herbert Asquith had referred to disparagingly as 'sparrows twittering'. But Emily was unperturbed, and did not spare the rod when it came to Smuts:

'We have a great crusade before us. We will try and undo all that you and those like you have done, the woe, the ruin, the misery you have wrought, and yet you write "we have the same ideals". You will take long to convince me of that. Men have indeed shown their absolute inability to guide and govern this fair world, without woman's civilizing and moderating influence to guide them.'[22]

She was outraged because he and Louis Botha had heeded Britain's request in August and taken South Africa into the war. He, Smuts, had let a glorious moment pass him by. 'So I mourn – not so much for the dead and dying as I mourn for England's lost prestige and South Africa's weakness in following her wrong.'[23] Those who had refused to take part in the war – the rebels – they were the ones who had acted nobly.

Jane Addams,[24] president of the Hague peace congress, invited Emily to attend the event. Emily was deeply touched by this gesture, but felt she was too ill to attend and would in any case find it difficult to get a permit to travel to The Hague.

Although she was in Italy, the British authorities were keeping her under surveillance. Sir Rennell Rodd, the British ambassador in Rome, had already complained about her to the Foreign Office: 'It would be better much better if these people [English pacifists] remained there [at home].' Emily had actually tried to convince people 'that we behaved in the most monstrous manner in South Africa,' he wrote.[25]

Out of 180 British women who applied to attend the congress, the government granted passports to only three. Women from Austria, Belgium, Canada, Denmark, Germany, the Netherlands, Hungary, Italy, Norway, Sweden and the United States attended, but not a single Frenchwoman managed to obtain permission.

At the congress, about thirteen hundred female peacemakers from warring and neutral countries came together to debate ways to end the war and prevent future conflict. The most important outcome was a resolution that they would all campaign for peace in their respective mother countries. This congress gave rise to the International Committee of Women for Permanent Peace, which became the Women's International League for Peace and Freedom[26] five years later.[27]

The foreword to the report on the proceedings of the congress came from Emily's pen, even though she had been unable to attend. Therein she quoted numerous organisations and individuals from across the world; she was clearly well informed about what was happening in socialist, pacifist and 'radical' organisations globally, and she had links with many of them.

The congress had been conceived spontaneously and 'lay in embryo in the hearts of many'. 'The Women's Congress unfurled the flag of Peace and – despite ridicule, disdain, opposition and disbelief – held it aloft before a bloodstained world.'[28]

The British branch of this movement was known as the Women's International League. In Britain, most of the suffrage activists, including Emily's old adversary Millicent Fawcett, supported the war. Emmeline Pankhurst and her daughter Christabel, too, were in favour of the war, but not Christabel's sister Sylvia. She ranged herself on Emily's side, and the two of them soon became friends.[29]

After the congress Addams and Dr Aletta Jacobs, the first female physician in the Netherlands, pacifist and a campaigner for women's suffrage, visited Emily in Rome. They offered her a position in the new organisation's offices in Amsterdam,[30] which Emily accepted.

Despite the efforts of various British government departments to keep track of Emily's movements, she returned to England without their knowledge and requested that her travel visas be renewed. She wanted to travel to Amsterdam via Bern in Switzerland and through Germany.

In Bern she succeeded in securing a meeting with Baron Gisbert von Romberg, the German ambassador in Switzerland, in an effort to bring about, if not peace, at least an amelioration of the effects of the war. 'It was a great relief talking things out with him . . . He reiterated that Germany would gladly withdraw her submarine warfare on mercantile ships if we would withdraw the food blockade.' Emily wrote to Jane Addams, asking her to request US President Woodrow Wilson put pressure on England with a view to achieving this. She realised that most of the so-called peace organisations did not desire peace, but a victory.[31]

Emily took up her position as acting secretary of the International Committee of Women for Permanent Peace in Amsterdam. She played a huge role in getting the organisation off the ground,[32] and worked in their office for three months.

Petronella van Heerden photographed in London in 1915 after she had visited Emily in Amsterdam.

Photo: By courtesy of Sarie

She made use of the opportunity to visit Petronella (Nell) van Heerden, who was studying medicine in Amsterdam. As a teenager in Philippolis, Nell had dropped in regularly on Emily and her companions at the weaving school. Keen that as many women as possible should hear Emily's peace message, she invited a number of prominent women to her flat.

Since Emily was unable to climb the four flights of stairs to the top, Petronella arranged for a litter in which she could be carried. Emily arrived wearing a black hat decorated with two big white ostrich feathers.[33] A short carpenter and a tall friend had to carry her, but as they rounded a corner something went awry and Emily slipped from the litter – Nell caught her in the nick of time. The meeting went off well nonetheless, and the Dutch women were impressed with Emily.[34] In October 1915, after three months in Amsterdam, Emily decided to return to London. This time the British authorities were on her track. The British Consul General in Rotterdam sent a telegram to his principals in London to alert them that 'the noted Pacifist' was on her way there, and provided detailed particulars of her passport and visa. When Emily and her servant Lucy arrived at the docks in Tilbury, a member of Scotland Yard was waiting for them. The women were searched and questioned.

Emily laughed off the incident in a letter to Aletta Jacobs. 'Lucy and I quite enjoyed being undressed at Tilbury. It was a new experience and as I tell her she will one day relate the adventure to her grandchildren.'[35]

After three weeks in England, Emily left once again for Switzerland and, she hoped, Italy. Whenever she crossed national borders, it was clear that the officials had been expecting her. Each time she was questioned.[36] In Switzerland the British ambassador, Evelyn Grant Duff, inquired from his principals whether he should allow her to travel to Italy.

A hitherto unpublished photo of Emily, taken in 1915 on the veranda at
the Hobhouse family home Hadspen, Somerset, England.

Photo: Private collection

Finally she obtained provisional permission; grudgingly, Emily
solemnly signed a document in which she promised 'not to
indulge in propaganda of any sort, especially propaganda in
favour of peace and not to remain in Italy a longer time than is
necessary to settle my personal affairs'.[37]

The British authorities decided that while this was all well and
good, it was the very last time she would be allowed to travel
outside Britain.

Emily stayed in Italy until April 1916 before returning to
Switzerland, where she attended an international conference of
anti-war socialists in the Alpine village of Kienthal. It became
known as the Second Zimmerwald Conference, where forty-three

'radical socialists' from eight countries gathered. (One of them was Vladimir Lenin, who would in the following year, 1917, play a leading role in the October Revolution that led to a communist one-party state in Russia.) Emily signed the register as an observer.[38]

Around this time she articulated her fundamental antipathy to war in a reasoned yet passionate manner in her diary:

Holding as I do, that war is not only wrong in itself, but a crude mistake, I stand wholly outside its passions and feel, while it lasts, a spectator of a scene I deplore, but with which I am in no sense part. I give and have given, and will give nothing to any fund to aid war or warriors . . .

I believe it useless to soften or civilize war – that there is no such thing as 'civilized war'; there is war between civilized people certainly, but as we now see that becomes more barbarous than war between barbarians. I believe that the only thing is to strike at the root of the evil and demolish war itself as the great and impossible Barbarity.

Hence all the Governments concerned in making this war are to blame in my eyes, none better than the others, though possibly some worse. They follow blindly an outworn and impossible system that must be swept away. I blame them all and am against them all equally . . .

I am not a harbinger of Peace itself yet hope I am a harbinger of the Spirit of Peace.[39]

17

Agent of peace

'A strangely moving experience to be sitting with the foreign minister of the country with which we are at death grips and having a heart to heart talk with what I believe was mutual confidence and respect.'

– Emily Hobhouse, about her conversation
with the German foreign minister, June 1916

While Emily was in Switzerland, she attended a meeting of the International Women's Union for Permanent Peace where she briefed the women on the congress in The Hague.

Following a report on this in the Swiss newspaper *Der Bund*, Sir Evelyn Grant Duff, the British ambassador in Switzerland, raised the alarm by notifying the Foreign Office in London.[1] Emily had violated her undertaking not to engage in any 'peace propaganda', he said. 'We shall do anything that is possible to put an end to [the woman's] activities.'[2] The authorities in London decided Emily was a 'peace crank', and on 27 May 1916

Emily's journey through Belgium and Germany, 1916

1 **6 June:** Bern to Basel

2 **7 June:** Wiesbaden to Cologne

3 **8 June:** Via Aachen (Aix-la-Chapelle) to Brussels

4 **9 June:** Brussels

5 **10 June:** Antwerp and Malines (Mechelen)

6 **11 June:** Charleroi

7 **12 June:** Louvain

8 **13 June:** Aerschot (Aarschot)

9 **14 – 16 June:** Brussels

10 **17 – 18 June:** Berlin via Cologne, Magdeburg and Potsdam

11 **21 June:** Ruhleben and Charlottenburg

12 **23 June:** From Berlin to Stuttgart, Singen, Zürich, Bern

13 **24 June:** Bern

14 **25 June:** Pontarlier, Le Havre to Southampton

15 **28 June:** London

N

W   E

S

North Sea

ENGLAND

NETHERLANDS

GERMANY

BELGIUM

FRANCE

SWITZERLAND

AUSTRIA-HUNGARY

ITALY

0   100   200   300   400km

Sir Edward Grey, the Foreign Secretary, ordered that her passport be withdrawn and that she had to return to England forthwith. It was now Grant Duff's responsibility to track her down and ensure that Grey's instructions were carried out.[3]

Emily was in Bern, where she had another meeting with Baron von Romberg, the German ambassador who also held a ministerial portfolio. She explained to him that she had to go to Germany and Belgium to see the wartime living conditions of civilians for herself. She also wanted to visit the British civilians in the internment camp at Ruhleben, on an old racing track near Berlin.

She had to wait several days for the good news that her request had been granted,[4] she had meanwhile received a seemingly innocent letter from Grant Duff in which he asked her to come to the British embassy.

Smelling a rat, Emily knew she had to leave Bern as soon as possible. She hurried back to von Romberg, who issued her a humanitarian passport that allowed her to visit the conflict areas. Within a few hours she and her servant Phoebe caught a train to Basel in Switzerland[5] where they met the courier, a certain von Rosenberg, who took them to the German border.

As they crossed the border, Emily was struck by the artificiality of such man-made barriers: 'Nature had no barrier – the earth and stones and grass were the same – one step only made the difference between the country of a friend and of an enemy. No barrier but man or at least governments had put up landmarks saying "here is all mine, there is all yours".'[6]

Shortly afterwards, Emily bought a newspaper at a station. The headline news read: 'KITCHENER IS DEAD' – and it was not as a result of natural causes.

The sixty-six-year-old British war secretary had been aboard

HMS *Hampshire* on a secret mission to Russia, reportedly at the invitation of Tsar Nicholas II.

On 5 June the *Hampshire* had departed on its voyage from Scapa Flow at the Orkney islands off the coast of Scotland.[7] Owing to the stormy weather, the ship had to change course twice. Between seven and eight o'clock that evening, there was a tremendous explosion that nearly ripped the ship in two.

According to the few survivors, in the frenetic chaos on the deck someone had called: 'Make way for Kitchener!' But no one had seen him trying to reach one of the few lifeboats. On the contrary, he had apparently calmly remained standing on the deck, in his khaki uniform.[8] Within fifteen minutes of the explosion – which later investigations attributed to a German sea mine – the *Hampshire* went down with more than six hundred people on board. Of the fourteen men who managed to reach the coast, two died. In the days that followed, corpses continued to wash up on the shores of the Orkneys but there was no sign of Kitchener.[9]

In the train en route to Cologne, Emily read about the demise of her old nemesis with mixed feelings, as she later recalled:

> A crowd of memories rushed back upon me and I felt regret that I should not be able to make him learn (what however he knew well enough) that Belgium was not devastated and destroyed as he destroyed South Africa – the Free State and the Transvaal . . . My opinion was that though no special military loss, Kitchener was a loss to peace prospects being probably the only man in England who was impervious to public opinion and with shoulders broad enough to bear that hostile opinion if he thought we could gain no military decision and must make peace by negotiation.[10]

In the hotel in Cologne that evening, Emily had her first taste of the effects of food shortages during this war. Supper consisted of a small cupful of watery soup, three thin slices of bread, and a few stewed cherries.

The next day, she and Phoebe travelled for three hours by train via Aachen to Brussels. With the exception of a small salient around Ypres, the whole of Belgium was occupied by the Germans. It was clear that much blood had been spilt in the country. According to several reports, the slightest sign of resistance on the part of the Belgians had been met with extreme violence. Women, even children, had been shot and homes torched. In Brussels Emily met her new escort, the thirty-two-year-old Baron Falkenhausen, Freiherr von Friedensthal, in his long, blue military overcoat.[11] She was struck by the eyes of the German soldiers when they saluted their officers. They had to look von Friedensthal – and all other officers – straight in the eyes when saluting, and Emily tried to gauge their expressions.

The soldiers' eyes were charged with feeling, almost pathetic and pleading; in one or two cases the expression showed hatred, in others the eyes were sad and those of men in physical pain. 'These constant recurring glimpses into the inmost souls of scores of men move me to tears and haunt and will haunt me for years.'[12]

Von Friedensthal informed her that her visit was subject to strict conditions. He had to accompany her at all times. She had to return to the Astoria Hotel in Brussels every evening. She was not allowed to buy anything in a shop on her own. She was forbidden to speak to any Belgians. Emily was dumbfounded. With these restrictions, she would be unable to establish the true state of affairs beyond what her eyes could tell her.

Nevertheless, she was allowed to visit a soup kitchen for the city's residents. The food appeared good but insufficient. Though the people were neat in appearance and orderly, they seemed hungry and weak, with wan faces and dark rings around their eyes. 'Not ill like the Boer women – but getting ill.'[13]

Back at the hotel, Emily was conscious of antagonistic stares because she was in the company of a German officer. It was an uncomfortable situation for both, with the baron also feeling the effect of the Belgians' antagonism towards the German occupiers.

In the port city of Antwerp, the docks were completely deserted. In Malines, Emily picked up bits of glass from the cathedral's shattered stained-glass windows. Here she also saw damaged houses, historic buildings of which only the skeletons remained. Houses had been destroyed in Charleroi too, but most parts of the city were unscathed. In Louvain, in the rain, she saw the ruins of the famous university library that had been deliberately burned, as well as the badly damaged cathedral.

She was reminded of Bernard Shaw's observation: 'You can have glorious wars or you can have glorious cathedrals, but you can't have both.'[14]

Louvain had been partially destroyed by the Germans in August 1914 because they believed it to be a hotbed of guerrilla activities. More than 240 civilians had been executed on the main square.[15]

Yet she kept feeling that her inability to speak freely to the inhabitants prevented her from getting the full picture of civilian life under German occupation.

In Aerschot, which Emily visited on 13 June 1916, she saw signs of war damage here and there. Frozen and wet through with rain, she sought shelter at an inn and asked to sit in front of the fire. For the first time in her life she drank half a glass of gin with hot water as a preventative measure against a threatening cold. To her delight, she was served a good meal consisting of an omelette and vegetables.[16]

Emily's lumbago troubled her, but she pressed on after managing to buy a woollen vest. Her suede jacket, too, was of great help against the cold.

On 17 June Emily received the joyous news that she was allowed to travel to Berlin. Contrary to the rules, she went shopping on her own and bought eggs, cheese, butter, biscuits, wine and chocolate for the journey.[17]

The station at Cologne was packed with German soldiers when their train passed through at half past ten that evening. The baron tried to hoodwink her by saying that the station was always so full of men, but on two occasions now she had seen so many *soldiers* assembled here. She said nothing, although she knew the troops were streaming to the Western Front. The following day Emily travelled through Magdeburg and Potsdam to Berlin.

Emily stayed at the Fürstenhof Hotel. The breakfast of excellent coffee, hot milk, a bread roll, two slices of 'war bread', a pat of butter, jam and sugar (which she never used) was sufficient for her needs.

The military commandant in Berlin gave her permission to move around freely. At last! 'I felt a great desire to get away and be alone . . . I was half in a dream and half dead with fatigue.'[18]

Emily knew the German foreign minister, Gottlieb von Jagow, whom she had befriended in Rome when he was the German ambassador there. He was now in Berlin, and she sent him a note to thank him for his assistance in making her visit possible. He responded immediately, inviting her to come to his office on Wilhelm Street that same day, 19 June, between six and seven o'clock in the evening.

Emily had to climb several flights of stairs to the office. A number of men were waiting to see von Jagow, but on her arrival he received her warmly and immediately invited her into his office. The room looked out on a garden; he was seated on a chair and she on a sofa.

'He was very simple and natural and wholly unofficial in manner . . . I felt lifted into some sphere aloof from our blood-stained World. That I should sit in the foreign office of Berlin ere the war ended, I had always felt – it had been a piece of second sight to me and there I was and it all looked familiar and as if I had seen and known it before.'

She found it 'a strangely moving experience to be sitting with the foreign minister of the country with which we are at death grips and having a heart to heart talk with what I believe was mutual confidence and respect. Only I was tortured by my feeling of utter mental incompetence – partly from an empty brain, the result of over fatigue and partly from a sense I was not trained enough maybe in public matters and diplomacy to make the most of a chance so unusual and so striking. I had the right spirit, but body and mind lacked power and knowledge.'[19]

Their conversation lasted for half an hour. According to von Jagow, Germany no longer wanted to continue fighting but would do so if they had to, even if it had to take years. No one was gaining from the war any more. The Germans wanted peace, but they feared that the English were not inclined to pursue it. 'We know England is not beaten,' he said. 'It is true Germany has had great victories, but she has had great defeats; England may not have had great victories, but neither has she suffered great defeats. We know full well that England is not defeated.'[20]

That evening Emily realised that it would be in the interest of England – and of the peace effort – if a British statesman such as Grey or Lord Robert Cecil, rather than she, were to hold talks with von Jagow. Early the next day she wrote to von Jagow: maybe they could first meet and talk as men so that a basis could be found for a discussion as statesmen. 'Such a plan seems to me more sensible than continued slaughter and if you agreed and wished I could make a similar suggestion to them in London.'[21]

Von Jagow wrote back the same day and agreed with her that provisional peace negotiations had to be unofficial. But now the chess game started: while he was in favour of talks, he was unable to see the benefit of such a meeting at the present time because of the attitude of the British leaders. Any steps towards peace that were initiated by Germany would be interpreted in England as a sign of 'our inability to continue the war and would have, in consequence, the effect of giving a new encouragement to the war-party in your country'. England had to take the first step.[22]

Emily was ready with her move: von Jagow did not have to worry, she assured him; she would make the suggestion of a meeting sound as if it came from her. If she should find that the British leaders were favourably disposed towards the idea, she would send him a message via Switzerland with von Romberg. 'You see it would give me confidence in making the suggestion in England if I knew that you would not reject it on your side. That knowledge, however, would be for myself alone.'[23]

She would make it quite clear to the British leaders that the Germans' desire for peace was based on 'reason and humanism' and not prompted by a shortage of arms, food, funds or soldiers on their side.

Van Jagow replied that he would not reject informal talks, but they should not be misinterpreted.

On the battlefield, there was no question of any slackening. The Battle of Verdun in France, between German and French forces, had started in February and lasted until 16 December

– the longest single battle (in the form of numerous offensives) of the war. About 360,000 French soldiers and nearly 340,000 Germans died in a bloody conflict during which the German offensive against Verdun was repulsed.

While this battle was still going on, the British and French forces launched an offensive against the Germans at the river Somme on 1 July – with the objective of requiring them to move men away from Verdun and thereby relieving the pressure on the French. Ironically, this offensive eventually claimed considerably more casualties than the Battle of Verdun, though it was shorter and lasted only four and a half months. More than one million soldiers died in the Battle of the Somme, which was a greater setback to the Germans than to the Allied Powers.

On 21 June, Emily was finally able to visit the Ruhleben camp, near Spandau outside Berlin, where British civilian men were interned at the horse-racing track. It brought back memories of her South African experiences.

> It was curiously stirring to be in a camp again – with all its sordidness and its artificiality – its neatness and its squalor – its dun colour and monotony, its forlorn efforts to find amusement and occupation – its shabbiness and the worn strained faces of the inmates.
>
> Only in this camp there were no children, no raging sickness, no starvation, no skeletons, no deaths. The problem was different to that which faced me sixteen years before in South Africa.[24]

Emily met a Captain Powell, the leader of the men, who asked for her help to get those over the age of forty-five out of the camp and the country before winter arrived. She promised to do all in her power to achieve this.

Patiently, she walked through the whole camp and talked to dozens of men, shook their hands and comforted them. She visited the kitchen where she tasted some of the food, and inspected the hospital and the barracks. She also spoke to the camp authorities and listened to their 'boring explanations'.

As she spoke to many 'lads' as well as older men, she became 'more and more sure that the problem was mental and psychological, not material. Some of the younger men also showed signs of great strain . . . I thought the men kept their barracks very dirty and told them so. Their excuse was "no time" yet there were hundreds of merchant seamen there well accustomed to keeping the deck of a ship spotless.'[25]

On her departure from the camp that afternoon, many of the men came to say goodbye to Emily. 'It gave a horrible pang to go away and leave them there – such a forlorn and despairing atmosphere hung about them. It was one of the most painful moments in my life and as such will always be remembered and the whole issue is stamped indelibly on my mind . . . I was almost dead with exhaustion.'[26]

But the gruelling day had not ended yet for the fifty-six-year-old Emily, who then paid a visit to the sanatorium in Charlottenburg for people suffering from psychiatric conditions. Here she spoke in a muted voice to the sixty-odd patients, who were in a wretched state.

The next day Emily took the train to Berlin and from there to Switzerland. She saw a giant Zeppelin floating in the sky.

18

'Traitor!'

'Is there no means of bringing to justice a lady who goes abroad for the purpose of betraying her country?'
    – John Butcher, House of Commons, 31 October 1916

A long, bureaucratic questionnaire awaited Emily at the British consulate in Bern when she went to apply for a visa for her and Phoebe to travel to London. Out of courtesy, she decided to pay Sir Evelyn Grant Duff, the British ambassador, the visit he had requested before her hasty departure from Bern.

When she walked into his office, he did not shake her hand but immediately went on the attack: 'Miss Hobhouse, have you directly or indirectly by word or letter been undertaking peace propaganda? Have you attended any peace meetings, conferences or congresses? Have you been consorting with Pacifists, Socialists or Germans?'[1]

Emily did not respond. She only said that she had visited the Ruhleben camp.

She could see now why people had told her that Grant Duff was a 'poor little creature in a state of such excitement as hardly to be considered normal'. He looked like a 'little cock-sparrow giving itself airs'.[2]

Grant Duff started shouting at her: 'You have been to Germany – enemy territory – without British permission! You have broken the law!' France would not allow her entry, she would be imprisoned there, and England would not allow her to leave the country ever again, he threatened.

Emily was not intimidated by his bluster. Surely what she had done was not so serious. And what specific law had she contravened?

The ambassador was not interested in hearing about her visit to Ruhleben, but she briefed him on it nonetheless – and also stated that she had information that needed to be conveyed to the British government. She would not disclose to him what it was but said she would convey it to Sir Edward Grey, the Foreign Secretary.[3]

The 'conversation' was over. Grant Duff opened the door for Emily – and kept his hands firmly behind his back.

He sent a telegram to London at once, informing the Foreign Office that Emily had admitted she had been in Germany and that she 'has information to lay before His Majesty's Government which she declined to divulge to me'.[4]

Emily decided the best way to get a message through to von Jagow would be via the physician and suffragist Dr Aletta Jacobs in Amsterdam. She also spoke to Baron von Romberg, the German ambassador, who promised that if she did not get a passport he would help her to get into the Netherlands.

Emily wrote two letters, one to Aletta and one to von Jagow – letters that would become part of a huge drama.

She informed Aletta that she would be unable to write freely once she was back in England and told her about her travels through Belgium and Germany, specifically her visit to Berlin where she had talked to von Jagow. 'From this, much I hope may develop. I am to keep open a line of communication with him. Will you help? – say nothing.'

This request was followed by the kind of instructions one might expect from a spy: 'If you have a letter from me (or card) from home, beginning as above 'Dear Friend' and signed by me – but either allusive or with not much meaning for you, will you put it into an envelope, but do not post it – take it to the ambassador at The Hague, to forward urgently. If, through the same hand, any word or letter should come back to be forwarded to me, will you re-write it, if necessary in your own hand and sign it with your name, unless it should reach you from the Legation (von Romberg) in a form in which it could be forwarded.'[5]

On 25 June 1916 Emily wrote a letter to von Jagow about her meeting with Grant Duff in which she told him he could communicate with Aletta and gave him the latter's address in Amsterdam.

Grant Duff was very angry, but I soothed him as one does a child, and I think he will let me go. Under the new French regulations the fact of my visit had to come out otherwise he had no idea of it . . . I have a reliable friend there [in Holland] whom I have instructed to deliver any letter or postcard she receives from me worded allusively to the German Minister at The Hague to be forwarded to you. If this postcard spoke of Edward or Edward's brother, you would know it meant Grey or one of his colleagues. Should you wish to send me any word in reply, she could send it to me instructed by your Minister . . . She [Aletta] is absolutely reliable but of course I told her nothing.[6]

Two days after her meeting with Grant Duff, when Emily arrived at his office to collect her visa, the officials insisted on more passport photos. Finally she found a place that promised to have the photos ready within three hours. These photos were given to her in a big, square envelope that Emily put in the green linen bag in which she always carried her papers. The bag also contained the letter to Aletta that she intended to post just before her departure.

At the consulate, she gave the big envelope with photos to Phoebe to hand over to the authorities, while she waited. Emily wanted to read through her letter to Aletta once more to ensure that everything was correct. To her dismay, however, it was no longer among all the other documents in the green linen bag. She was convinced that it had been in there. (The glue on the envelope with the photos must have stuck to the letter to Aletta, which outlined all her plans for staying in contact with von Jagow.)

Phoebe was away for a long time.

At last she returned with the passports and the letter to Aletta. But she had bad news: the officials had found and read the letter!

Phoebe related that they had first taken the letter, disappeared into an office and locked the door. She had heard the rattling of a typewriter, which might mean that they had copied it. On their return, they had told her nonchalantly that they did not think the letter was meant for them.

When Emily took it out, the marks of a typewriter ribbon were clearly visible. There was no doubt that its contents had been copied. The British government was aware of her plans!

Emily and Phoebe left for England at once, but at Pontarlier in France all Emily's possessions were searched and her writing paper confiscated – fortunately not her diaries. They then proceeded by train to Le Havre, where she was stopped and her passport was examined. When the officials saw her name, they checked it and produced an index card (no. 85) – they had a record of her.

Emily was scrutinised from head to toe, and then had to remove some of her clothes and submit to being searched. At last she and Phoebe were allowed to continue their journey.

Emily's notes on her visits to Germany and Belgium. She was staying in the Westminster Palace Hotel in London at the time. 'General slow enfeeblement. Tubercular trouble', 'As I sat with von Jagow it came into my head – if only it could begin', 'Difficulties vanish – unities appeared.'

Photo: Courtesy of Jennifer Hobhouse Balme

On 28 June 1916 Emily was back in London. Eager to effect the release of the older men in the Ruhleben camp and get peace negotiations going, she notified Foreign Secretary Sir Edward Grey that she wished to see him. But his advisers dissuaded him from granting her an audience.

In the meantime Grant Duff wrote Sir Edward a letter marked 'SECRET' in which he told him about Emily's letter to Aletta, enclosing a copy. In his opinion, Emily's actions in Berlin and Belgium had been illegal, and she had even preached to him about Ruhleben. This letter was the key to an international pacifist conspiracy in which militant women were involved, he believed. In addition, Emily was in contact with von Jagow, so much so that they were now using a code.[7]

Hereafter the Home Office's police unit also became involved in the case, in the person of Basil Thomson, head of the CID at New Scotland Yard, who was the liaison with the War Office.

Thomson, nicknamed 'the Spy-catcher', had an aversion to female suffrage activists, Irish nationalists, Marxists and Jews. He summoned Emily to the offices of New Scotland Yard to be interrogated.

When she arrived, he had her sit down on a low chair opposite him. Not long before Emily, the female spy Mata Hari had also sat in that chair as he interrogated her. A lack of evidence had led to her release, but she was later executed by the French. Sir Roger Casement too had occupied that chair – only a day before Emily's interrogation he had been found guilty of high treason and sentenced to death for his involvement in the Irish nationalist rebellion of April 1916 – the Easter Rising – and was hanged shortly afterwards.[8]

The chair had conspicuously low armrests. The reason for this was that apparently, when people lied, they pressed down subconsciously on these supports to straighten their posture.

Thomson clearly knew about Emily's letter to von Jagow, even if he didn't know its contents. After this interrogation he wrote a report in which he said that, as far as he was concerned, any conclusions of Emily's about the war were not important. The Germans probably regarded her as an unofficial peace envoy from whose visit to von Jagow they would expect limited useful results.

> Up to a point she was evidently speaking the truth.
>
> I am expecting today or tomorrow a draft of a letter that she wrote to von Jagow from Switzerland, in her handwriting, which has come into our agent's hand, but what she did omit to tell me is that she was given an address in Amsterdam to which she is to communicate when she wishes to write to von Jagow. Probably it will be possible to intercept the letter, but one cannot be sure, and therefore she ought to be treated with great reserve.[9]

When the letter to von Jagow was obtained, Thomson's chief at the Metropolitan Police, C. F. Dormer, concluded that Emily was a dangerous spy. The police recommended that the Home Office should have her arrested as she was communicating with England's enemies.[10] This led the British authorities to decide finally that no official should grant Emily an audience.

Emily, unaware of this, was still determined to speak to Grey, but his secretary informed her that she should rather write a letter. 'I write to assure you that I bear no message from von Jagow and am in no way an emissary of the German Government, a thing which I am sure would not be acceptable to you.' She considered it her duty, however, to convey to him certain information that she could not put in writing.[11]

Grey did not respond to her letter. Again Emily wrote to him, and again he ignored her.

She then appealed to Lord Robert Cecil, Grey's under-secretary of state for foreign affairs, who also served in the cabinet as Minister of Blockade. Could he arrange to let the Belgians get more food? They were having a difficult time, and some women and children were already enfeebled. Tuberculosis was rife, she informed him.[12]

Cecil, too, had gatekeepers. Emily was 'a mischievous pacifist', two of them warned him. 'This lady is a person with whom we must be very much on our guard. She acts as a German agent and there is a question of her being interned . . . her intervention is unnecessary.'[13]

Thomson came to the conclusion that Emily was a 'silly, mischievous old woman, but not disloyal to the country'.[14] Finally Arnold Rowntree, a Liberal MP, persuaded Cecil to speak to Emily about the camp. She had to make an appointment with Guy Locock, an assistant under-secretary in Cecil's office, but after five attempts at phoning him she threw in the towel and sent him her suggestions in writing. It is uncertain whether he received them, but the plan that was eventually implemented corresponded largely to her suggestions.[15]

Emily proposed that the camps be abolished as nothing was to be gained by keeping them but moral and mental decay. Men of fifty and over should have the choice of: 1. repatriation with their wives; or 2. internment in a neutral camp and the wives should receive an allowance, or 3. To remain in a small camp with a choice of employment.

Men who are medically unfit of forty-five and fifty years should have the same choice. All the men of military age should be in a neutral camp (in a neutral state) and be allowed to work. And each country should pay the neutral state an agreed sum as is done with military convalescents.

Leonard Hobhouse, Emily's younger brother.

Photo: Courtesy of Jennifer Hobhouse Balme

Emily's plan proposed that all British male prisoners of war above the age of fifty, as well as those who were younger and medically unfit, be exchanged for prisoners held by England. After a parliamentary debate in July 1916 Cecil announced that negotiations were being conducted about an exchange of prisoners of war – they proposed to repatriate men over fifty and those over forty-five who were ill.[16]

Emily tried to explain to her brother Leonard what she had seen and experienced in Germany and Belgium in the aftermath of the conflict; that the men in the camp at Ruhleben were depressed and that their problems were not so much material as psychological. In her view, being prisoners of war was harder for civilians as they were less adaptable than soldiers.[17]

Leonard had initially advocated British neutrality but as the conflict intensified he started supporting military action against Germany – even the use of poison gas. He wrote several articles in the *Manchester Guardian* in which he, among other things, referred to 'the mazes of German mysticism, militarism and megalomania which had plunged the civilised world into war'.

Emily's beloved nephew, Oliver Hobhouse, in uniform.
He was initially in the infantry during World War
One, but later joined the air force. For her, so opposed
to the war, this was a huge disappointment.

Photo: Courtesy of Jennifer Hobhouse Balme

For Leonard, his son Oliver's active participation in the war was a cause for pride, but for Emily it was a cause for heartache.[18] As she had often done in the past, Emily targeted the influential people of the day – including those who stood outside politics. She set her sights on the head of the Anglican Church, Randall Davidson, the Archbishop of Canterbury.[19] He agreed to see her on 2 August 1916.

Emily confided in Davidson and told him about everything she and von Jagow had discussed and agreed. She confessed that she was feeling trapped and powerless because she had to keep silent. Someone, a strong leader, had to take the lead with regard to the message of peace, she pleaded. 'If the tide of militarism is rising, as it seemed, at least the Christian Church should say: "This cannot be tolerated, thus far and not further." '[20]

But the archbishop seemed unmoved by Emily's moral appeal. Her information about the conversation with von Jagow was worthless if they were unable to speak about it freely, he said. Von Jagow had to give her permission to say that he was indeed willing to discuss peace.

Thanks to a Swiss friend, Dr Theodore Kocher, Emily managed after a considerable struggle to get a message through to von Jagow, whom she called 'Henry'. But von Jagow's eventual reply was a firm 'NO!'[21]

Emily still had her hopes pinned on the archbishop: 'I pray it may be, for words fail to express how strongly I feel, that we are all wrong to continue this slaughter, as in the end Negotiation must be resorted to . . . My hope in telling you what I did was just this – that the knowledge that our opponent would support and forward such effort would give irresistible power – and multitudes at home and abroad would rise up and call you blessed . . .'[22]

She tried to convince Davidson to come to the fore as a religious leader for the sake of peace and to use his influential position by taking an anti-war stand.

Once again her message did not seem to fall on fertile soil. He did not wish to go into the question of what was right and wrong at this point, Davidson informed her, and 'there are greater things in heaven and earth than peace, eagerly as we long and pray that peace may come if it be of a righteous kind'.[23]

Having evidently decided that the public might show understanding for her actions, Emily wrote an article for *The Nation* and the Union of Democratic Control's newsletter UDC under her name, with the title 'Interview with a High Official of The German Foreign Office'. Another article of three thousand words, in which she wrote extensively about her visit to Belgium, appeared in the UDC newsletter and in Sylvia Pankhurst's paper, the *Women's Dreadnought*, in October 1916.

Without mentioning von Jagow's name, the first article was essentially an account of Emily's conversation with the German foreign minister.

Now everyone knew where she had been and what she had done: she had visited enemy territory in wartime and spoken to a high-ranking German official who had declared: 'We do not wish to continue fighting, but if we must we can.'[24]

I heard this most forcibly from the lips of a high official of the [German] Foreign Office. He told me that Germany wished for peace and was willing to enter into negotiations to that end, but he reiterated that he feared there was no such disposition of English statesmen. He said he could not conceive that any country could gain anything by a continuance of the war.[25]

The first page of the article Emily wrote in the *Woman's Dreadnought*, a socialist and feminist newspaper.

He reminded me of the fact – very real to them if not understood here – that twice Germany had plainly set forth to the world that she desired peace. He said the only reply to those statements of her willingness had been insults. He felt that under these circumstances it was for our side to make the next move.

Emily was immediately accused by readers of *The Times* of being a propagandist for the Germans as she had visited their country under their protection. Charge her with high treason, some urged in letters to the paper.[26]

Emily's world started changing dramatically on 26 October 1916. In the House of Commons, Lord Robert Cecil was bombarded with questions. Was he aware that a Miss Emily Hobhouse, a British subject, had been enabled to travel hundreds of miles through Germany and Belgium? Did she have permission to do so? Was it with the knowledge of the British government? Had she left the country under false pretences?

At least there was also a 'sympathetic' question: might her visit to German high officials not be 'of great service' to Britain?[27]

Cecil replied that the government had had no knowledge of the matter until Emily's arrival in Switzerland. He gave the assurance that the government 'never issued a passport to enable any British subject to go to Germany . . . I presume she had a passport before she went abroad.'

Had she travelled under false pretences? 'No, Sir, I should not like to say that . . . No doubt she obtained a passport to go to an Allied or neutral country. What she did after that I do not know. I have no reason to suppose she made false statements to us.'[28]

He added, however: 'I think it is highly undesirable that any British subject should pay visits to German high officials.'

Five days later there were more parliamentary debates, this time in both the House of Commons and the House of Lords. Again Emily was the topic of discussion, and again Cecil was driven into a corner – not out of sympathy with Emily. Was he going to take any further action in this matter, he was asked.[29] 'I imagine Miss Hobhouse will not be allowed again to leave the country,' was the reply.

John Butcher, a Conservative MP, asked: 'Is there no means of bringing to justice a lady who goes abroad for the purpose of betraying her country?'[30]

That was not a question the Foreign Office could answer, Cecil replied, but if Butcher so desired, he could put it to the legal advisers of the Crown.

Charles Trevelyan of the Liberal Party, a co-founder of the UDC, asked if it was not the case that immediately on her return to the country, Emily had 'offered to give every possible information she had to the government'.

Cecil then blatantly lied by saying: 'I do not know anything about that . . .' What he did know, he continued, was 'that the general opinion of the House – and I believe of the country – is that Miss Hobhouse's activities have not been in the interests of this country'.[31]

In the House of Lords, the aged Lord Courtney came to Emily's defence and said that, as a friend of humanity, she had been moved to go into Germany 'to ascertain something which might be of use, not to Germany, not to her own country above all countries, but . . . to her own country and all of Europe'.

That action, 'be it wise or otherwise, a noble act of supreme tenderness,[32] or a foolish act of self-belief' was her 'offence', Courtney argued. She had merely tried to 'ascertain some things which she thought might be useful for the restoration of international peace'.[33]

On the same day, 1 November, the debate was continued in the House of Commons after Ronald McNeill of the Conservative Party had received a reply to a question he had put to the Attorney General, Sir Frederick Smith. Regarding Emily's activities, McNeill asked whether legislation existed that would make what she had done a criminal offence. Smith replied that there was no such legislation, but he suggested that the Defence of the Realm Act be amended. And if people read carefully, they would see that what Emily had written in the press was her own opinion, and it was not possible to establish its veracity. For the duration of the war, however, she would not be allowed to leave the country again, and 'she will not enjoy similar opportunity in the future of disparaging the cause of the Allies'.[34]

On 7 November the Defence of the Realm Act was amended[35] so that no British subject would in future be allowed to travel to enemy territory without permission from the authorities.

The press reported the debates in detail, and most papers castigated Emily with scathing commentary. Her role during the Anglo-Boer War was raked up again and one paper referred to 'the indefatigable zeal with which she bore testimony against her own countrymen'.[36] She was even called a traitor.

In a letter to *The Times*, Emily wrote that when she was journeying back to England from her winter home in Italy, the idea of visiting Germany only came to her after she had arrived in Switzerland. 'I went to Germany quite simply and openly, contravening no law; I went under my own name with a "humanitarian pass" in the interest of truth, peace and humanity; and I am proud and thankful to have done so.'[37]

In the midst of these events, Stephen Hobhouse, the son of Emily's cousin Henry V, was imprisoned for six months as a conscientious objector; he had refused to participate in military activities. The attendant publicity made Emily an even more controversial figure. On top of that, the German government used her report on Belgium as propaganda.[38]

Nevertheless, the government decided not to prosecute her. On the one hand, there was probably not enough evidence against her, and on the other, they did not want to make a martyr out of a pacifist who was held in high esteem by a group of influential Liberals.[39]

Though it was indeed an offence to make false statements about the war, according to the Attorney General, they could not prove that what she had written about Belgium and Germany was false.[40] Yet most Britons now despised Emily even more.

In the autumn of 1916 Emily received an invitation to address an informal meeting of the Women's International League (WIL) at a flat in London. Come and tell us about your visit to Belgium and Germany, the invitation read. They were clever enough not to hold the meeting in the WIL's offices, so that it could not be regarded as official.[41]

On her arrival at the flat of Emmeline Pethick-Lawrence, a well-known suffragette, Emily was given a rather cool reception. Emmeline and others such as Sylvia Pankhurst, a friend of Emily, had earlier broken away from the Women's Social and Political Union (WSPU) that had become too militant for their taste.

When Sylvia arrived at the meeting, she saw a frail, elderly woman sitting apart on a chair. To her shock she realised that this was none other than Emily, whom she had last seen ten years ago. Yet she looked as if she had aged more than ten years during this time. Emily seemed 'saddened and was obviously labouring under a painful agitation'.[42]

The WIL women were both curious about what Emily had seen at the war front and outraged because she had contravened the law of the land in the process. These women had been Emily's fellow campaigners in the struggle for women's suffrage, but now the war and Emily's radical choice to take pity on the victims on the enemy's side as well had created a gulf between them.

The women made it quite clear to Emily that they did not approve of her projects in Germany and Belgium, that she acted alone and not on behalf of the WIL. The questions they asked were mostly critical and hostile.

As usual, however, Emily stated her case with great resoluteness and conviction. 'It seemed as she spoke that we were in Court for the trial of crimes and she the prisoner in the dock,' Sylvia reported. 'When she ceased no one questioned her, no one commented on her experience.'[43]

One of the women made the suggestion, which was probably well intentioned but inappropriate nonetheless, that Emily could perhaps become a member of the British branch of the WIL. Sylvia cringed.

Emily was clearly wounded by this empty gesture. She did something that was rare for her: she stood up from the meeting and shuffled out of the room, muttering an audible 'No!'.

Sylvia hurried home to apologise to Emily in writing. 'It felt like Peter denying Christ,'[44] she wrote.

19

Millions of meals

'A morning spent looking into the faces of a thousand ashen-faced children leaves a numbed feeling – a sense of things as they should not be, impossible to define.'

– Emily to Tibbie Steyn, 1919

In early 1917 General Jan Smuts and Lord Alfred Milner were invited to join the new British War Cabinet. Smuts had been in command of the Allied forces' offensive in German East Africa until the year before, while it was Milner's first political appointment since 1905.

The War Cabinet was constituted after Prime Minister Herbert Asquith had lost the support of the cabinet and resigned in December 1916. David Lloyd George, leader of the Liberal Party, formed a coalition government, mainly with the support of Conservatives, which led to a split in the Liberal Party.

Although Germany had proposed a negotiated peace on 12 December 1916, Lloyd George declared that it was important to fight to the end in order to give Germany a 'knockout-blow'.[1]

Both Smuts and Milner accepted the invitation to serve in Lloyd George's cabinet. They and four others were ministers without portfolio. Smuts arrived in London in early January 1917 and eventually stayed in England for more than two years.

Emily wrote to him as the 'Pacifist and Anti-Imperialist I am prouder than ever to be'.[2]

Smuts, for his part, remarked to his wife Isie that 'Miss Hobhouse is all for making peace (by negotiation) and is a little troublesome and, of course, as always tactless, so that her whole family, even her brother is against her'.[3] While he considered Emily 'quite sweet', 'her letters are much exaggerated. But she is, of course, as always, a little mad.'[4]

In the meantime Emily had moved to Baron's Court on St Dunstan's Road in London where she lived fairly close to Smuts, but he never visited her there. He preferred the company of Margaret Clark Gillett and her husband Arthur instead. Isie Smuts had also stopped writing to Emily after she had apparently angered the 'Oubaas' (Old Boss, a term of endearment).

Emily did not leave Smuts alone and offered herself again as a bridge between the warring countries, mainly England and Germany. 'War is the wrong way of settling differences – and indeed it never settles anything for long,' she wrote:

A Pacifist – a true one I mean – sees all this clearly and calmly.

A bridge is needed – let me be that bridge. I have begun to build it – and am not afraid to cross it alone to begin with. Each side is sensitive – the greatest tact and gentleness is needed. Lloyd George would trust me I know and you would and the Germans will. I ask nothing better of life than to make a bridge across the gaping chasm that divides two countries that I love.[5]

She also suggested he should help get British conscientious objectors released from prison. For Smuts, Emily was 'a pacifist of a very troublesome kind'.[6]

When Prime Minister Louis Botha and his wife Annie visited London, Emily only saw Mrs Botha briefly on one occasion but not Botha himself. 'They dropped me entirely. As I had previously thought of General Botha as a real personal friend I felt it very acutely . . .'[7]

Emily's passionate pacifism was probably the cause of the growing gulf between her and the two former Boer generals. She could not afford to lose Smuts's friendship however, because he looked after her financial affairs and house in South Africa.

Her once close friendship with Olive Schreiner was also a thing of the past. In May 1918 they saw each other at a tea party in London, but Schreiner was 'as cold, distant and repellent as she could possibly be. She did all that she could to cold-shoulder and keep me out of the conversation and this in the house of people to whom I had introduced her.'[8] Later she heard that Olive was furious because Emily had not severed all ties with Smuts. According to what Emily had heard, Olive had literally prostrated herself before Smuts and begged him with tears in her eyes to end the slaughter of the war.[9]

Peace would not come through victory, Emily wrote to Smuts in January 1918; victory would come through peace. Three things had to be accepted: 'Acknowledge that guilt lies equally among all. Meet and discuss on equal terms. No nation deserves to gain anything by the war.'[10] Then it would be possible for a community of 'equal nations' to arise from the ashes of the war.

In 1916 the warring powers were in a stalemate after neither side, despite the loss of millions of soldiers' lives, had succeeded in gaining a significant advantage. During 1917, however, two important developments changed matters. In April, the United States entered the war after Germany had attacked US ships in the Atlantic Ocean. Seven months later the Bolshevik Revolution broke out in Russia, whereupon Russia withdrew from the Allied offensive. Hostilities continued in 1918, but gradually the scales tipped against the Central Powers. The Germans lost a number of important battles and slowly retreated. On both sides soldiers became disheartened, especially after the outbreak of a devastating flu pandemic. Several instances of mutiny occurred in the defence forces of Germany and Austria-Hungary.

In the autumn of 1918 the war came to an end after several of the countries of the Central Powers signed peace agreements with the Allies. At 'the eleventh hour of the eleventh day of the eleventh month' (11 November 1918) an armistice came into effect. It was only on 28 June 1919, however, that the Treaty of Versailles was signed after months of peace negotiations. In terms of this peace settlement, the Austro-Hungarian Empire was broken up into several countries and a heavy war debt was imposed on Germany, which also had to relinquish some of its territory. The Ottoman and Russian Empires also came to their ends in this time.

The war had claimed the lives of about eleven million soldiers and seven million civilians, while twenty million people had been wounded. Food was scarce, and everyone suffered the effect of the shortages.

During the last months of the war, from August 1918, Emily spent much time in Chelsea with Lady Courtney, whose husband had died a few months earlier.[11] Lady Courtney made a banner of blue silk on which a dove and an olive branch were depicted, which was meant to be displayed when peace arrived. On 12 November 1918, the day after peace had been declared, she wanted to have it put up among other banners at the city hall, but the city clerk refused as 'we are not ready to offer Germany the olive branch'.

'We are not pro-Germans here,' he scoffed.

'Nor Christians either apparently,'[12] Lady Courtney retorted.

In the aftermath of the war, famine, disease and poverty were rife in many countries. Emily's eyes and heart were instinctively focused on the alleviation of suffering. 'What is wanted is medicines, disinfectants, soap, bedding, linen, milk and all kinds of foods. And an army of doctors and nurses to cope with disease,' she wrote to Smuts.[13] The situation was similar to the need in South Africa eighteen years before.

Friends in Switzerland informed her of a plan to bring starving Viennese children to Switzerland to recuperate there. She approached Edith Durham, Lady Clare Annesley, Joyce Tarring and T. R. Bridgewater, and together they collected four hundred pounds.[14] Emily became the cofounder of the Swiss Relief Fund for Starving Children.

This fund sent children from Germany, Austria, Czechoslovakia and Hungary to sanatoriums in Olivella and other places near Lake Lugano in Switzerland to regain their health. When the Save the Children Fund (which still exists today) was founded in April 1919, Emily's organisation officially became part of it.

Emily also founded the Russian Babies' Fund, of which she was chair; the membership of the committee included several medical doctors. Her brother Leonard also assisted Emily with this project. The fund sent baby food, milk, clothing and soap to the childrens' hospital in the Russian city of Petrograd (the present-day St Petersburg).[15]

In September 1919, fifty-nine-year-old Emily and Joyce Tarring, an acquaintance, travelled to Leipzig in Germany and

Vienna in Austria on behalf of the Save the Children Fund to gain first-hand information about the conditions and the needs of children in particular.[16]

She felt hurt that Smuts, who was now prime minister in South Africa, who also wanted a report on the conditions in Vienna, did not send her to do the investigation even though he knew that she was equal to the task. He sent Dr Hilda Clark, Margaret's sister, instead.[17] Yet it was thanks to Smuts that she was able to obtain a passport again, after it was withdrawn after the German drama.

It did not take Emily and Joyce long to establish that there were at least thirty thousand children in Leipzig who were in dire need of food. The local authorities did not provide any food to the children, and the distress was overwhelming.

'It so paralysed me that I could only retain any power of action by shutting my eyes and pretending there was only Leipzig,'[18] she wrote to the Quakers in London, who were helping to raise money for the cause. Most people were surviving on food parcels from England and whatever they were still able to exchange on the black market. In the hotel were Emily stayed, too, there was neither meat nor eggs.

Emily appealed for help to Jane Addams, her old acquaintance from the Women's International League for Peace and Freedom. She also received support from sympathisers in London, from American and British Quakers, Swiss friends and members of the local community in Leipzig, and later also in Vienna.

The distress was depressing but there were also small joys: 'The children – especially the little ones of 6 or 7 who have had no milk for years and never proper nourishment are in great need of this help. We give them a thick sandwich of bread and sausage, bread and cheese, or bread and meat of some kind, and with it a steaming large cup of cocoa made with condensed milk or of hot fresh milk. To see them drink that milk is in itself a joy.'[19]

She stated in a telegram sent in November 1919 that she hoped to feed ten thousand children daily in Leipzig at a cost of a thousand US dollars per day.[20] These children were being fed thanks to donations made by the American Quakers via the Friends' War Victim Relief Fund, when Emily had launched an independent and urgent fund-raising campaign.

She wrote to Jane Addams, 'We have a strong feeling that it is best to begin in one town even if only a section of the children in that town can be fed say 25–50,000 is better than none. So it seems better to do one town if we cannot do all. We are all so afflicted by a feeling of paralysed effort when we confront the huge child-distress of Germany, and the power of action only returns by concentrating one's limited mind and means on one town . . .'

She wrote that the children who received food were afraid of eating too much and gaining too much weight, as they believed they might then be excluded from the feeding scheme.

'We can only look for help to America . . . I am astounded and abashed by my own tenacity . . .'[21]

Emily decided that her requests for aid and the report she had to compile for the Save the Children Fund would carry more weight if a medical doctor could add his impressions and conclusions. With this in mind, she asked a Swiss doctor, Dr Fritz Schwyzer, to accompany her to Vienna and Leipzig.

In Vienna they found thousands of famished people; the elderly looked emaciated, pale and sad; the workers showed signs of starvation. Women with children, in particular, were in a wretched condition. Tuberculosis was rife. 'Nearly everyone save the profiteers are hungry.'[22]

One ray of light was that about 105,000 children in this city were being fed daily thanks to donations from the United States.

In Leipzig, however, there was no food for the 85,000 school-age children. 'A morning spent looking into the faces of a thousand ashen-faced children leaves a numbed feeling – a sense of things as they should not be, impossible to define.'[23] All the schools were closed because there was no coal to heat the buildings. About 30,000 of the children were malnourished.

Thanks to a donation from a baron Emily initially had one hundred pounds per week available for six months with which only one thousand children could be fed per day, but she did not give up hope. She stayed on in Leipzig throughout the hungry winter.

To Sir William Goode from the British Ministry of Food she wrote that 'thousands must die and thousands more sicken if cows are taken away'. Pleading with him, she wrote: 'I implore you to use your power to prevent this disaster.'

With the help of various prominent people in Germany, such as the Director of Education, the Director of the Deutsche Bank, academics, hospital doctors and friends, the feeding scheme was given a huge boost. The doctors examined the children to determine who needed to be fed first.

The American Quakers purchased food in Switzerland and Denmark to prevent a further depletion of supplies in Germany.[24] The Danish Red Cross as well as members of the public in England and Denmark contributed financially, and by April 1920 this scheme was no longer part of the Save the Children Fund. The project now belonged to Emily and the city fathers of Leipzig.

Some of the schoolchildren in Leipzig who were fed between January
1920 and July 1922 thanks to Emily's project. Ultimately, 11,000
children were part of the feeding scheme for which she raised
£49,000. About 5.5 million meals were provided with this money.

Photo: Courtesy of Jennifer Hobhouse Balme

In January 1920 Emily started feeding 225 children in 4 schools in Leipzig; by May 1920 the numbers had already increased to 34 schools and 11,000 children.[25] According to a report by Dr Schwyzer who had examined thousands of children, close to 40 per cent of the children in Leipzig were underweight and stunted.

Some children were unaccustomed to hot food and had to be taught to eat it, according to Drs Poetter and Kuntze, two hospital doctors in Leipzig. In August 1920 the following supplies were purchased: rice, flour, sugar, condensed milk, peas, beans, onions, shortening, pasta, chocolate, sago, eggs, cheese, dried mushrooms, sausage and potatoes.

But the need was still enormous, and the money too little. Emily thought of her friends in South Africa. In June 1920 she requested help from Tibbie Steyn in Bloemfontein, who immediately launched a public appeal in the press: 'Want and misery in Germany and Austria'. 'We dare not close our ears to the cry for help, nor dare we forget . . . [about Emily's work in the concentration camps]. Therefore I ask the mothers and daughters of South Africa to render assistance at once.'[26]

As a result of Emily and Tibbie's pleas, the Union government undertook to contribute an amount equal to that raised by Tibbie. The British government refused to contribute, saying that they had 'no money for her [Emily]'.[27]

About eight hundred pounds was collected by South African children, whereupon Tibbie and Emily decided to use this money to give nine thousand children in war-ravaged Europe a Christmas gift: a pair of warm socks or gloves or handkerchiefs, accompanied by a card. In addition, each child received a sweet honey-bread roll.[28] Emily also donated one hundred pounds to a hospital that had no linen.

In the end, more than fifteen thousand pounds was raised for the fund in South Africa. Of this amount, five thousand two hundred had been donated by the government.[29] One of the recipients, Ruth Wagner from the 16th Elementary School in Leipzig, wrote this thank you letter, one of the many Emily preserved in her scrapbook:

> Dear Miss Hobhouse, In the name of my school fellows. I thank you for the good food we receive for so long a time. I have already got quite thick cheeks, because the meals are to my taste especially when we have milk with chocolate. We are also very pleased with the beautiful gift to the children . . .
>
> When I speak my evening prayers I pray that God may bless your health. We would have a great joy to see you once in our school, when you could see how we enjoy your meal.
>
> God blessing be with you.

At the beginning of 1921 Emily was ill and weak, and a doctor recommended that she stay in bed for at least a month. She went to recuperate in Bude, a coastal village in the north of Cornwall where the Hobhouse family used to go on holiday. Her condition did not improve, however, and she insisted on being pushed around the town in a wheelchair while she made arrangements for children to be sent to Italy and Switzerland for holidays with families in those countries.[30]

She continued working and became so ill that she ended up in a hospital in Rome that was run by French nuns. She was ill for months, and later went to convalesce at Lake Lucerne and also at the home of her brother Leonard in London. Too weak to return to Leipzig, she remained involved with the feeding scheme from a distance.[31]

Emily wrote to Tibbie on 24 January 1922 that the Quakers could not help any more, as they had no funds left. Her fund committee in Germany was appealing to the richer German cizitens, and funds were coming in – the money placed where it would bear interest. The exchange rate at the time, she stated, was one pound to 800 German Marks.

The depot with all the food and clothes they collected was now called 'The South African and Quaker depot,' Emily said. Fifteen thousand pounds from South Africa helped keep the feeding scheme going until the summer of 1922.

Emily's bookkeeping records show that from January 1920 to January 1921 her scheme provided 3.4 million hot meals for children, and from January 1921 up to the end of the scheme in March 1922 another 1.4 million. The children also received milk or cocoa. Ultimately, £46,700 and 1 million Deutschmarks were collected for the massive project to buy 1.2 million kilograms of food.[32] There was no office, and only two paid employees –supervisor Ida Mansfeld, who organised the purchases, and helper Ann Fischer. Little of the money that was raised was spent on administration.[33]

Emily's project was wound up in Leipzig in July 1922. The amount of about 248,000 Deutschmarks still left in the fund was transferred to the Emily Hobhouse Foundation, which was run from Leipzig to send children to country areas in the summer.

At the fund's last meeting in the city hall in Leipzig on 13 July 1922, a report on the project read as follows:

By bringing about charitable gifts and donations, Miss Hobhouse had done such immeasurable good that her memory should never be forgotten in Leipzig . . . In the end, the meals that were supplied numbered more than 5.5 million. More than 130 double railway trucks carrying 10 tons each were required to transport the supplies for the children's feeding.

According to the doctors and teachers . . . the physical and psychological condition of the children improved substantially as a result of the school-feeding system.[34]

A signed studio photo of Emily in September 1922, at the age of sixty-two. A Mr E. Stockenström met Emily in 1921 at a symphony concert in Europe. He was struck by 'her proud bearing, the slender figure, almost six foot tall, the attractive facial features, the striking elegance of her posture and gestures, the amiability of nature and character that could be clearly read on the face and, above all, the remarkable intelligence and eloquence'.

Photo: Anglo-Boer War Museum

The feeding scheme relieved much suffering and saved thousands of lives, but most of Emily's post-war ideals were not realised, or at least not quickly. One of these was full suffrage for women.

During 1918 the British Parliament passed the Representation of the People Act 1918. Women over thirty years old received the vote if they were either a member or married to a member of the Local Government Register, a property owner, or a graduate voting in a university constituency. The Act enfranchised 8.4 million women, but Emily was excluded on all counts as she was unmarried, did not own property in England and was not a graduate.

Ten years later, in March 1928, the Act was revised, these restrictions were lifted, and women began to enjoy full electoral equality. In South Africa, white women were able to vote from 21 May 1930.

Emily was eligible to vote in the 1922 election, however, after she had bought a house in St Ives. But the opportunity to vote did not excite her, as the candidates were again 'the old lot and it leaves me cold'.

'Who on earth is there to vote for?' she remarked to Leonard. It is not known whether she voted or not.

20

A house by the sea

'Will the spirit go on living when the final decay comes? I ask myself. I like [Maurice] Maeterlinck's thought: "The dead live again every time we remember them".'

— Emily to Tibbie Steyn, September 1922

In 1921, the ever-travelling — and now sixty-year-old — Emily, who had been moving from one hotel to another flat all her life, realised that she had to find a fixed abode. She was always on the road: between England, Italy, France, Germany, Switzerland . . . without anywhere to come home to.

Earlier, in South Africa, she had felt this intense need for a place of her own when she bought the house in Bellevue, Johannesburg. But this was not where she wanted to spend her last years, and she had in any case sold the house at some point between 1919 and 1922.

Then she saw a house that was for sale in the seaside village of St Ives in Cornwall, on England's south-west coast. It was just over 60 miles from St Ive where she had grown up.

'It is Italy in England – foreign parts without travel,' she wrote excitedly to Smuts.[1] It was a 'dear little house, so bright & sunny – low and red roofed and with a magnificent view of seas & cliffs ... over 1000 years my mother's family has lived in this neighbourhood and we feel part and parcel of the rocks and soil,' she wrote to Tibbie Steyn.[2] Smuts had supported Emily during the feeding scheme – they never stopped their correspondence.

Warren House[3] was next to the Porthminster Hotel, with a magnificent view over the bay and a beautiful garden. With three reception areas, seven bedrooms, dressing rooms, a kitchen, bathroom and other rooms, the house was far from modest.[4]

From Emily's description of the house and Tibbie's intimate knowledge of her good friend of many years, she knew that Emily would not be able to afford it. Tibbie raised the matter of South African help diplomatically: 'Don't refuse it as we shall be so disappointed. We have so set our hearts on your purchasing a little home.'[5]

Emily accepted the offer, deeply grateful for this 'unique sign of an affectionate remembrance – still fresh and living after twenty long years'.[6]

In South Africa, Tibbie made a nationwide appeal in the press for people to repay a debt of honour to the angel of the concentration camps. She also had a pamphlet printed with this request: 'I have felt for a long time that we have never given Miss Hobhouse any tangible token of our appreciation for all that she did for us ... I want to give everyone the opportunity to donate, and therefore I only ask for a contribution of 2/6 [half-a-crown].' The house would enable Emily 'to spend the evening of her life quietly, happily and free of care in a home of her own'.[7]

Despite a positive reaction, the money that was raised was insufficient. Jan Smuts and Annie Botha, the wife of General

Louis Botha (who was deceased by that time), put their hands in their pockets and made up the shortfall.[8] Even though the friendship between Emily and Annie had cooled, she still cared enough for Emily to support her on this occasion. Within just three months, the full purchase price of £2,300 was collected and paid over.

On 18 July 1921, an excited Emily wrote to Tibbie that she had spent her first night at Warren House. Her first guest happened to be a South African: Frank Reitz, the son of former president F. W. Reitz, who had helped her put down carpets, hang paintings and unpack the boxes with goodies that she received annually from well-wishers in South Africa for her birthday.[9]

'I am haunted by very tender thoughts of thousands of South Africans. I can still hardly believe it.'[10] Emily referred to these gifts as 'Wonder Boxes'. They contained preserved and dried fruit of all kinds, jams, rusks, finely minced biltong (which she preferred), honey, chutney and biscuits.[11] The arrival of gifts from South Africa was a highlight on her calendar every year. 'I can only say that the overflowing gratitude shown to me by the mass of Boer people, thousands of whom have never seen me, must be almost if not quite unique.'[12]

She made a point of serving some of the treats whenever she hosted a South African visitor at her home. Sometimes she would give 'a pot of preserve, or dried fruit or biscuits' as a gift. As far as possible, she sent each donor a thank you note.[13]

It was here, in Warren House, that Emily was finally able to reread all her letters and papers and the few diaries she had kept, and put them in order. The process gave rise to intro-spection on which she wrote a few paragraphs to 'my South African friends', which were included in her draft autobiography:

Emily in 1922 outside Warren House, St Ives. On the
table is a bottle of the jam South African women used
to send her in Wonder Boxes on her birthday.

Photo: Anglo-Boer War Museum

As I read over the old letters and papers of sixty years, the first
thing that strikes me is the many mistakes I have made – the
frequent misjudgement of men and things. Viewing all in the
light of riper experience I see in a flash how much better I
could have acted, or written or spoken. Is this, I wonder, a
universal experience? Strange that I have muddled through.
[Edmund] Waller must have felt this when he wrote:

> The soul's dark cottage, battered and decayed,
> Lets light through chinks that time has made.
> Stronger by weakness, wiser men become
> As they draw near to their eternal home.

Emily with her own cart, in St Ives.

Photo: Courtesy of Jennifer Hobhouse Balme

Secondly, I am struck by how pain passes, whether physical, mental or spiritual. Gashes may be left, but they do heal. One reads with surprise the burning words written under pressure of some torture through which one has passed.

And thirdly, how often I have been misunderstood – almost entirely from my lack of ability to explain myself, through lack of ready words, or through lack of courage. Clinging to the love of Truth and a passion for Justice. Will the spirit go on living when the final decay comes? I ask myself. I like [Maurice] Maeterlinck's thought: 'The dead live again every time we remember them.'

Partly by hand and partly by means of a typewriter, Emily wrote her autobiography in the form of long letter to Tibbie Steyn, with an explanation of the choice of this format: 'This curious feeling of wanting some sympathetic person to whom to speak with the pen persists and you see an instance in this memoir which I felt I could not write except in the form of a letter to yourself.'

Her constant letter-writing throughout her life also required a (psychological) explanation, Emily felt. 'Possibly this is the result of a solitary life. The greater part of mine has been spent in silence, without mental or spiritual companionship, often without even the relief of a servant to speak to. The human desire for interchange of speech is strong, and was, I think the force which inspired my constant letters. My pen was my tongue.'[14]

The autobiography started at the year 1899 (four years after her father's death) and ended, unfinished, at 1908 after she had established the weaving schools.

As a scrupulous record-keeper, Emily had copied and preserved some of her most important letters on separate sheets of paper. These records now came in handy as she wrote about those eventful years in South Africa, sometimes in bed with the typewriter resting on her knees.

She made two copies of the unfinished autobiography – one for her nephew Oliver and another for Gladys Steyn, a daughter of Tibbie. The various chapters were ordered and neatly enfolded in brown paper.

After a while – as if her priorities had changed – she put the autobiography aside for the time being and worked on her translation of the diary Alie Badenhorst of Hartebeestfontein had kept about her experiences during the Anglo-Boer War. Alie had made an indelible impression on Emily when they met one another in 1903. In Emily's translation of the work from Afrikaans into English, she was at pains to retain the simplicity and honesty of the document that had moved her so much. 'I've tried to put it into very simple English that suits her very simple Taal.' She believed that Alie's unvarnished account would convey the inhumanity of war in a striking fashion.

But the writing sapped her strength: 'The work is very hard and at times I turn sick and faint, but then I take a few minutes in the garden among my plants and so go back refreshed.' She was anxious for the book to be done 'for I feel certain it will take a place in the history and literature of your country and even amongst the diaries of the world . . .'[15]

The English version of *Tant' Alie of Transvaal* appeared in 1923. A total of fifteen hundred copies were published but the book did not sell well, presumably because the British public was no longer interested in reading about this war.[16]

While Emily was still busy with *Tant' Alie*, she started working on another book: *War Without Glamour* – a unique work for its time as it consisted of women's stories, told by themselves, of what they had experienced first-hand in the Anglo-Boer War. The stories had been written down at the request of Emily, who had met many of these women in 1901.

Half of the stories were in 'Boer-Dutch', which Emily translated into English. In the case of the others, where women had made a brave attempt to write down their stories in English for Emily, she edited their language. This book, which may well have been the first of its kind in the world, appeared in 1924.

Though Emily was very happy in Warren House, it had not been a very practical decision to buy such a big house for her as a solitary person. Emily planted Orange River lilies in the garden, which provided her with much joy and in all probability also pleasant memories. The location and view must have played a huge role in her happiness. But by the end of 1922 Emily was incapable of climbing stairs and was using the study on the ground floor as a bedroom. She was also having problems with servants, but was incapable of getting by without one.

At last the reality of her diminishing powers and a demanding house came home to Emily. Probably most reluctantly but without a practical alternative, she sold Warren House in July 1923 and moved to a much smaller house at 7 Tor Gardens, Campden Hill, in the London suburb of Kensington.

By this time Emily was a semi-invalid, but her social conscience gave her no rest. The post-war distress in Germany kept haunting her: 'It responds to something inside myself which was accusing me of not using my renewed vitality (I can hardly say strength) for the good of the sufferers of this world's tragedy.'[17]

As she had always done before, Emily decided to investigate the conditions for herself and determine what she could do to alleviate the suffering of 'the enemy'. For the last time.

By the end of October 1923 she was in Hamburg, and thereafter in Heidelberg and Berlin. She saw and experienced how worthless the Deutschmark had become as a result of the sky-high inflation. People were spending every cent they had on food. There was no money for meat; expensive meals consisted of potatoes and turnips. The shops were mostly empty.

Some days Emily was unable to walk. She enlisted the help of a student to push her around in a wheelchair.[18] Then she suffered another setback: in Heidelberg she fell down a flight of stairs, head first, and sustained such serious injuries that she was forced to return home. 'The work here [in Germany] has been intense I am near the end of my tether so I must tear myself away,'[19] she wrote.

She hoped to touch the conscience of her good friend Jan Smuts with a plea that he should go and see the conditions for himself. 'See the abject misery of the middle class intellectual Germany and then you won't rest.'[20] Although she herself was struggling to make ends meet, Emily still sent money to Germany for the relief of distress.

It must have come as a consolation that the people of Leipzig had not forgotten her. Shortly after her move to London, the German ambassador in Britain sent an address and a porcelain plaque with which the city paid tribute to her.[21] It was 'a token of the gratitude – of the residents of Leipzig for the tireless and warm kindliness you showed towards them in relieving the distress and hardship they suffered as a result of the war'.[22]

The porcelain plaque given to Emily by the City of Leipzig in recognition of her relief work among children of that city in the aftermath of World War One.

Photo: Jennifer Hobhouse Balme collection

On 24 December 1924 the city council of Leipzig sent a moving letter:

> Tonight on Christmas Eve, where all to whom good has been done are grateful to their benefactors and would like to thank them, we remember your help to us in earlier years, and our thoughts are with you. We think back to the years when we suffered terrible distress after the war, and how you rendered assistance to us, how you raised money to feed our hungry children and how you helped all who suffered in the need of the time. In those terrible years you became the helper and the friend of the city . . .
>
> In memory of your humanitarian activities aimed at the improvement of our city we have displayed the bust [of Emily] . . . in the lobby of our city hall, where it is accessible to the public.[23]

Earlier, in June 1924, Emily had followed the general election in South Africa with great interest.

Before the election J. B. M. Hertzog's National Party (NP) had formed an alliance with Colonel F. H. P. Creswell's Labour Party; the coalition was known as the Pact.[24] Their major opponent was the South African Party (SAP) of Jan Smuts, who had been prime minister since 1919.

A small percentage of the eligible voters were coloured and black men who met property and literacy requirements. This system only applied in the Cape, however. Owing to the Smuts government's harsh action during the 1922 labour unrest, the leaders of the South African Native National Congress (renamed in 1923 to the African National Congress) asked their supporters to vote against the SAP. Meanwhile the NP was supported mainly by voters outside the business community and by farmers.

The Pact won the election, and Hertzog became prime minister. The new government immediately took steps to look after the interests of white farmers, mineworkers and civil servants in particular.

Emily had initially been in favour of a change of government as she believed Smuts put imperial interests above those of South Africa, but when she saw how Hertzog and the NP were deploying their racial policy, she changed her tune.

'Personally I believe that segregation of any of either race or colour and class is the wrong policy and one which can only lead to discontent and ultimate disaster,'[25] she wrote to Tibbie. The races of the world had to start mixing systematically,[26] though not necessarily in marriage, she wrote on a later occasion.

During this time an old adversary emerged again: Millicent Fawcett, with her autobiography *What I Remember*. In the chapter on South Africa, which Emily described as 'scandalous' and full of falsehoods,[27] Fawcett repeated her old view that with the concentration camps Kitchener only had the best intentions of ending the war.[28] Also that the Boer women and children often accompanied the men on commando and were already in a weak condition because of poor food by the time they arrived at the camps. She referred mockingly to Boers' poor English and had little sympathy with their suffering.

The British monarchy rewarded Fawcett with a high honour: Dame Grand Cross of the Most Excellent Order of the British Empire. Whether the award had been intended as such or not, it was a slap in the face to Emily.

On 13 May 1925, while Emily was working through her papers and letters pertaining to South Africa, she heard the news of

Alfred Milner's demise. He had died of sleeping sickness at the age of seventy-one.

That same day she wrote to Tibbie:

Today comes the tidings of Lord Milner's death. It was told me through the wireless set in this quiet room, told as things are told by broadcasters in what often seems a curiously intimate way, as if told for your ear alone. It felt as if I wanted to say back that I was sorry, very sorry. For as a man it was impossible to help liking Milner; his charm was irresistible and I had liked him very much.

Twenty five years soften all dislikes, especially those of only a public nature, and though my arrest and deportation must never be forgiven because it was an offence against English rights and freedom, yet I myself had sought him out and met him during the Great War in 1917 as one of the few of our statesmen who then took the wiser views. We met then in the friendly spirit of those with the same object at heart . . .

One after the other they pass, all the actors on your South African Scene, and you and I, dear friend, will soon quit the stage . . .[29]

21

The last yearnings

'. . . though it is the late hour and little of life remains in me, I do feel some sort of re-institution in the public mind of England and documentary evidence of it, would do more than anything else to brighten the remaining time.'

           – Emily to Tibbie Steyn, 1 May 1926

Emily was constantly in search of a place where she hoped to recuperate.

In November 1925 she and her maid, Ella, moved to a cottage in East Wittering near Chichester in West Sussex. She actually needed a nurse but could not afford one.[1]

The change in her frame of mind is discernible in her writing. She wrote in early February 1926 to Tibbie:

All the morning as the slow dawn crept on, I have lain listening to the long melancholy moaning of the sea as the waves break upon the shingly shore. It seemed as if daylight and Ella would

One of the last photos of Emily. It was taken
when she was already in her sixties.

Photo: Courtesy of Jennifer Hobhouse Balme

never come. Yet tonight thank Heaven I had no pain or cough but only that weakness which often seems to me worse than pain. To raise myself in bed becomes an effort and I can no longer get up, light my stove and make my coffee as I want.

It has been a week of great suffering and at times helpless weakness. It is a great responsibility for poor little Ella. I am sorriest for her. Some days I get up for a few hours. It is the extreme of washing that nearly kills me every day. My pulse races, mere flicker of a pulse as it is and breathless and giddy I have to keep stopping and resting. I was in despair about myself at first being so much weaker & more suffering than when I took to my bed.[2]

A month later Emily and Ella were on the Isle of Wight, at Godshill, where they stayed at Godshill Park House. She had hoped that the weather there would help her to recover from the pleuritis that kept her chained to her bed, but unfortunately it was 'cold, grey and damp'.[3] One of her lungs no longer functioned and she had difficulty swallowing.

As if it were a birthday gift, the sun shone briefly on 9 April – Emily's sixty-sixth birthday. And there was also a letter of congratulation from Tibbie. Two days later she wrote back:

> Believe me, since my dear old aunt's death, no one has filled an equal place in my life. With her I never felt I was a bore, and with you also I have a kindred belief that your heart & sympathy is open to me at all times & on all questions.
>
> That is such a restful feeling and believe me when I tell you, you have thus done more than anyone else to solace the loneliness of my declining years. A thousand thanks cannot express what I feel.[4]

Emily had sold Tor Gardens, and had no accommodation in London to which she could return. The previous abode she had only rented temporarily. Her furniture and other possessions were still in storage. She was dependent on others to inspect flats on her behalf and notify her by post of their findings. The bedrooms and bathrooms of most of the places were on the first floor, and she had been unable to climb stairs for years.

Emily had never sought credit or recognition. But now, in the twilight of her life, she had one compelling yearning – not for fame or praise, but for the righting of a wrong.

Tibbie, she knew, would understand. She marked the letter of 1 May 1926 'Private'.

My work for the Camps in the South African War brought down upon my head the scorn and contumely of almost the entire country [England]. I was libelled in the press and held up as a rebel – a liar, unpatriotic, hysterical and worse. One or two papers like the *Manchester Guardian* raised voices in my defence, but the fight was unequal and the mass of people received an impression of me which was wholly untrue.

This did much to blight my existence. I was ostracised in society. People turned their backs on me if they heard my name. For years and years this continued – and in addition I lost many old friends of my girlhood who took different views.

I always felt that the harm thus done to me would only be cured by the public utterance of some highly thought of public man who with a few words would strip off the lies and re-instate me in the public eye.

To a small extent this, was done by Sir Henry Campbell-Bannerman, when after my arrest and deportation in November-October 1901 he was speaking at a public dinner in Bath. His speech, however, was never widely read – few knew the kind words he said and J. A. Spencer who recently wrote his biography carefully left out all that made C. B. so popular amongst Liberals of that period.

Later, however, in 1906 when C. B. came into power at the head of a huge Liberal majority, he had every opportunity of uttering a few effective words which would have re-instated me in the public mind and have removed the injustice from which I suffered. The Liberals had not scrupled to make use of me while they were in opposition and that alone, I felt ought to have make them ready to speak a few words on my behalf in the day of their power and success. But not one word was ever said . . .[5]

Also on the occasion of the unveiling of the Women's Monument in 1913 this was not done, as the *Cape Times* had again reported negatively on her, and everything this newspaper wrote was repeated in England in *The Times* as supposedly being the prevailing opinion in South Africa, Emily wrote.

Neither Louis Botha nor Jan Smuts 'said a word in public to refute the lies nor to place my activities (which they had always applauded) in the true light'. She had 'felt it very deeply' that Botha 'did nothing'. Likewise, Ramsay MacDonald, an old acquaintance, did nothing to restore her reputation when the Labour Party came to power in 1924 and he became prime minister.

She realised that the public had a short memory; 'the Boer War has faded to a mere passing incident of which few retain any recollection and those of us who then laboured are dead as snails'.

But lately, when I heard Genl Hertzog was coming to London I wondered if any occasion of public speech or writing would arise when perhaps he (if he felt he could conscientiously do so) would in a few simple words say something that would, by proving South African esteem for me, shew that England need not be ashamed of me. He might even put it more positively.

Believe me dear Friend, I do not seek for praise or for notoriety. I only yearn for justice, to be relieved of the weight I have borne for 25 years being unjustly looked down upon and despised as a rebel – unpatriotic – a liar, hysterical notoriety seeker and many other rich epithets as the Chamberlain Press employed.

It struck me that you, who know him so well – might perhaps convey to your Premier [Hertzog] who I believe is the soul of chivalry – the story I have here written to you and suggest to him if he thought proper to say something when in England. I do not think Botha or Smuts had the moral courage to be my champion. Especially since 1917 when my visit to Germany in 1916 increased in some circles my unpopularity.

Those two dear valiant men feared to be seen with me and kept aloof. Botha indeed I never once saw. Smuts used to see me now and then but would never come under my roof. Maybe he was right. Yet he did not avoid the company of other pacifists.

Now I have told you this story and though it is the late hour and little of life remains in me, I do feel some sort of re-institution in the public mind of England and documentary evidence of it, would do more than anything else to brighten the remaining time. Few know what a heavy burden it has been to 'carry for quarter of a century.'[6,7]

In between, Emily worked on her autobiography. She was keen to get hold of documents about her arrest in Table Bay and deportation from South Africa. 'I need it badly,' she wrote to Betty Molteno.[8]

And the reason was clear: 'I really can't last long. I only wanted to finish my memoires – thus I should die with contentment.'[9]

To make matters worse, there was a nationwide postal strike. It was a disaster for someone like Emily for whom letters were a fountain of life.

'Life is just paralyzed. I am crushed to earth. Posts are few or nil. Not a newspaper can be get. Darkness has fallen like a pall upon me. Plans have melted away.

'Life seems like some shifting or quaking sands. All is vague and uncertain around you.'[10]

The search for a flat or a house yielded nothing. Oliver had not taken her needs into account; in her condition, she was unable to live in a place he found for her. All her life Emily had been independent and self-reliant but now, heartsore, she appealed for help in a letter to Tibbie:

> . . . O do you know that from the depths of my soul, burdened by this terrible bodily weakness, this loneliness, this poverty, cries go out to the unseen Powers to send me some help in the darkness. If it could be some kind capable friend who would just take me in hand, gently lay me on one side and say: 'Now be still & be calm. I will undertake all for you and arrange everything & when all is ready put you into the new home with your own furniture about you.' In fact I long for a good fairy to act while I lay quiescent.[11]

Then, good news. In Kensington, at 13 Bedford Gardens House, there was a suitable flat that was available for at least a few months.

Emily, who rarely showed signs of religiousness, directed her gratitude heavenwards: 'So the words that spring to my lips to say are those of praise and thanksgiving, and worried and weak as I still am I can say, Praise the Lord O my soul and all that is within me, praise His Holy Name.'[12]

But the rental of £252 per year was a cause of anxiety, as there would be little left over for food, clothing and Ella's wages – let alone medical costs.[13] It made Emily deeply depressed.

'I do not mind poverty and have always been able & proud to live economically – but then I was well and strong. It is my bodily condition [that] makes the difficulty – how to pay my way. The anxiety is so great & continuous that for this reason & this alone I want to depart hence & be no more seen.

'Life is sweet in itself & still replete with interest & work for me

– but under these circumstances I do not want to live on,' she confessed to Tibbie.

On the Christian calendar it was Whitsuntide, something of which Emily as a parson's daughter was well aware. On Whitsunday Ella opened the window of her bedroom wide to let in the rather weak sunlight so that Emily could sit and write in her bed.

From before sunrise, the hymn she learnt years ago in the church choir at St Ive had been running in her head:

> Come Holy Ghost our souls inspire;
> and lighten with celestial fire
> thou the anointing Spirit art,
> who dost thy sevenfold gifts impart.
> Thy blessed unction from above
> is comfort, life, and fire of love;
> enable with perpetual light
> the dullness of our blinded sight.[14]

Emily began to immerse herself once more in the biblical events.

> I can realize how the disciples after the Ascension when their leader and teacher was gone felt themselves groping in the dark and craved to be "enabled with perpetual light". And that is my feeling.
>
> All are gone to whom I looked up to and whose guidance I would follow and my chief prayer is now also for Light; perpetual light. In all the darkness and perplexities that surrounds one I crave for light and guidance . . .[15]

In visibly shaky handwriting – especially on the last two pages where some of the lines lie aslant across the page – Emily wrote her last letter to Tibbie on 30 May.

The first page of the last letter, as far as it is known, that Emily
wrote. It was addressed to Tibbie Steyn on 30 May 1926.

Photo: Free State Archives Repository

She was no longer in full control of the English language she
could use so masterfully. The most important parts read as
follows:[16]

Dear Mrs Steyn,

I am disappointed in myself – to find it is Sunday morning
when I usually look forward to my chat with you and behold,
I feel fit for nothing. And I know it is many months since I
felt so utterly weak and incapable even if doing what is a
pleasure to me.

Emily's signature at the end of her last letter.

Photo: Free States Archives Repository

Thank Heaven it is the final Sunday here [on the Isle of Wight] and I hope much from the more stimulating air of London . . .

Tuesday is coming. Once the journey is over my nerves may calm down a little – at present I am all of a shake and cannot lift a teacup with security. Ella must hold it to my mouth. I upset everything.

Doctor said it is not real palsy and it will pass away as I get generally stronger, but sad to say I do not get stronger and these shakes seem at present to get worse.

I am trying the much advertised YeastVite which he [the doctor] told me he believed to be quite harmless and useful in certain cases. I began yesterday but hitherto with no relief as promised.

Many letters from South Africa this week. A long one from Oom Jannie. Who tells me he has given up his American trip as proposed no longer feels energy enough . . .

We have had 4 warm days.

It was wonderful! I was able to sit outdoors a few hours the cold has returned so no more. But it was doing my lung good – more air was beginning to penetrate and made me feel more natural . . .

I am anxious to know if you got safely the very long letter I wrote you very confidential. It was posted during the strike. Please read it slowly and carefully to yourself – and let me know if you understand exactly my point and views viz my desire is merely to be put right in the eyes of my fellow Englishmen and women.

I do not want praise or laudatory expressions of any kind. Only I do wish for justice or at least by some wise strong words the removal of my injustice such as at present marks upon my name. I think dear kind Genl. Hertzog will understand to make themselves think I was in no sense a rebel or unpatriotic.

Rather I felt that I laboured for the highest, honouring England in labouring to recover and present the Boer Women and Children. England had been proud of her reputation and humanity and of the humane treatment of prisoners of war much more the women and children of P.O.W.'s was incumbent on her. It was also embodied in the Hague convention, which she England, had signed.

I believe on the Continent this view was widely taken. I want it accepted by the English people as a whole. I know a few Liberals hold it. My deeds were as I believe highly patriotic, strange how the *Daily Mail* and its fellows have darkened the right of our people. It needs a strong clear voice to pierce the veil of lies which has blinded our people since '99 [1899].

Lovingly Yours

Emily Hobhouse

On 1 June 1926, Emily departed on what would turn out to be her last journey. The trip to Bedford Gardens House in Kensington, in the back of a Daimler ambulance, lasted ten hours.

There was a last flicker of life. She asked friends 'to come and discuss the urgent questions of the day'. But when some of them arrived it was 'to find her dying'.[17]

During his last visit to Emily, Leonard comforted his sister: 'You were always brave.'

'Yes, too brave,' she replied with typical selfmockery.

He thought that these words should be her epitaph, but that was not to be.[18]

On 8 June 1926 Emily died peacefully in London at the age of sixty-six years.

A 'deep growth' was found in her chest. On the death certificate, Dr J. M. Hurley specified pleuritis, heart failure and a form of internal cancer as causes of death.[19] Emily's request was that she be cremated.[20] Like many of her choices, it was an uncommon one for the time.[21]

She had a romantic image of this practice, as is apparent from a remark she made twelve years earlier: 'I like to think of cremation and then the scattering of one's ashes to the four winds, the confined spirit free to join the universal spirit of life and keep up the sum total of things.'[22]

Emily had stipulated that Oliver and her niece Dorothea Thornton could decide together on what should happen to her ashes, but had added that Dorothea knew 'I owe a debt to South Africa'.[23] There was no debate about the final destination of her remains. The Women's Monument committee in Bloemfontein accepted the family's offer without hesitation.

Three days after her death, a service was held for Emily in the St Mary Abbots church in Kensington. The coffin was covered with summer flowers. Among those who attended the service were Leonard Hobhouse and his son Oliver, Sir Charles Hobhouse, Emily's cousin Henry Hobhouse, Margaret Clark Gillett and her husband Arthur, Lady Courtney, Ruth Fry[24] and Tibbie's daughters Gladys and Emmie, and a daughter of Jan Smuts. No prominent statesman or politician – not even from the ranks of the Liberal Party.[25]

The Scripture readings were from Psalm 90 and 1 Corinthians 15, with hymns of praise 193 and 537 and the Nunc Dimittis:

Lord, now lettest thou thy servant depart in peace according to thy word.

For mine eyes have seen thy salvation,

Which thou hast prepared before the face of all people;

To be a light to lighten the Gentiles and to be the glory of thy people Israel.[26]

Three days later, Emily was cremated at the Golders Green Crematorium in London. There were no mourners or a clergyman present. A certain J. Baker, presumably the undertaker, signed the register and put the wooden casket on the train to Southampton.[27]

From there it was transported across the Atlantic Ocean aboard the *City of Dunkirk*.

22

Thousands say goodbye

'Here was a great war, in which hundreds, thousands of men were engaged, in which the greatest Empire on earth was exerting all its strength and force. And an unknown woman appears from nowhere and presses the right button; and the course of our history in South Africa is permanently altered. For the future of South Africa the whole meaning and significance of the Anglo-Boer War was permanently affected by this Englishwoman.'

– Jan Smuts, 27 October 1926

One by one, people had been walking into the Tweetoring Church in Bloemfontein from early that morning. The pulpit was dwarfed by the masses of flowers in the front of the church.

Directly in front of the pulpit stood a wooden bier, a moveable frame, covered in dark purple cloth edged with a silver border. On top was a cushion with the same covering.[1] Dozens of wreaths were heaped against the pulpit, which was also draped in purple and decorated with lilies and proteas.

A small oaken casket rested on the cushion.[2] Big white lilies lay on either side of the casket, which bore the inscription: 'Emily Hobhouse. Died June, 1926. Age 66 years'.

From all over the country, people, mostly women, came in silence to spend some time at the casket, and then left the church where Emily's ashes lay in state before the funeral that would take place the next day. Towards evening, a male guard of honour positioned themselves at the casket.

A small group of women held an all-night vigil in the church.

By half past eight the next morning, the day of Emily's funeral on 27 October 1926, the church was already packed to capacity for the service that would only start in an hour and a half's time.

Emily Hobhouse's ashes (in the casket on the bier in front of the pulpit) lying in state in the Tweetoring Church in Bloemfontein, a day before her funeral.

Photo: Free State Archives Repository

A section of the crowd of thousands of people who
attended Emily's funeral ceremony at the Women's
Monument in Bloemfontein on 27 October 1926.

Photo: Free State Archives Repository

Four hundred women from across the country who had been
in the concentration camps and/or weaving schools had places
of honour in the front pews along with General Jan Smuts,
leader of the South African Party and a good friend of Emily,
and his wife Isie; Dr D. F. Malan, minister of the interior,
education and public health; General Jan Kemp, minister of
agriculture; Caroline Murray and Tibbie Steyn.[3] Prime Minister
J. B. M. Hertzog was unable to attend, as he was at the Imperial
Conference in London.[4]

While the funeral march played, six young girls in mauve
dresses and veils walked in at half past nine and formed a guard of
honour next to the bier. As the Reverend John Daniël Kestell
(also known as 'Father' Kestell) started the service, the six girls
kneeled reverently.

The funeral procession arrives at the monument. In front are six children named after Emily, including a boy (with the name Emile Hobhouse), followed by the girls carrying the bier with the casket; behind them, are 200 schoolgirls and then 400 women delegates.

Photo: Free State Archives Repository

After the service, the mourners set off in a long, silent procession in a southern direction, out of the city. The doors of all shops and other enterprises in Bloemfontein were closed. Flags flew at half-mast. The Free State capital had come to a standstill.

Heading the procession were hundreds of men on horseback who had been in the concentration camps as boys during the Anglo-Boer War, followed by an orchestra from the Department of Railways and Harbours. Behind them came the bier with the casket that was carried by six girls, followed by another six children who had been named after Emily, two hundred schoolgirls in mauve dresses whose faces were covered by veils, and students in togas. Then followed the four hundred women delegates and the other official guests who included administrators and judges,

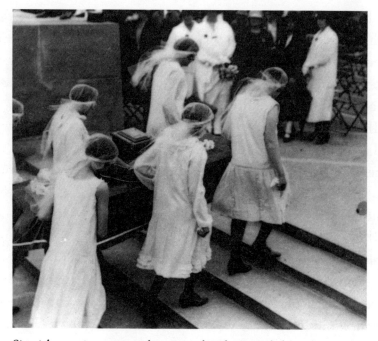

Six girls wearing mauve dresses and veils carried the oaken casket
with Emily's ashes to the base of the Women's Monument.

Photo: Free State Archives Repository

friends and other interested individuals, the cars with the guests
of honour and, right at the end, another group of men on
horseback.[5]

Thousands of people stood lining the streets up to the monument two miles outside the city. As the procession passed, they
joined it. At the hill, at the monument, thousands of men, women
and children had stood waiting since early that morning.
Loudspeakers had been erected so that no one needed to miss out
on any aspect of the proceedings.

This was the first – and to date the only – state funeral in South
Africa for a foreigner. The copies of newspapers that carried
reports on this historic day were all sold out.[6] The six girls carried

the bier to the base of the Women's Monument in front of the high obelisk where a niche had been prepared for the casket, directly below the sculpture group Emily had helped to design. The two hundred girls came forward and solemnly lay their palm branches at the base of the monument.

The crowd sang Psalm 146:3, which was followed by a prayer and a choir singing an Afrikaans version of Handel's 'Largo'. An angel of solace. An interpreter of our woes. Our advocate before the world. The healer of our wounds. The mother of the motherless.

This was how Dr Malan described Emily when his turn came to give an address. 'She went childless into her grave, but there are thousands who owe her their lives ... Therefore she is being buried among our heroes in the bosom of the women of our nation.'Emily Hobhouse was our own, and also, in the deepest sense of the word, one of *her* nation's own. Who would deny that she salvaged the honour of her own nation in South Africa?'[7]

Smuts, too, delivered a moving address in which he said, among other things, that one impression that remained with him of Emily's life and work was 'that of the power and profound influence of women in the affairs of the world'. 'How often in the great happenings of history a woman appears at the decisive moment, and in her weakness turns the flowing tide of events!'

A second impression of Emily he related to the dying words of the British nurse Edith Cavell before she had been shot as a spy during the First World War: 'Patriotism is not enough.'

As 'great and noble and pure an emotion' as patriotism is, it is not enough, Smuts said.

Let us not forget Emily Hobhouse. She was an Englishwoman to the marrow, proud of her people and its great mission and history. But for her patriotism was not enough. When she saw her country embark on a policy which was in conflict with the higher moral law, she did not say: 'My country, right or wrong.' She wholeheartedly took our side against that of her own people, and in doing so rendered an imperishable service, not only to us, but also to her own England and to the world at large.

For this loyalty to the higher and great things of life she suffered deeply. Her action was not understood or appreciated by her own people . . . Emily Hobhouse will stand out in our record as a trumpet call to the higher duty, to our duty and loyalty to the great things which do not merely concern us as a nation, but which bind together all nations as a great spiritual brotherhood . . . More than anything in our history the example of Emily Hobhouse reminds us that we are not merely citizens of South Africa, but that we belong also and above all to the greater city of God.[8]

After the speeches, the daughter of Johanna Osborne of the lace-making school released a flock of white doves as the casket with Emily's ashes was placed in the niche. Above the niche stood Anton van Wouw's mournful figures from the scene that Emily had witnessed at the station in Springfontein in April 1901.

A stream of people came up to lay wreaths at the foot of the modest memorial plaque inscribed with the words 'Hier rus Emily Hobhouse. 27 Okt. 1926' (Here rests Emily Hobhouse. 27 Oct. 1926). After the crowd had sung Psalm 118:7, the mounted men gave the mourning salute.

'It was a great occasion. We buried her like a princess,' Smuts wrote to Emily's beloved nephew, Oliver Hobhouse.[9]

23

Love in a notebook

She 'had the face of a Madonna, but she fights like the devil.'
— Lieutenant-Colonel J. F. Williamson of the
Royal Army Medical Corps about Emily, 1901

For years Emily carried the small leather notebook with her in which she regularly made notes, mostly jotting down poems and quotations.

It started around Christmas 1899, shortly after the outbreak of the Anglo-Boer War and before she had begun agitating vehemently against it. Until the book was finally filled with writing from one end to the other, including the back page. Sometimes in pencil, mostly in pen. On the front she wrote down who had to inherit it one day: her confidante Johanna Osborne.

The notebook reveals much about Emily – not only because of what she wrote in it in terms of her own thoughts and feelings, but also through the excerpts from poems and other writings she copied in it.

An undated photo of Emily. She wrote in her later
years, 'I like [Maurice] Maeterlinck's thought: "The
dead live again every time we remember them." '

Like the single line from Shakespeare's Henry VI: 'A heart
unspotted is not easily daunted.'

And this quotation: 'We women miss life only when we have to
confess, we have never met the man to reverence.'

Because she was in essence a solitary person, and her active
involvement in the great issues of her time meant that she had to
relinquish a carefree existence for the sake of those pursuits, the
notion of a vulnerable Emily who yearned to be loved does not
occur to me.

And yet this was the case. Her love affair with the American John Carr Jackson who won her heart and then, as her fiancé, abandoned her, is testimony to that.

No wonder that the quotation from *Diana of the Crossways* by George Meredith and the reference to reverence appealed so strongly to her. The man in her life had to be someone she could look up to, who deserved respect. 'Caro' was evidently not such a man.

Then Jaap de Villiers came onto the scene, and Emily could barely conceal her attraction to him – in writing, at least – because 'undoubtedly he is the man with ballast, uncommon brains and force of character'.[1] He could certainly lay claim to 'reverence', and with his 'dark grey eyes, full of feeling and of humour and a sweet smile' he was physically attractive to boot.

Was it with him in mind that she copied this poem by Adelaide Anne Procter in the notebook?[2]

> It is not because your heart is mine – mine only –
> Mine alone;
> It is not because you chose me, weak and lonely,
> For your own;
> Not because the earth is fairer, and the skies
> Spread above you
> Are more radiant for the shining of your eyes –
> That I love you!

But in the end nothing came of the relationship between her and Jaap either. He was not the knight in shining armour after all, as he married a 'ninny'. Emily – strong, resolute and individualistic – was clearly not his kind of woman.

Her yearning for a lover and a spouse, for children and a home of her own, remained unfulfilled. Despite the proud bearing there was a trace of sadness in her pale blue eyes, especially in later years.

Yet she achieved miracles – not only measured by the thousands of lives she saved, but also by the breaking down of prejudices and the sincere caring she radiated by taking on the almost impossible and unthinkable. Who else would have even considered crossing the ocean in the midst of a war to a completely unfamiliar country, with hardly any money, for the purpose of assisting the enemy's women and children?

Or in the midst of a world war, without any mandate whatsoever, to start discussions about peace at the highest level and in great secrecy with the enemy, a 'great power' at the time? And ultimately provide 5.5 million meals to hungry children – again, those of 'the enemy'?

Achieving what she did required boundless optimism, courage and bravery, as well as heaps of creativity, organisational know-how and perseverance, and the ability to work with money – and people – while constantly navigating a minefield of politicking and moral dilemmas.

Probably the best description of Emily came from her brother Leonard:

> The root cause of her achievement lay in the whole-heartedness with which she would throw herself into the pursuit of an end which had firmly seized her imagination. She then displayed an initiative and resourcefulness, a contempt of danger and disregard of social consequences which carried her through seeming impossibilities . . . In the rarer gift of moral courage she was supreme, owing it at bottom to that simplicity of faith . . . and to a certain haughtiness which was natural to her, but which she came to use with deadly effect on the lesser forms of false patriotism.[3]

Emily had a single-minded purposefulness and a zeal for work that few people, men or women, could match. Although she was sickly since the age of about forty-one and even had to be carried around at times, she steamed ahead. 'Rather wear out than rust out' was her motto.

This apparently inexhaustible energy she poured into various causes in the course of her life. Pacifism. Feminism. Liberalism, later socialism and internationalism. Women's suffrage. Human rights – long before it became fashionable.

And always impelled by the desire to alleviate pain and suffering, and eliminate deprivation.

With these convictions and sentiments, she was inevitably opposed to patriarchy, racism and jingoistic nationalism. This brought her into contact – and also conflict – with some of the great men of her time: Milner, Kitchener, Grey, Cecil, Brodrick and also her good friend Jan Smuts. She did not let any of them stop her.

Emily was not without flaws. She could scarcely tolerate opposition. She was often stubborn, and some of her best friends considered her tactless. She easily rubbed people up the wrong way, with the result that good friendships ran aground. The watch before her mouth was absent at times. Because only the best was good enough for her, she was hard to please.

Ironically, one could say of her what she had remarked about Petronella van Heerden: 'Too uncompromising of course to succeed in life, but some of that will wear off with experience.' As someone who was far ahead of her time and who did not flinch from going against the stream, she was a controversial figure in many eyes, especially in her beloved England. At home she was reviled and ostracised, but in South Africa and among many people in Germany she was regarded with goodwill and held in the highest esteem.

Leonard related that a man once asked Emily: 'Are you the Miss Hobhouse?'

Trumping him in typical fashion, and with a hint of self-mockery, she retorted: 'Well, I rather thought I was that Miss Hobhouse.'[4]

Sketch: Ruan Huisamen, 2015

References

There are two original copies of the draft autobiography. Both were written by hand by Emily and she also typed sections when she acquired a typewriter in later years. She worked on it from 1922 until shortly before her death. One copy she left in her will to Advocate Gladys Steyn, the daughter of her friend Rachel Isabella 'Tibbie' Steyn, with the instruction that it be published, and she bequeathed £500 to Gladys for this purpose. She also left £500 to Oliver Hobhouse for the same purpose. It is not known why the book was never published. Maybe because the autobiography was unfinished, or maybe because they were satisfied with the book on Emily's life that Ruth Fry published in 1929. Gladys subsequently donated the autobiography and other letters of Emily's to the Free State Archives Repository in Bloemfontein.

1. From slave ship to freedom flight

1. *Royal Cornwall Gazette.*
2. Ibid.

3. E. Hobhouse, List of paupers, St Ive parish.
4. J. Hobhouse Balme, *To Love One's Enemies*, p. 11.
5. W. S. Trelawny, Will of W. S. Trelawny.
6. A. R. Fry, *Emily Hobhouse: A Memoir*, p. 21.
7. R. Dunning, Hobhouse family history.
8. W. Minchinton, 'The Virginia Letters of Isaac Hobhouse, Merchant of Bristol', *The Virginia Magazine of History and Biography*, p. 281.
9. Ibid.
10. Ibid., p. 288.
11. R. Dunning, Hobhouse family history.
12. A. R. Fry, p. 23.
13. J. Hobhouse Balme, p. 7.
14. A. R. Fry, p. 27.
15. Ibid., p. 25.
16. Ibid., p. 28.
17. Ibid., pp. 28–9.
18. J. Hobhouse Balme, p. 8.
19. Ibid., p. 9.
20. A. R. Fry, p. 31.
21. Ibid., p. 32.
22. Ibid., pp. 20–1.
23. J. Hobhouse Balme, p. 9.
24. Ibid., p. 13.
25. Ibid.
26. A. R. Fry, p. 34.
27. G. Bishop, *A Parish Album of St. Ive*.
28. British Listed Buildings 1985, Chantry, St Ive: English Heritage Building.
29. J. Hall, *That Bloody Woman: The Turbulent Life of Emily Hobhouse*, p. 11.
30. Ibid.

2. Into the wide world

1. J. Hobhouse Balme, *To Love One's Enemies*, p. 13.
2. A. R. Fry, p. 43.

3. J. Fisher, *That Miss Hobhouse*, p. 31.

4. A. R. Fry, p. 44.

5. J. Fisher, p. 29.

6. A. R. Fry, p. 49.

7. Ibid., p. 45.

8. Ibid., p. 49.

9. J. Hobhouse Balme, p. 14.

10. A. R. Fry, pp. 46–7.

11. Ibid., p. 52.

12. J. Fisher, pp. 33–4.

13. Ibid., p. 34.

14. A. R. Fry, p. 55.

15. J. Hall, pp. 19–20.

16. J. Hobhouse Balme, p. 15.

17. J. Hall, p. 21.

18. J. Fisher, pp. 36–7.

19. J. Hobhouse Balme, p. 16.

20. J. Fisher, pp. 38–9.

21. A. R. Fry, p. 60.

22. J. Hobhouse Balme, p. 17.

23. About the dress, too, little is known. Although Emily was very outspoken about many issues, she recorded virtually nothing about matters of the heart.

24. J. Hall, pp. 23–4.

3. A vision that grows like a seed

1. E. Hobhouse, 'Autobiography: First Draft Chapter for 1900', p. 2.

2. Ibid.

3. T. Pakenham, *The Boer War* p. xxi

4. B. S. Seibold, *Emily Hobhouse and the Reports on the Concentration Camps during the Boer War, 1899–1902*, pp. 32–3.

5. T. Pakenham, *The Scramble for Africa*, p. 558. For the purpose of this book, therefore, the citizens of the Zuid-Afrikaansche Republiek (Transvaal) and the Orange Free State are referred to as Boers, as this was the common parlance of the time.

6. T. R. H. Davenport, p. 51

7. B. S. Seibold, p. 33.

8. Ibid.

9. F. Pretorius, p. 9.

10. T. Pakenham, p. 9.

11. Ibid., p. 558.

12. Ibid., p. 559.

13. B. S. Seibold, p. 34.

14. T. Pakenham, *The Scramble for Africa*, p. 559.

15. Ibid., p. 559.

16. Ibid., p. 560.

17. Ibid., pp. 564–5.

18. E. Hobhouse, 'Autobiography: First Draft Chapter . . .', pp. 3–4.

19. The author refers to the Anglo-Boer War in order to reflect the common parlance of the time.

20. F. Pretorius, p. 13.

21. A. Davey, *The British Pro-Boers, 1877–1902*, p. 78.

22. Ibid., p. 79.

23. E. Hobhouse, 'Autobiography: First Draft Chapter . . .', p. 3.

24. A. Davey, p. 78.

25. E. Hobhouse, 'Autobiography: First Draft Chapter . . .', p. 4.

26. J. Hobhouse Balme, *To Love One's Enemies*, p. 32.

27. E. Hobhouse, 'Autobiography: First Draft Chapter . . .', p. 6.

28. Ibid., p. 7.

29. F. Pretorius, p. 25.

30. Ibid., p. 27.

31. A. Grundlingh and B. Nasson (eds), *The War at Home: Women and Families in the Anglo-Boer War*, p. 32.

32. Ibid., pp. 32–3.

33. E. Hobhouse, 'Autobiography: First Draft Chapter . . .', p. 8.

34. Ibid., pp. 8–9.

35. J. Hobhouse Balme, p. 42.

36. E. Hobhouse, 'Autobiography: First Draft Chapter . . .',. p. 10.

37. *The Times*, 1900, 'Peace Meeting in Liskeard; Uproarious Proceedings – speakers refused hearing, platform stormed'.

38. E. Hobhouse, 'Autobiography: First Draft Chapter . . .', p. 11.

39. Ibid., p. 12.

40. Ibid.

41. Ibid., p. 13.

42. Ibid.

43. Ibid., p. 14.

44. Ibid., p. 15.

45. F. Pretorius, *Verskroeide Aarde*.

46. A. Grundlingh and B. Nasson, p. 32.

47. S. Raath and P. Warnich, 'From a concentration camp to a post-apartheid South African school: A historical-environmental perspective in developing a new identity', *Y&T* [online]. 2012, n.7 [cited 2017-09-08], pp.139–67.

48. E. Hobhouse, 'Autobiography: First Draft Chapter . . .', p. 20.

49. Ibid.

50. Ibid., p. 16.

51. Ibid., p. 26.

52. E. Hobhouse, letter: 1900-12-30 to 1901-01-01.

53. E. Hobhouse, 'Autobiography: First Draft Chapter . . .', p. 17.

54. Ibid., p. 17.

55. A. Grundlingh and B. Nasson, p. 37.

56. J. Hobhouse Balme, p. 62.

57. The author went to great lengths to confirm the colour of Emily Hobhouse's eyes and hair, as well as her height. In an interview with Jennifer Hobhouse Balme, a direct relative, Emily was described as follows: she had 'pale blue eyes and she was about five foot seven inches, and she most definitely had fair hair'. There are also descriptions of her appearance from Emily herself and other people.

58. T. Pakenham, *The Boer War*, p. 503.

59. J. Hobhouse Balme, p. 262.

60. Mary was a daughter of Hendrik Cloete of the famous Groot Constantia estate that belonged to the Cloete family.

61. E. Hobhouse, 'Autobiography: Chapter III, Cape Town & Arrived There'.

62. Ibid., p. 3.

63. Ibid., pp. 3–4.

64. Ibid., p. 5.

65. Henry Hobhouse V (1854-1937), heir of the Hobhouse estate and the mansion Hadspen House, in Somerset, England, was MP for East Somerset from 1885 to 1906. He was married to Margaret Heyworth Potter, a sister of Beatrice Webb, the social reformer, and Kate Courtney. There are friendly letters between Henry V and Milner in a private collection.

66. B. S. Seibold, p. 31.

67. E. Hobhouse, 'Autobiography: Chapter III . . .', p. 6.

68. Ibid., p. 7.

69. E. Hobhouse, letter: 1901-01-08.

70. E. Hobhouse, 'Autobiography: Chapter III . . .', p. 6.

71. Ibid.

72. Roos was a prominent figure in the Cape Colony and founded an Afrikaans Christian women's organisation, the Afrikaanse Christelike Vrouevereniging, in 1904.

73. E. Hobhouse, 'Autobiography: Chapter III ', pp. 12–13.

74. Ibid., p. 14.

75. Charles Fichardt fought with General Cronjé at Paardeberg and was one of 1200 men who escaped. His family had a business in Bloemfontein, where he was elected mayor in 1897.

76. E. Hobhouse, 'Autobiography: Chapter III', p. 12.

4. Looking into the depths of grief

1. E. Hobhouse, 'Autobiography: Chapter IV, The Camps', p. 1.

2. Ibid., p. 3.

3. E. Hobhouse, letter: 1901-01-26.

4. Queen Victoria died on 22 January 1901, while Emily was on the train. She did not write much about her feelings regarding the Queen's demise in her autobiography. The only mention she made of the event was a reference to an old Sotho woman who had told her in February that she was sad about Victoria's death. Emily also stated that she had wished Victoria would say something about the war on her sickbed to bring it to an end.

5. E. Hobhouse, 'Autobiography: Chapter IV . . .', p. 4.

6. Ibid.

7. A. Grundlingh and B. Nasson, p. 36.

8. Ibid., p. 68.

9. E. Hobhouse, 'Autobiography: Chapter IV . . .', p. 5.

10. F. Pretorius, p. 68.

11. E. Hobhouse, 'Autobiography: Chapter IV . . .', p. 6.

12. Ibid.

13. Ibid., pp. 6–7.

14. Ibid., p. 29.

15. Ibid., p. 7.

16. F. Pretorius, p. 113

17. Ibid., p. 114.

18. E. Hobhouse, *The Brunt of the War and Where it Fell*, pp. 319–20.

19. Emily certainly spoke to thousands of people during the Anglo-Boer War and in the course of her travels through the country in 1903. She put basic questions to women, wrote down their responses and then elaborated on this information.

20. E. Hobhouse, 'Autobiography: Chapter IV . . .', p. 10.

21. Ibid.

22. Emily did not publish the photograph of Lizzie in her book *The Brunt of the War and Where it Fell* (1902), as she believed it to be too 'painful for reproduction'. It was thanks to Emily that the world did take notice of Lizzie. But she added in her book that this raised the question of the extent to which it was right to shy away from an image, no matter how painful it might be, of the suffering experienced by others which had been caused by a series of events for which we were partially responsible. Emily wrote that the now well-known photograph, which was even discussed in Parliament, had not been taken by the camp doctor, as Chamberlain had said, but by a Mr De Klerk who had given her the photograph. Emily's documentation contains an explanation of what exactly happened to Lizzie.

23. E. Hobhouse, *The Brunt of the War*, p. 214.

24. E. van Heyningen, *The Concentration Camps of the Anglo-Boer War: A Social History*, p. 149.

25. E. Hobhouse, 'Autobiography: Chapter IV . . .', p. 11.

26. Ibid., p. 7.

27. Rachel Isabella 'Tibbie' Steyn (1865–1955) was five years younger than Emily. She was born at Philippolis and her father, the Reverend Colin McKenzie Fraser, was of Scottish descent, although he was a minister of the Dutch Reformed Church. Her mother was Isabella Paterson. Tibbie married Theunis (M.T.) Steyn in 1887. (E. Truter, *Tibbie: Rachel Isabella Steyn (1865–1955): Haar lewe was haar boodskap*, pp. 1–2, 25.)

28. E. Truter, *Tibbie: Rachel Isabella Steyn (1865–1955)*, p. 51.

29. T. Pakenham, p. 506.

30. J. Hobhouse Balme, *To Love One's Enemies*, p. 97.

31. E. Hobhouse, 'Autobiography: Chapter IV . . .', p. 20.

32. Ibid.

33. J. Hobhouse Balme, pp. 97–8.

34. E. Hobhouse, 'Autobiography: Chapter IV . . .', p. 37.

35. J. Hobhouse Balme, pp. 111–13.

36. Years later, in 1924, Emily received a note from Eunice van Schalkwyk (née Ferreira) to thank her for this education. After Emily had paid for her first year at the school, she had obtained a state bursary, completed her school education and trained as a teacher. 'It was thanks to you that I received an education. Eternally grateful for this,' she wrote. Could Emily please send her a photo of herself? She had cut one from a newspaper, but it was blurred.

37. E. Hobhouse, 'Autobiography: Chapter IV . . .', p. 25.

38. Ibid.

39. Ibid., p. 26.

40. Ibid.

41. Ibid., p. 27.

42. J. Hobhouse Balme, p. 119.

43. Ibid., p. 133.

44. F. Pretorius, p. 31.

45. E. Hobhouse, letter: 1901-02-18 to 1901-02-22.

46. E. Hobhouse, 'Autobiography: Chapter IV . . .', p. 32.

47. Ibid., p. 33.

48. Ibid., p. 36.

49. Ibid., p. 42.

50. Ibid., p. 43.

51. Although Emily was friends with many Quakers and they regularly provided halls in which she could address meetings, Emily was raised in the tradition of the Church of England. Many writers and researchers refer to her as a Quaker, but that is not correct.

52. E. Hobhouse, 'Autobiography: Chapter IV . . .', p. 45.

53. According to the researcher Stowell Kessler (*The Black Concentration Camps of the Anglo-Boer War, 1899–1902*, p. 281), the black camps were 'not less harsh than the white camps. Indeed the study shows that in all areas of life these camps were much more severe and the deprivations were much greater. The misery in these laagers of suffering was the result of the deliberate neglect by the military and high level civilian leaders.'

54. E. Hobhouse, 'Autobiography: Chapter IV . . .', p. 48.

55. Ibid., p. 49.

56. Ibid., p. 50.

57. Ibid., p. 52.

58. Ibid.

59. Ibid.

60. E. Hobhouse, letter: 1901-03-08.

61. E. Hobhouse, 'Autobiography: Chapter IV . . .', p. 60.

62. Ibid.

63. Ibid., p. 61.

64. Ibid., p. 63.

65. Ibid.

66. Ibid., p. 63.

67. During the first and second visit of the later Women's Commission five hundred people died in the Mafeking camp. The commission, headed by Millicent Fawcett, travelled through the country in luxury and had been despatched to visit the camps in the wake of the appearance of Emily's report.

68. E. Hobhouse, 'Autobiography: Chapter IV . . .', p. 63.

69. Ibid.

70. Ibid., pp. 64–5.

71. Ibid., p. 66.

72. Ibid., p. 75.

73. Ibid., p. 71.

74. Ibid.

75. E. Hobhouse, letter: 1901-04-22.

76. E. Hobhouse, 'Autobiography: Chapter IV . . .', p. 71.

77. E. Hobhouse, *The Brunt of the War*, p. 121.

78. Ibid., p. 122.

79. E. Hobhouse, 'Autobiography: Chapter IV . . .', p. 71.

80. E. Hobhouse, *The Brunt of the War*, p. 123.

81. Ibid., p. 124.

82. Ibid.

83. Ibid.

84. E. Hobhouse, p. 123.

85. E. Hobhouse, p. 75.

86. E. Hobhouse, 'Autobiography: Chapter IV . . .', p. 76.

87. Ibid., p. 77.

88. Ibid., p. 78.

89. Shortly after Milner's arrival he was raised to the peerage as Lord Milner.

90. E. Hobhouse, letter: 1901-01-17.

91. Afrikaans-Dutch.

92. E. Hobhouse, 'Autobiography: Chapter IV . . .', p. 81.

93. Ibid.

94. R. van Reenen, *Heldin uit die vreemde*, p. 64.

95. E. Hobhouse, 'Autobiography: Chapter IV . . .', p. 14.

5. Reviled, but not defeated

1. W. K. Hancock, *Smuts, Volume 1: The Sanguine Years, 1870–1919*, p. 180.

2. E. Hobhouse, *The Brunt of the War*, p. 126.

3. B. S. Seibold, p. 31.

4. The first wife of Emily's Uncle Edmund (an older brother of her father), Bishop of Nelson in New Zealand, was Mary Elizabeth Brodrick, a cousin of Brodrick's grandfather.

5. E. Hobhouse, 'Autobiography: Work in England', p. 12.

6. E. Hobhouse, Recommendations to St John Brodrick.

7. T. Pakenham, *The Boer War*, p. 502.

8. J. Hall, p. 94.
9. C. Headlam (ed.), *The Milner Papers: South Africa 1899–1905, Vol. II.*, p, 227.
10. E. Hobhouse, 'Autobiography: Work in England', p. 4.
11. Ibid., p. 5.
12. W. K. Hancock, p. 180.
13. E. Hobhouse, 'Autobiography: Work in England', p. 12.
14. Ibid.
15. T. Pakenham, p. 508.
16. S.B. Spies, *Methods of Barbarism?*, p. 9.
17. Hansard, 1901: 'South African War – Mortality in Camps of Detention'.
18. Ibid.
19. Ibid.
20. Ibid
21. B. S. Seibold, p. 74.
22. *Cheltenham Looker-On*, p. 584.
23. *The Times*, 26 July 1901, p. 6.
24. The organisation searched for and marked graves during the war.
25. M. Hasian (Jr.), *Restorative Justice, Humanitarian Rhetorics, and Public Memories of Colonial Camp Cultures*, pp. 84–5.
26. Ibid.
27. E. Hobhouse, 'Autobiography: Work in England', p. 5.
28. E. Hobhouse, *The Brunt of the War*, p. 143.
29. E. Hobhouse, 'Autobiography: Work in England', p. 14.
30. J. Hobhouse Balme, *To Love One's Enemies*, p. 262.
31. Ibid., pp. 238–9.
32. S. J. Brodrick, letter/report: 1901-06-27.
33. J. Hobhouse Balme, p. 252.
34. E. Hobhouse, letter: 1901-07-11.
35. J. Hobhouse Balme, p. 278.
36. E. Hobhouse, 'Autobiography: Work in England', p. 7.
37. T. Pakenham, p. 515.
38. *Cape Times*, 22 Jul. 1901.
39. R. van Reenen (ed.), *Emily Hobhouse: Boer War Letters*, p. 452.
40. J. Hall, p. 113.
41. E. Hobhouse, pamphlet: 'Appeal of Miss Hobhouse to Mr Brodrick'.

42. Ibid.

43. Ibid.

44. 'The nationalists misunderstood Emily Hobhouse. They saw her as a friend of the Boers and enemy of her own country . . . Emily protested when she saw that her own nation was depriving the Boers of their natural rights; life, health, liberty, property. She regarded it as her duty to bring to light the truth about the situation in South Africa, so that the British infringement of the Boers' human rights should be stopped . . . out of love for her motherland she wished to save it from making a tragic mistake.' (B. S. Seibold, p. 156.)

45. E. Hobhouse, 'Autobiography: Arrest & Deportation', p. 2.

6. 'I feel ashamed'

1. A. R. Fry, *Emily Hobhouse: A Memoir*, p. 167.

2. E. Hobhouse, report: 'A letter to the Committee of the South African Women and Children Distress Fund'.

3. E. Hobhouse, 'Autobiography: Arrest & Deportation', p. 1.

4. Ibid.

5. E. Hobhouse, 'Autobiography: Arrest & Deportation', p. 4.

6. J. Hobhouse Balme, *To Love One's Enemies*, p. 333.

7. E. Hobhouse, 'Autobiography: Arrest & Deportation', p. 2.

8. Ibid., p. 4.

9. Ibid., p. 2.

10. J. Hobhouse Balme, p. 343.

11. E. Hobhouse, p. 3.

12. Ibid.

13. F. Beer, *The Angel of Love: Emily Hobhouse*, p. 14.

14. E. Hobhouse, 'A letter to the Committee . . .'

15. Ibid.

16. E. Hobhouse, 'Autobiography: Arrest & Deportation', p. 7.

17. J. Hall, p. 129.

18. C. Murray, report: 'Arrest and Deportation'.

19. Ibid.

20. B. Molteno, 'Statement re Miss Hobhouse's removal from the Avondale Castle'.

21. E. Hobhouse, 'Autobiography: Arrest & Deportation', p. 8.

22. B Molteno, 'Statement . . .'

23. Ibid.

24. E. Hobhouse, 'A letter to the Committee . . .'

25. Ibid.

26. E. Hobhouse, 'Autobiography: Arrest & Deportation', p. 10.

27. J. Hall, p. 138.

28. E. Hobhouse, 'Autobiography: Arrest & Deportation', pp. 6–8.

29. Ibid.

30. Ibid.

31. C. Murray, letter: 1902-02-28.

32. J. Hobhouse Balme, p. 360.

33. Ibid.

34. Ibid.

35. M. Hobhouse, letter.

36. E. Hobhouse, 'Autobiography: Arrest & Deportation'

7. Vindicated

1. B. S. Seibold, p. 109.

2. J. Hobhouse Balme, *To Love One's Enemies*, p. 396.

3. Ibid., p. 403.

4. E. van Heyningen, 'Fools Rush In: Writing a history of the concentration camps of the South African War', *Historia*, p. 17. The War Office had published a number of these 'Blue Books' from November 1901 after serious questions were raised about the war in the House of Commons. The reports mostly defended the actions of the government of the day.

5. R. van Reenen, *Emily Hobhouse: Boer War Letters*, p. 462.

6. Hansard, 1902.

7. Ibid.

8. Ibid.

9. T. Pakenham, The Boer War, p. 509.

10. B. S. Seibold, pp. 147–9.

11. It was Milner who took the women more seriously and insisted that their recommendations be implemented. (E. van Heyningen, 'Fools Rush In . . .', p. 192).

12. E. van Heyningen, 'Fools Rush In . . .'.

13. E. van Heyningen, *The Concentration Camps of the Anglo-Boer War*, pp. 195–6.

14. E. Hobhouse, 'Autobiography: Chapter VIII, 1902', p. 9.

15. B. S. Seibold, p. 112.

16. E. Hobhouse, *The Brunt of the War*, p. 350.

17. Ibid., p. 351.

18. Ibid., pp. 352–3.

19. S Kessler, pp. 243–4.

20. There is no clarity or consensus among historians, about the exact number of camp deaths. According to calculations by P.L.A. Goldman in 1913, 22,074 children, 4177 women (16 years and older) and 1676 men (total: 27,927) died in the camps for white people (Transvaal archives section of the National Archives Repository in Pretoria, South Africa; Folder/R.S. Goldman). According to other research by Celeste Reynolds, about 34,000 white people died in and en route to concentration camps, or as a result of privation suffered in the veld (http:// celestereynolds.weebly. com). The researchers I.R. Smith and A. Stucki estimate the number of white deaths at 25,000 ('The Colonial Development of Concentration Camps, 1868–1902'). Likewise, there is uncertainty about the number of deaths in the black camps. Officially, according to the records of the British military authorities, a total of 14,154 black people died, 80 per cent of whom were children (P. Warwick and S.B. Spies, *The South African War: The Anglo-Boer War, 1899–1902*). The researcher Stowell Kessler, however, puts the total at about 25,000 people (*The Black Concentration Camps of the Anglo-Boer War 1899–1902*).

21. Encyclopedia Britannica (online): 'South African War'.

22. E. Hobhouse, 'Autobiography: Chapter VIII, 1902', pp. 12–13.

23. E. Hobhouse, *The Brunt of the War*, p. xv.

24. Ibid., p. o.

25. Ibid., p. xvi.

26. B. Nasson, The South African War, 1899-1902, p. 232.

27. Ibid.

28. E. Hobhouse, 'Autobiography: Chapter VIII, 1902', p. 14.

8. Peace – and loss

1. E. Hobhouse, 'Autobiography: Chapter IX, Quieter Days – 1902–1903', p. 1.
2. J. Hall, p. 156.
3. C. Muller, *500 jaar: Suid-Afrikaanse geskiedenis*, p. 368.
4. The British were not in favour of changing the agreement. (C. Muller, p. 368.)
5. E. Hobhouse, 'Autobiography: Chapter VIII, 1902'. Here Emily is quoting from the White Paper 1902, Cd.1284.
6. E. Hobhouse, 'Autobiography: Chapter VIII, 1902', p. 20.
7. Ibid., p. 16.
8. Ibid., p. 17.
9. Enteraden Ltd, 'Cheyne Court and Rossetti Garden Mansions – History'.
10. E. Hobhouse, 'Autobiography: Chapter IX, Quieter Days – 1902–1903', p. 3.
11. Ibid., p. 6.
12. Ibid., p. 7.
13. Ibid., p. 8.
14. Ibid.
15. In 1910 he became Baron de Villiers and the country's chief justice.
16. E. Hobhouse, 'Autobiography: Chapter IX, Quieter Days – 1902–1903', p. 12.
17. Ibid.
18. R. van Reenen, *Emily Hobhouse: Boer War Letters*, p. 181.
19. E. Hobhouse, 'Autobiography: Chapter IX, Quieter Days – 1902–1903', p. 9.
20. O. Schreiner, letter: 1903-04-03.
21. Olive's brother William was premier of the Cape Colony from 1898 to June 1900. Her husband, Samuel ('Cron') Cronwright-Schreiner, adopted her surname to support her campaign of equal rights for women, but he dropped it again after her death. She was also a renowned social commentator and wrote thousands of letters. Later, by the time of her death in 1920, she and Samuel were estranged and he destroyed many of her letters. (L. Stanley and A. Salter fedsj; *The*

World's Great Question: Olive Schreiner's South African Letters, 1889–1920, p. xii.)

22. E. Hobhouse, 'Autobiography: Chapter X, Beaufort-West & Olive Schreiner', p. 1.
23. Ibid., p. 4.
24. Ibid., p. 6.
25. E. Hobhouse, 'Autobiography: Chapter XI, O.R.C. Once More'.
26. L. M. Thompson, *The Unification of South Africa, 1902–1910*, p. 13.
27. R. van Reenen, *Emily Hobhouse: Boer War Letters*, p. 480.
28. Ibid.
29. P. Kapp, 'War and Reconstruction: Four Comparative Case Studies', *Scientia Militaria*, p. 117.
30. 'In the end the British government paid the war debt and the reconstruction money (reparations). The British denied that the payments were compensation and tried to defend them as free grants or reconstruction loans. A bitter dispute arose about the amounts that were paid out, the way in which claims were submitted, and the clumsy and unsympathetic way in which the claims were administered.' (P. Kapp, p. 112.)
31. W. K. Hancock, p. 173.
32. Ibid., pp. 192–3.

9. A country of skulls and bones

1. J. Smuts, letter: 1903-10-25.
2. E. Hobhouse, 'Autobiography: Chapter XI, O.R.C. Once More', p. 3.
3. Ibid., p. 2.
4. Rykie van Reenen wrote that it might have been Zacharias Enslin of Heilbron, but he was in the prisoner-of-war camp in Bermuda (R. van Reenen, *Emily Hobhouse: Boer War Letters*, p. 480). Emily did not mention his first name in her account.
5. Emily mentioned that these people were among those she encountered who had the most food (E. Hobhouse, 'Autobiography: Chapter XI . . .', p. 5).
6. E. Hobhouse, 'Autobiography: Chapter XI . . .', p. 6.
7. Ibid.

8. Ibid., p. 7.

9. Ibid.

10. Ibid.

11. Ibid., p. 9.

12. Ibid., p. 11.

13. Ibid., pp. 9–10.

14. Ibid., p. 11.

15. Ibid., p. 14.

16. E. Hobhouse, 'Autobiography: Chapter XI . . .', p. 14.

17. The act introduced censorship in peace time and prohibited criticism of the government. The authorities were also allowed to detain people for twenty-one days without trial. (R. van Reenen, *Emily Hobhouse: Boer War Letters*, p. 481.)

18. E. Hobhouse, 'Autobiography: Chapter XI . . .', p. 17.

19. Ibid.

20. Ibid., pp. 16–17.

21. Ibid.

22. Ibid., p. 11.

23. Ibid.

24. H. Giliomee, *The Afrikaners*, p. 268.

25. E. Hobhouse, 'Autobiography: Chapter XIII, In the Transvaal; Heidelberg and the Volksvergadering', p. 1.

26. Ibid.

27. W. K. Hancock, p. 183.

28. E. Hobhouse, 'Autobiography: Chapter XIII . . .', p. 2.

29. Ibid.

30. W. K. Hancock, p. 117.

31. E. Hobhouse, 'Autobiography: Chapter XIII . . .', p. 2.

32. Ibid., p. 4.

33. Ibid.

34. Ibid., p. 6.

35. Ibid., p. 11.

36. Ibid., p. 8.

37. E. Hobhouse, *War Without Glamour; Or, Women's War Experiences Written by Themselves, 1899-1902*, p. 5.

38. Ibid., pp. 142–6.

39. E. Hobhouse, 'Autobiography: Chapter XIII . . .', p. 11.
40. E. Hobhouse, 'Autobiography: Chapter XIII . . .', p. 15.
41. Ibid.
42. Ibid.
43. Ibid., p. 16.
44. Ibid.
45. Ibid., p. 17.
46. E. Hobhouse, 'Autobiography: Chapter XIV: First Visit to General and Mrs Smuts; Pietersburg and Warm Baths', p. 1.
47. Ibid.
48. E. Hobhouse, 'Autobiography: Chapter XIV . . .', p. 6.
49. Ibid.
50. Ibid., p. 2.
51. Ibid., p. 6.
52. Ibid.
53. Ibid., p. 8.
54. Ibid.
55. Ibid., p. 11.
56. Ibid., p. 12.
57. J. Hobhouse Balme, *To Love One's Enemies*, p. 487.
58. R. van Reenen, *Emily Hobhouse: Boer War Letters*, p. 250.
59. Ibid., p. 253.
60. Ibid., p. 254.
61. Ibid., p. 255.
62. Ibid.
63. Ibid.
64. Ibid.
65. E. Hobhouse, letter: 1903-08-23.
66. Ibid.
67. J. Hobhouse Balme, p. 489.
68. Military correspondence, 1903.
69. E. Hobhouse, 'Autobiography: Chapter XV, Repatriation and The Three Million', p. 2.
70. Ibid., p. 3.
71. Ibid., p. 1.
72. E. Hobhouse, letter: 1903-08-16.

73. E. Hobhouse, letter: 1903-08-22.

74. Ibid.

75. E. Hobhouse, 1903, speech: 22 August. This speech, one of the few that have been preserved, is in the archives of the Anglo-Boer War Museum in Bloemfontein.

76. R. van Reenen, *Emily Hobhouse: Boer War Letters*, p. 492.

77. Ibid., p. 494.

78. Ibid., p. 492.

79. E. Hobhouse, letter: 1903-09-12.

80. E. Hobhouse, letter: 1903-09-23.

81. Ibid.

82. E. Hobhouse, letter: 1903-09-06.

83. Ibid.

84. E. Hobhouse, 'Autobiography: Chapter XV . . .', p. 5.

85. E. Hobhouse, letter: 1903-09-12.

86. Ibid.

87. E. Hobhouse, letter: 1903-09-27.

88. E. Hobhouse, letter: 1903-09-30.

89. W. K. Hancock and J. van der Poel (eds), *Selections from the Smuts Papers: Volume II – June 1902 – May 1910*, p. 133.

90. E. Hobhouse, letter: 1903-11-17.

91. E. Hobhouse, letter: 1903-10-04.

92. E. Hobhouse, letter: 1903-11-23.

93. Ibid.

94. E. Hobhouse, letter: 1903-11-26.

95. E. Hobhouse, letter: December 1903.

96. J. Smuts, letter: 1903-10-25.

97. *De Zuid-Afrikaan*, 1903-11-05. p. 6.

98. W. K. Hancock and J. van der Poel, *Smuts Papers Vol. II*, p. 139.

99. R. van Reenen, pp. 298–9.

100. Ibid.

10 The Smuts letter blunder

1. W. K. Hancock, pp. 185–6.

2. R. van Reenen, *Emily Hobhouse: Boer War Letters*, p. 324.

3. Ibid.

4. E. Hobhouse, 'Autobiography: Boer Industries'.

5. C. Muller, *500 jaar*, p. 366.

6. W. K. Hancock and J. van der Poel (eds), *Selections from the Smuts Papers: Volume III – June 1910 – November 1918*, p. 144.

7. Ibid., pp. 147–8.

8. Ibid.

9. Ibid.

10. Ibid., p. 149.

11. Ibid., pp. 155–6.

12. W. K. Hancock, pp. 185–6.

13. W. K. Hancock and J. van der Poel, *Smuts Papers Vol. III*, p. 168.

14. Ibid.

15. Ibid., p. 150.

16. Ibid.

17. W. K. Hancock and J. van der Poel, *Smuts Papers Vol. III*, pp. 158–9.

18. Ibid., pp. 161–2.

19. Ibid., pp. 163–4.

20. Ibid., p. 166.

21. L. Stephen (ed.), *Dictionary of National Biography*, pp. 272–3.

22. Testimonial, Lady Courtney, 1904. 'Testimonial to Miss Emily Hobhouse'

23. Emily sent many letters from this address in London.

24. Subscribers to the Fund, 1904, letter.

25. There still exists a beautiful pendant made from diamonds from the Jagersfontein mine that the Free State Boers had given to Emily. In her will, Emily left this pendant to Johanna Osborne (née Rood), who became the principal of the lacemaking school in Koppies. Johanna, in turn, bequeathed it to the Anglo-Boer War Museum in Bloemfontein.

26. W. K. Hancock and J. van der Poel, *Smuts Papers Vol. III*, pp. 175–6.

27. Ibid., p. 180.

28. 'Margaret Clark (1878–1962) was the third daughter of William Stephens Clark (1839–1925) and Helen Priestman Bright Clark (1840–1927). She graduated from the University of Cambridge (Newnham) in 1901. She maintained links with South Africa

throughout her life, in particular with the family of General Jan Smuts (1870–1950) (whose daughter was later to marry Margaret's nephew Bancroft Clark).' (C. Berry, report: 'Papers of Margaret Clark Gillett', 2010-08-19.)

29. W. K. Hancock and J. van der Poel, *Smuts Papers Vol. III*, pp. 183–4.
30. E. Hobhouse, 1905, diary: 'Journal of Emily Hobhouse': 1 Jan. 1905 – 6 April 1905.
31. Ibid.
32. A. R. Fry, p. 232.
33. E. Hobhouse, 1905, diary.
34. E. Hobhouse, 'Autobiography: Boer Industries'.
35. E. Hobhouse, 1905, diary.
36. E. Hobhouse, 'Autobiography: Boer Industries'.
37. Ibid.
38. For years Lord Hobhouse gave Emily and her sisters £40 annually and assisted her financially in other ways. She inherited £3720 from his estate. (J. Hall, p. 187.)
39. E. Hobhouse, 1905, diary.
40. Ibid.

11. Blossom like a rose

1. E. Hobhouse, diary: 'Journal of Emily Hobhouse': 1 Jan 1905 – 6 April 1905.
2. 'Small cards, called flick cards, are used to flick the ends of a lock of fibre, or to tease out some strands for spinning off.' ('Carding', Wikipedia.)
3. E. Hobhouse, diary: 12 Feb.
4. E. Hobhouse, diary: 19 Feb.
5. M. Clark, diary: Margaret Clark: 23 Jan. 1905 – 8 Oct. 1905, 11 Feb.
6. E. Hobhouse, 1905, diary: 18 Feb.
7. R. van Reenen, *Emily Hobhouse: Boer War Letters*, p. 353.
8. Ibid., p. 506.
9. M. Clark, diary: 2 March.
10. Ibid.

11. Ibid.
12. E. Hobhouse, 1905, diary: 8–9 March.
13. E. Hobhouse, letter: 1905-01-30.
14. E. Hobhouse, 1905, diary: 14 March.
15. R. van Reenen, *Heldin uit die vreemde*, p. 95.
16. Ibid.
17. Ibid.
18. M. Clark, diary: 3–4 April.
19. E. Hobhouse, 1905, diary: 25 March.
20. Ibid., 6 April.
21. M. Clark, diary: 15 April.
22. E. Hobhouse, 1905, diary: 31 March.
23. M. Clark, diary: 20 April.
24. Ibid.
25. J. Hobhouse Balme, *To Love One's Enemies*, p. 508.
26. M. Clark, diary: 23 April.
27. Ibid., 29 April.
28. E. Hobhouse, 'Autobiography: Langlaagte and After'.
29. Ibid., p. 3.
30. J. Farrer, letter: 1905-04-28.

12. Elusive happiness

1. E. Hobhouse, 'Autobiography: Langlaagte and After'.
2. Ibid.
3. M. Clark, diary: 2 June.
4. Ibid., 1 June.
5. Ibid., 27 May.
6. Ibid., 29 May.
7. E. Hobhouse, letter: 1905-06-25.
8. E. Hobhouse, letter: 1905-07-02.
9. R. van Reenen, *Emily Hobhouse: Boer War Letters*, p. 381.
10. E. Hobhouse, letter: 1905-07-02.
11. L. M. Thompson, The Unification of South Africa, 1902-1910, p. 21.
12. E. Hobhouse, 'Autobiography: Chapter XXVII, Bellevue 1906-1907'.

13. E. Hobhouse, letter: 1905-07-09.

14. R. van Reenen, *Heldin uit die vreemde*, p. 99.

15. J. Hobhouse Balme, *To Love One's Enemies*, p. 522.

16. M. Clark, diary: 14 July.

17. E. Hobhouse, letter: 1905-07-23.

18. E. Hobhouse, letter: 1905-08-06.

19. M. Clark, diary: 23 Aug.

20. Ibid., 28 July.

21. Ibid., 27 Aug.

22. R. van Reenen, *Boer War Letters*, p. 507.

23. E. Hobhouse, letter: 1905-09-16.

24. E. Hobhouse, 'Autobiography: Langlaagte and After'.

25. R. van Reenen, *Heldin uit die vreemde*, p. 99.

26. M. Clark, diary: 4 Oct.

27. Ibid., 8 Oct.

28. E. Hobhouse, letter: 1905-12-25.

29. Ibid.

30. R. van Reenen, *Boer War Letters*, p. 383.

31. None of the sources I consulted mentioned the number of the house she owned. In the end I was able to trace it with the help of the Johannesburg Heritage Foundation that confirmed it as no. 91. The house has since been demolished, but it could still be found on the valuation roll of 1922 in Emily's name. At that time the stand was worth £80 and the property £1440.

32. E. Hobhouse, 'Autobiography: Chapter XXVII, Bellevue 1906–1907'.

33. Ibid. The pages were not numbered.

34. Ibid.

35. Ibid.

36. Ibid.

37. Ibid.

38. Ibid.

39. E. Hobhouse, 'Autobiography: Langlaagte and After'.

40. L. M. Thompson, p. 23.

41. E. Hobhouse, 'Autobiography: Langlaagte and After'.

42. R. van Reenen, *Boer War Letters*, p. 512.

43. E. Hobhouse, 'Autobiography: Chapter XXVII, Bellevue 1906-1907'.

44. Ibid.

45. C. Muller, p. 370.

46. Ibid., pp. 369–70.

47. E. Hobhouse, 'Autobiography: Chapter XXVII, Bellevue 1906–1907'.

48. M. Clark, Undated summary of M.C.'s time in SA.

49. E. Hobhouse, letter: 1906-04-04.

50. A. Walsh, 'Miss Hobhouse's Work in South Africa', *The Advocate of Peace*.

51. E. Hobhouse, letter: 1906-06-23.

52. Ibid.

53. E. Hobhouse, 'Autobiography: Chapter XXVIII, 1907 Jo'burg – London – Jo'burg – Pretoria'.

54. Ibid.

55. M. Clark and E. Hobhouse, report: 'Transvaal and Orange River Colony – Spinning, Weaving as Boer Home Industries'.

56. Ibid.

57. Ibid.

58. E. Hobhouse, 'Autobiography: Chapter XXVIII, 1907 Jo'burg – London – Jo'burg – Pretoria', p. 8.

59. Ibid.

60. Ibid, p. 9.

61. Ibid.

62. Ibid.

63. J. Hobhouse Balme, *To Love One's Enemies*, p. 518.

64. Ibid., p. 520.

65. M. Clark, Undated summary of MC's time in SA.

66. E. Hobhouse, 'Autobiography: Chapter XXVIII', p. 14.

67. R. van Reenen, *Boer War Letters*, p. 378.

68. J. Hall, p. 193.

69. According to some stories Emily apparently asked Jaap to marry her, but this is not confirmed in Emily's documents. Jaap told Tibbie's grandson 'that it was the most terrible moment in his life to jilt her face to face in this way', Elbie. Truter wrote in her doctoral thesis and

book on Tibbie's life ('Rachel Isabella Steyn, 1905–1955', p. 34).
Emily had been raised in a conservative fashion, and it is doubtful
whether she would have done something like that.

70. R. van Reenen, *Boer War Letters*, p. 525.
71. E. Hobhouse, 'Autobiography: Chapter XXVIII', p. 9.
72. J. Hobhouse Balme, p. 518.
73. A. R. Fry, p. 256.
74. J. Hobhouse Balme, *To Love One's Enemies*, p. 521.
75. This painting is now part of the collection of the Ditsong National
    Museum of Cultural History in Pretoria, previously the Transvaal
    Museum.
76. A. R. Fry, pp. 255–6.
77. W. K. Hancock and J. van der Poel, p. 409.
78. C. Smith, 'Halssnoer van Emily Hobhouse terug in Vrystaat',
    Volksblad.
79. Ibid.
80. J. Hobhouse Balme, p. 523.

13. A living flame

1. D. C. Kaminski, 'The Radicalization of a Ministering Angel: A
   Biography of Emily Hobhouse, 1860–1926', p. 254.
2. J. Hobhouse Balme, *To Love One's Enemies*, p. 525.
3. W. K. Hancock and J. van der Poel, p. 536.
4. J. Hobhouse Balme, p. 525.
5. A. Rosen, *Rise up, Women! The Militant Campaign of the Women's
   Social and Political Union*, p. 113.
6. J. Purvis, 2002. *Emmeline Pankhurst: A Biography*, p. 5.
7. R. Baksh and W. Harcourt (eds), *Oxford Handbook of Transnational
   Feminist Movements*, p. 705.
8. D. C. Kaminski, p. 242.
9. W. K. Hancock and J. van der Poel, p. 536.
10. Ibid.
11. E. Hobhouse, letter: 1909-10-22, *Cambridge Independent*.
12. D. C. Kaminski, p. 240.
13. Ibid.

14. D. C. Kaminski, p. 249.
15. Ibid.
16. Ibid.
17. E. Hobhouse, letter: 1909-10-08.
18. W. K. Hancock and J. van der Poel, p. 605.
19. D. C. Kaminski, pp. 252–3.
20. Ibid., p. 253.
21. Ibid., p. 254.
22. Ibid., pp. 255–6.
23. E. Wessels and V. Heunis, report: 'Die kantskool by Koppies', pp. 3–4.
24. Ibid., p. 5.
25. Ibid., p. 6.
26. E. Hobhouse, letter: 1909.
27. E. Wessels and V. Heunis, p. 6.
28. A. du Plessis, 'Kantskole het meisies uit kampe ná die oorlog opgehef', *Volksblad*.
29. E. Hobhouse, letter: 1909-10-08.
30. Ibid.
31. A. R. Fry, p. 261.
32. E. Hobhouse, letter: 1909-11-19.
33. J. Hall, p. 205.
34. Ibid.
35. D. C. Kaminski, p. 261.
36. L. M. Thompson, pp. 458–9.
37. E. Hobhouse, letter: 1910-06-19.
38. W. K. Hancock and J. van der Poel, p. 32.
39. Ibid.
40. J. Hobhouse Balme, *To Love One's Enemies*, p. 532.
41. What possessed the South African Nationalist government to name a Daphne-class submarine after Emily Hobhouse is anybody's guess. Emily would have refused such a suggestion in horror, The SAS *Emily Hobhouse* was launched in 1972 and renamed the SAS *Umkhonto* in 1995.
42. J. Hobhouse Balme, *To Love One's Enemies*, p. 532.
43. O. Schreiner, letter: 1903-04-03.

44. A. Terblanche, *Emily Hobhouse*, p. 306.

45. W. K. Hancock, p. 285.

46. W. K. Hancock and J. van der Poel, p. 57.

47. J. Hall, p. 206.

48. A. Terblanche, p. 309.

49. W. K. Hancock and J. van der Poel, p. 54.

50. Ibid., p. 56.

51. E. Truter, 'Rachel Isabella Steyn, 1905–1955', pp. 59–60.

52. Ibid., pp. 61–2.

53. R. van Reenen, *Boer War Letters*, p. 513.

54. Ibid.

55. R. van Reenen, *Heldin uit die vreemde*, p. 105.

56. R. van Reenen, *Boer War Letters*, p. 513.

57. E. Truter, p. 63.

58. J. Hobhouse Balme, p. 534.

59. Nowadays the Monument and the Anglo-Boer War Museum pay homage to all who were involved in the war and died in the concentration camps, including the black women and children. A new Garden of Remembrance honours 34,000 women and children – white and black – who died in the camps.

60. W. K. Hancock and J. van der Poel, p. 127.

61. S. Marschall, 'Serving Male Agendas', *Women's Studies*, p. 1016.

62. R. van Reenen, *Boer War Letters*, p. 393.

63. T. Cameron and S.B. Spies (eds), *Nuwe geskiedenis van Suid-Afrika in woord en beeld*, p. 232.

64. E. Hobhouse, letter: 1913-06-09.

65. Lists: UK Outward Passengers, 1890-1960.

66. E. Hobhouse, letter: 1913-06-09.

67. R. van Reenen, *Boer War Letters*, p. 396.

68. Ibid., p. 394.

69. E. Truter, p. 66.

70. R. van Reenen, *Boer War Letters*, pp. 397–8.

71. Ibid., p. 399.

72. G. Fraser, telegram: December 1913.

73. W. K. Hancock and J. van der Poel, p. 137.

74. Ibid., p. 138.

75. E. Truter, p. 67.
76. J. Smuts, letter: 1913-12-10.
77. E. Hobhouse, letter: 1913-12-06.
78. E. Hobhouse, letter: 1913-12-08.
79. R. van Reenen, *Boer War Letters*, p. 401.

14. A prophetic warning

1. N. Kruger, *Rachel Isabella Steyn: Presidentsvrou*, p. 98.
2. Ibid.
3. Ibid.
4. Monument Committee, telegram: 1913-12-17.
5. E. Hobhouse, 1913, speech: 16 December.
6. She is quoting Pericles, an Athenian statesman.
7. Jeremiah 31:16.
8. She is quoting Oscar Wilde, in *De Profundis*. (E. Hobhouse and K. Bekker, 'Uit die konsentrasiekamp na die Vrouemonument', in *Om te skryf*, pp. 7-126 to 7-134.)
9. Matthew 5:43-45.
10. The Bloemfontein concentration camp.
11. '. . . then deep calleth unto deep'. *De Profundis* (From the depths) is based on Ps. 130.
12. '. . . all the world is kin' – the reference is not clear, but Hobhouse was exposed to nineteenth-century religious literature which is today mostly unknown.
13. 'Facing east' suggests looking towards the rising sun; 'facing west' suggests the end of one's life.
14. Mark 3:25.
15. Bright, a British MP, said in the British context: 'The nation in every country dwells in the cottage', and here the cottage is represented by the farmhouse. (E. Hobhouse and K. Bekker, p. 7-132.)
16. Pericles.
17. Ibid.
18. Monument Committee, telegram: 1913-12-17.
19. E. Truter, pp. 70–1.

15. Gandhi, Emily and the leaders

1. T. R. H. Davenport, p. 116–17
2. South African History Online: 'Gandhi and the Passive Resistance Campaign 1907–1914'.
3. W. K. Hancock, p. 343.
4. C. Corder and M. Plaut, 'Gandhi's Decisive South African 1913 Campaign: A personal perspective from the letters of Betty Molteno', South African Historical Journal, p. 29.
5. Ibid., pp. 30–2.
6. Ibid., p. 34.
7. E. S. Reddy, *Gandhiji's Vision of a Free South Africa*.
8. C. Corder and M. Plaut, p. 43.
9. Ibid., p. 45.
10. W. K. Hancock and J. van der Poel, p. 152.
11. The author was unable to track down the first-hand correspondence between Emily and Gandhi. It is also not in the large collection of Emily's letters in the possession of Jennifer Hobhouse Balme in Canada.
12. W. K. Hancock and J. van der Poel, p. 155.
13. C. Corder and M. Plaut, p. 33.
14. E. S. Reddy, p. 83.
15. Ibid.
16. Ibid., pp. 79–80.
17. Ibid., p. 85.
18. Ibid.
19. J. Hobhouse Balme, *To Love One's Enemies*, p. 541.
20. Ibid.
21. Ibid.

16. Into another battle

1. S. C. Tucker, *The Great War, 1914–1918*, p. 1.
2. Ibid., pp. 2–3.
3. H. Strachan (ed.), *The Oxford Illustrated History of the First World War*.
4. E. Hobhouse, letter: 1914-08-06.'

5. L. T. Hobhouse, letter: 1914-08-05.
6. L. T. Hobhouse, letter: 1914-08-08.
7. W. K. Hancock and J. van der Poel, p. 185.
8. Ibid., p. 186.
9. L. T. Hobhouse, letter: 1914-08-26.
10. P. Warner, *Kitchener: The Man behind the Legend*, p. 175.
11. Ibid., p. 176.
12. D. C. Kaminski, p. 289.
13. Emily's image as a pacifist was presented in a negative light in South Africa too. In 1948 a biography in Afrikaans titled *Emily Hobhouse* was published under the pseudonym Annette Terblanche (Martie van den Heever). She wrote: 'With the outbreak of the First World War in 1914, Miss Hobhouse again advocated the unpopular cause of Pacifism.' (A. Terblanche, p. 325.)
14. E. Hobhouse, letter: 1914 October, 'To Women throughout Europe'.
15. H. Giliomee, p. 381.
16. W. K. Hancock and J. van der Poel, p. 206.
17. H. Giliomee, p. 383.
18. W. K. Hancock and J. van der Poel, p. 206.
19. E. Hobhouse, letter: 1915-04-09.
20. E. Hobhouse, letter: 1915, 'To the Women of Germany and Austria: Open Christmas Letter', *Jus Suffragii* (The Right of Suffrage).
21. Ibid.
22. Ibid.
23. Ibid.
24. Jane Addams was awarded the Nobel Peace Prize in 1931.
25. J. Fisher, p. 237.
26. The organisation still exists today and celebrated its centenary in 2015.
27. D. C. Kaminski, p. 295.
28. E. Hobhouse, foreword: 'International Congress of Women, The Hague 28 April to 1 May'.
29. D. C. Kaminski, p. 296.
30. J. Hobhouse Balme, *Agent of Peace: Emily Hobhouse and Her Courageous Attempt to End the First World War*, pp. 28–9.
31. E. Hobhouse, letter: 1915-07-05.

32. D. C. Kaminski, p. 295.

33. A. Bouwer, 'Elf babas land gelyk', *Sarie Marais*.

34. Ibid.

35. J. Hobhouse Balme, *Agent of Peace*, p. 177.

36. C. MacMillan, letter: 1915-12-16.

37. D. C. Kaminski, p. 303.

38. J. Hobhouse Balme, *Agent of Peace*, p. 43.

39. E. Hobhouse, diary (Journal): Emily: 'Volume I, 1916'.

17. Agent of peace

1. D. C. Kaminski, p. 303.

2. Ibid.

3. Ibid., p. 304.

4. E. Hobhouse, diary: 'Vol. I, 1916', pp. 3–4.

5. Ibid., p. 5.

6. Ibid., p. 6.

7. P. Warner, p. 197.

8. Ibid., p. 201.

9. Ibid.

10. E. Hobhouse, diary: 'Vol. I, 1916', pp. 6–7.

11. Ibid., p. 11.

12. Ibid., p. 13.

13. Ibid., p. 36.

14. E. Hobhouse, 'Union of Democratic Control 1 October 1916', *Belgium To-Day*.

15. H. Strachan, p. 40.

16. E. Hobhouse, diary: 'Vol. I, 1916', p. 35.

17. E. Hobhouse, diary (Journal): Emily: 'Volume II, Belgium and Germany, 1916', p. 1.

18. Ibid., p. 4.

19. Ibid., pp. 9–10.

20. E. Hobhouse, 'Interview with a high official of the German foreign office', *The Nation*.

21. E. Hobhouse, letter: 1916-06-20.

22. G. von Jagow, letter: 1916-06-20.

23. E. Hobhouse, letter: 1916-06-21.
24. E. Hobhouse, diary: Vol. II, 1916, pp. 14–15.
25. Ibid., p. 17.
26. Ibid., pp. 17–18.

18. 'Traitor!'

1. E. Hobhouse, diary (Journal): 'Volume III, Visit to Germany and Belgium: The story of my visit to Germany during the Great War', 1916, p. 2.
2. Ibid.
3. Ibid., pp. 3–4.
4. D. C. Kaminski, p. 308.
5. E. Hobhouse, diary: Vol. III, 1916, p. 9.
6. E. Hobhouse, letter: 1916-06-25.
7. D. C. Kaminski, pp. 310–11.
8. J. Hall, p. 254.
9. D. C. Kaminski, p. 312.
10. Ibid., p. 313.
11. E. Hobhouse, letter: 1916-07-01.
12. E. Hobhouse, diary: 1 July – 14 July 1916.
13. D. C. Kaminski, p. 316.
14. J. Hall, p. 256.
15. J. Hobhouse Balme, *Agent of Peace*, p. 136.
16. D. C. Kaminski, p. 319.
17. E. Hobhouse, letter: 1916-07-16.
18. J. Hobhouse Balme, *Agent of Peace*, p. 142.
19. E. Hobhouse, notes: 'Lambeth, Aug. 2.16, 11.30 am'.
20. Ibid.
21. J. Hobhouse Balme, *Agent of Peace*, p. 154.
22. E. Hobhouse, letter: 1916-08-05.
23. R. Davidson, letter: 1916-08-10.
24. E. Hobhouse, 'Interview with a high official of the German foreign office', *The Nation*.
25. Ibid.
26. D. C. Kaminski, pp. 322–3.

27. Hansard, 1916: 'Miss Emily Hobhouse'.

28. Ibid.

29. Hansard, 1916: 'Miss Emily Hobhouse (Passport)'.

30. Ibid.

31. Ibid.

32. J. Hobhouse Balme, *Agent of Peace*, p. 166.

33. Ibid.

34. Hansard, 1916: 'Miss Hobhouse (Passport)'.

35. Ibid.

36. *Evening Telegraph*, 1916.

37. E. Hobhouse, 'Miss Hobhouse's Tour', *The Times*.

38. J.V. Crangle and J.O. Baylen, 'Emily Hobhouse's Peace Mission, 1916', *Journal of Contemporary History*, p. 740.

39. D.S. Patterson, *The Search for Negotiated Peace*, p. 254.

40. Ibid., pp. 254–5.

41. D. C. Kaminski, p. 339.

42. Ibid., p. 338.

43. Ibid.

44. Ibid, p. 340.

19. Millions of meals

1. J. Turner, *Britain and the First World War*, p. 123.

2. W. K. Hancock and J. van der Poel, p. 460.

3. Ibid., p. 471.

4. Ibid., p. 475.

5. J. Hobhouse Balme, *To Love One's Enemies*, p. 558.

6. D. C. Kaminski p. 343.

7. J. Hobhouse Balme, *To Love One's Enemies*, p. 558.

8. E. Hobhouse, letter: 1918-09-18.

9. W. K. Hancock and J. van der Poel, p. 460.

10. J. Hobhouse Balme, *Agent of Peace*, p. 172.

11. J. Hall, p. 266.

12. Ibid., pp. 266–7.

13. J. Hobhouse Balme, *To Love One's Enemies*, p. 563.

14. A. R. Fry, p. 278.

15. E. Hobhouse, pamphlet: 'Russian Babies' Fund'.
16. J. Hobhouse Balme, *To Love One's Enemies*, p. 563.
17. Ibid.
18. E. Hobhouse, letters: 'Friends – Various Relief Worker Letters'.
19. J. Hobhouse Balme, *To Love One's Enemies*, p. 571.
20. E. Hobhouse, telegram to Jane Addams 1919.
21. E. Hobhouse, letter: 1919-11-19.
22. F. Schwyzer and E. Hobhouse, report: 'Save the Children Fund'.
23. Ibid., p. 14.
24. J. Hobhouse Balme, *To Love One's Enemies*, p. 565.
25. A. R. Fry, p. 281.
26. E. Truter, pp. 151–2.
27. Ibid., p. 154.
28. Ibid., p. 155.
29. Ibid., p. 158.
30. J. Hobhouse Balme, *To Love One's Enemies*, pp. 567–9.
31. A. R. Fry, p. 284.
32. Ibid., p. 283.
33. Ibid.
34. Leipzig City Council, 1922, report.

20. A house by the sea

1. J. Hobhouse Balme, *To Love One's Enemies*, p. 569.
2. E. Truter, p. 165.
3. The house is now part of the hotel.
4. Advertisement, 1921, Sale of Warren House.
5. E. Truter, p. 166.
6. Ibid.
7. R.I. Steyn, Appeal from Mrs Pres. Steyn.
8. J. Hobhouse Balme, *To Love One's Enemies*, p. 571.
9. E. Truter, p. 167.
10. Ibid.
11. T. Steyn, 'Emily Hobhouse', *Die Huisgenoot*.
12. J. Hobhouse Balme, *To Love One's Enemies*, p. 574.
13. E. Hobhouse, letter: 1926-05-16.

14. E. Hobhouse, 'Autobiography: Introduction'.
15. R. van Reenen, *Boer War Letters*, p. 473.
16. Today editions of this book – Emily's English translation – are collector's items. In 1939 the book was translated into Afrikaans by M.E.R.
17. J. Hobhouse Balme, *To Love One's Enemies*, p. 577.
18. J. Hall, p. 282.
19. J. Hobhouse Balme, *To Love One's Enemies*, p. 578.
20. Ibid., p. 576.
21. This porcelain plaque still exists, as does the address written in ornamental writing, which was signed by the deputy mayor of Leipzig in 1923. The German Red Cross also awarded her their 2nd Class decoration, but its present whereabouts are unknown. In 1922 the German sculptor Mathieu Molitor made a marble bust of Emily, just under 60cm high, which was displayed in the new City Hall in Leipzig for many years. The statue disappeared without a trace after 1947. There is a second bust of Emily by Molitor in the Anglo-Boer War Museum in Bloemfontein, but this statue is not a good likeness of her. Emily did not like it either, but Tibbie Steyn reasoned: Rather this statue than no statue. (E. Truter, p. 128.)
22. Letter, German Ambassador, 1923-03-22.
23. Leipzig City Council, letter: 1924-12-24.
24. C. Muller, pp. 405–06.
25. J. Fisher, p. 266.
26. J. Hall, p. 284.
27. E. Hobhouse, 'Autobiography: Chapter VII, Attacks & Criticisms'.
28. M. G. Fawcett, *What I Remember*, p. 152.
29. E. Hobhouse, 'Autobiography: Chapter VII, Attacks & Criticisms'.

21. The last yearnings

1. E. Hobhouse, letter: 1926-02-07.
2. Ibid.
3. E. Hobhouse, letter: 1926-04-11.
4. Ibid.
5. E. Hobhouse, letter: 1926-05-01.
6. Ibid.

7. It is not known whether Tibbie ever had this conversation with Hertzog, but there is no indication that he carried out Emily's last wishes. (E. Truter, p. 192.)

8. E. Hobhouse, letter: 1925-05-27.

9. E. Hobhouse, letter: 1926-05-01.

10. E. Hobhouse, letter: May, 1926.

11. Ibid.

12. E. Hobhouse, letter: 1926-05-16.

13. E. Hobhouse, letter: 1926-05-23.

14. The words differ from those of the original hymn, but this was how Emily remembered them as she lay writing in her bed.

15. E. Hobhouse, letter: 1926-05-23.

16. As far as could be ascertained, this was the last letter Emily ever wrote; the day before, she had written a letter to Henry Hobhouse V. Tibbie would have received this letter, as well as the letter of 23 May, long after Emily's death.

17. A. R. Fry, p. 285.

18. J. Hobhouse Balme, *To Love One's Enemies*, p. 591.

19. J. Fisher, p. 269.

20. Will: Estate of the Will of Miss Emily Hobhouse.

21. Emily's estate came to £5621, most of which was bequeathed to Oliver, her brother Leonard's son. To Jan Smuts she left £100 – the sum she had borrowed from him. An amount of £500 was bequeathed to Gladys Steyn to ensure that Emily's autobiography was published; some money was also left to her sister Maud, her niece Dorothea Thornton, and servants. Johanna Osborne, who had established the lacemaking school at Koppies, inherited the necklace of seven yellow- and rose-coloured diamonds from the Jagersfontein mine that the Free State Boers had given to Emily (C. Smith, 'Halssnoer van Emily Hobhouse terug in Vrystaat', *Volksblad*).

22. W. K. Hancock and J. van der Poel, p. 177.

23. Will: Estate of the Will of Miss Emily Hobhouse.

24. *Manchester Guardian*, 1926.

25. Ibid.

26. Funeral notice, 1926. St Mary Abbots, Kensington.

27. J. Hall, p. 290.

22. Thousands say goodbye

1. *Die Burger*, 1926-10-27.
2. C. Murray, 'Impressive Memorial Service'.
3. *Die Burger*, 1926-10-28.
4. Hertzog sent a telegram with this message: 'We are with you and participate with you in demonstration of appreciation and homage to one who so nobly sacrificed herself in love for the women of South Africa. Emily Hobhouse is henceforth one with us in all our tributes of honour and affection.' (*The Friend*, 28 October 1926: 'Impressive Memorial Service'.)
5. Funeral programme, 1926. 'Plegtige teraardebestelling van Emily Hobhouse'.
6. C. Murray, 'Impressive Memorial Service'.
7. *Die Burger*, 1926-10-28.
8. *Manchester Guardian*, 1926, 'General Smuts's Speech'.
9. J. Hobhouse Balme, *To Love One's Enemies*, p. 587.

23. Love in a notebook

1. R. van Reenen, p. 379.
2. E. Hobhouse, 'Emily's notebook'.
3. D. C. Kaminski, p. 364.
4. A. R. Fry, p. 305.

Bibliography

Abbreviations

Emily Hobhouse: EH
Jennifer Hobhouse Balme collection: JHB
Free State Archives Repository: VAB

Books and draft autobiography

Baksh, R., and Harcourt, W. (eds), 2015. *The Oxford Handbook of Transnational Feminist Movements*. New York: Oxford University Press.

Beer, F., 2002. *The Angel of Love: Emily Hobhouse*. Liskeard: Polpentre Design and Print.

Cameron, T., and Spies, S.B. (eds), 1986. *Nuwe geskiedenis van Suid-Afrika in woord en beeld*. Cape Town: Human & Rousseau.

Davenport, T. R. H., 1988. *South Africa – A Modern History*. Bergvlei: Southern Book Publishers.

Davey, A., 1978. *The British Pro-Boers, 1877–1902*. Cape Town: Tafelberg.

Encyclopædia Britannica. 'South African War', available at: http://global.britannica.com/event/South-African-War.

Fawcett, M. G., 1924. *What I Remember*. London: T. Fisher Unwin.

Fisher, J., 1977. *That Miss Hobhouse*. London: Secker & Warburg.

Fry, A. R., 1929. *Emily Hobhouse: A Memoir*. London: Jonathan Cape.

Gandhi, M., 1926. 'Young India: A Great Heart', No. 27:157–1926, *Collected Works of Mahatma Gandhi*, Vol. 36, Jul. 1926 – Nov. 1926.

Gandhi, M., 1968. *The Selected Works of Mahatma Gandhi – An Autobiography – Vol. 2*. Ahmedabad: Navajivan Publishing House.

Giliomee, H., 2003. *The Afrikaners: Biography of a People*. Cape Town: Tafelberg.

Grundlingh, A., and Nasson, B. (eds), 2013. *The War at Home: Women and Families in the Anglo-Boer War*. Cape Town: Tafelberg.

Hall, J., 2008. *That Bloody Woman: The Turbulent Life of Emily Hobhouse*. St Agnes: Truran.

Hancock, W. K., 1962. *Smuts, Volume 1: The Sanguine Years, 1870–1919*. London: Cambridge University Press.

Hancock, W. K., and Van der Poel, J. (eds), 1966. *Selections from the Smuts Papers: Volume II, June 1902 – May 1910*. London: Cambridge University Press.

Hancock, W. K., and Van der Poel, J. (eds), 1966. *Selections from the Smuts Papers: Volume III, June 1910 – November 1918*. London: Cambridge University Press.

Hansard, 1901. 'South African War – Mortality in Camps of Detention', House of Commons Debates, 17 June 1901, Vol. 95 cc 573-629. London.

Hansard, 1902. 'South Africa – Conduct of the War', House of Commons Debates, 20 Jan. 1902, Vol. 101 cc 324-436. London.

Hansard, 1902. 'Concentration Camps', House of Commons Debates, 21 Jan. 1902, Vol. 101 cc 455-6455. London.

Hansard, 1902. 'South African War – Arrest of Miss Hobhouse', House of Commons Debates, 27 Jan. 1902 Vol. 101 cc 947-8947. London.

Hansard, 1902. 'Miss Hobhouse', House of Commons Debates, 28 Jan. 1902 Vol. 101 cc 1095-61095. London.

Hansard, 1902. 'Miss Hobhouse', House of Commons Debates, 6 Feb. 1902, Vol. 102 cc 509-10509. London.

Hansard, 1916. 'Miss Emily Hobhouse', House of Commons Debates, 26 Oct. 1916, Vol. 86 cc 1270-1. London.

Hansard, 1916. 'Miss Emily Hobhouse (Passport)', House of Commons Debates, 31 Oct. 1916, Vol. 86 cc 1493-6. London.

Hansard, 1916. 'Miss Hobhouse (Passport)', House of Commons Debates, 1 Nov. 1916, Vol. 86 cc 1745-7W. London.

Hasian, M. (Jr), 2014. *Restorative Justice, Humanitarian Rhetorics, and Public Memories of Colonial Camp Cultures*. Ebook: Palgrave Macmillan.

Headlam, C. (ed.), 1933. *The Milner Papers: South Africa 1899–1905, Vol. II*. London: Cassell & Co.

Hobhouse Balme, J., 2012. *To Love One's Enemies: The Work and Life of Emily Hobhouse*. Stuttgart: ibidem-Verlag.

Hobhouse Balme, J., 2015. *Agent of Peace: Emily Hobhouse and her Courageous Attempt to End the First World War*. Stroud: The History Press.

Hobhouse, E., and Bekker, K., 2013. *Uit die konsentrasiekamp na die Vrouemonument (Emily Hobhouse toespraak, vertaal deur Koos Bekker). Oorspronklike in: Om te Skryf*. Pretoria: Van Schaik, pp. 7-126 tot 7-134.

Hobhouse, E., 2007. *War Without Glamour: Or, Women's War Experiences Written by Themselves 1899–1902*. Warrington: Portrayer Publishers. (Facsimile edition of the 1924 edition published in Bloemfontein by Nasionale Pers Beperk.)

Hobhouse, E., 1902. *The Brunt of the War and Where it Fell*. Reprint ed. London: Methuen & Co.

Hobhouse, E., c. 1920s. 'Autobiography: Arrest & Deportation' (VAB: A156/3/11 Adv. Gladys Steyn and Mrs M. T. Steyn collection).

Hobhouse, E., c. 1920s. 'Autobiography: Boer Home Industries' (VAB: A153/3/11).

Hobhouse, E., c. 1920s. 'Autobiography: Boer Industries' (VAB).

Hobhouse, E., c. 1920s. 'Autobiography: Chapter III, Cape Town & Arrived There' (VAB: A156/3/11 Adv. Gladys Steyn and Mrs M. T. Steyn collection).

Hobhouse, E., c. 1920s. 'Autobiography: Chapter IV, The Camps' (VAB: A156/3/11 Adv. Gladys Steyn and Mrs M. T. Steyn collection).

Hobhouse, E., c. 1920s. 'Autobiography: Chapter VII, Attacks & Criticisms 1902' (VAB).

Hobhouse, E., c. 1920s. 'Autobiography: Chapter VIII, 1902' (VAB: A156/3/11 Adv. Gladys Steyn and Mrs M. T. Steyn collection).

Hobhouse, E., c. 1920s. 'Autobiography: Chapter IX: Quieter Days – 1902-1903' (VAB: A156/3/11 Adv. Gladys Steyn and Mrs M. T. Steyn collection).

Hobhouse, E., c. 1920s. 'Autobiography: Chapter X: Beaufort-West & Olive Schreiner' (VAB: A156/3/11 Adv. Gladys Steyn and Mrs M. T. Steyn collection).

Hobhouse, E., c. 1920s. 'Autobiography: Chapter XI: O.R.C. Once More' (VAB: A156/3/11 Adv. Gladys Steyn and Mrs M. T. Steyn collection).

Hobhouse, E., c. 1920s. 'Autobiography: Chapter XII – A Storm in a Teacup; A Visit to De Wet' (VAB: A156/3/11 Adv. Gladys Steyn and Mrs M. T. Steyn collection).

Hobhouse, E., c. 1920s. 'Autobiography: Chapter XIII: In the Transvaal; Heidelberg and the Volksvergadering' (VAB: A156/3/11 Adv. Gladys Steyn and Mrs M. T. Steyn collection).

Hobhouse, E., c. 1920s. 'Autobiography: Chapter XIV: First Visit to General and Mrs Smuts; Pietersburg and Warm Baths' (VAB: A156/3/11 Adv. Gladys Steyn and Mrs M. T. Steyn collection).

Hobhouse, E., c. 1920s. 'Autobiography: Chapter XV: Repatriation and the Three Million' (VAB: A156/3/11 Adv. Gladys Steyn and Mrs M. T. Steyn collection).

Hobhouse, E., c. 1920's. 'Autobiography: Chapter XXVII, Bellevue 1906-1907' (VAB).

Hobhouse, E., c. 1920's. 'Autobiography: Chapter XXVIII, 1907 Jo'burg – London – Jo'burg – Pretoria' (VAB).

Hobhouse, E., c. 1920s. 'Autobiography: First Draft Chapter for 1900' (VAB: A156/3/11 Adv. Gladys Steyn and Mrs M. T. Steyn collection).

Hobhouse, E., c. 1920s. 'Autobiography: Langlaagte and After' (VAB: A156/3/11 Adv. Gladys Steyn and Mrs M. T. Steyn collection).

Hobhouse, E., c. 1920s. 'Autobiography: Work in England' (VAB).

Hobhouse, E., c. 1920s. Notes at the beginning of 'Autobiography', loose pages (VAB: A153/3/11).

Hobhouse, E., c. 1925. 'Autobiography: Introduction' (VAB: A156).

Hobhouse, E., 'Emily's notebook' (VAB: A53 Johanna Osborne collection).

Kaminski, D. C., 1977. 'The Radicalization of a Ministering Angel: A Biography of Emily Hobhouse, 1860-1926'. PhD thesis, University of Connecticut.

Kessler, S., 2012. *The Black Concentration Camps of the Anglo-Boer War, 1899–1902*. Bloemfontein: The War Museum of the Boer Republics.

Kruger, N., 1949. *Rachel Isabella Steyn: Presidentsvrou*. Cape Town: Nasionale Pers Beperk.

McClintock, A., 1992. 'Olive (Emilie Albertina) Schreiner', in *British Writers*, edited by George Stade. New York: Charles Scribner's Sons. Available at: http://www.english.wisc.edu/ amcclintock/schreiner.htm.

McFadyen, Rev. P. and Chamberlin, Rev. D., 1997–2015. 'Edith Cavell 1865–1915 – A Norfolk Heroine' 1985, available at: http://www. edithcavell.org.uk (accessed 11 Aug. 2015).

Muller, C., 1977. *500 jaar: Suid-Afrikaanse geskiedenis*. 2nd edition. Pretoria and Cape Town: Academia.

Nasson, B., 1999. *The South African War, 1899–1902*. London: Arnold.

Padel, O. J., 1988. *A Popular Dictionary of Cornish Place-Names*. Penzance: Alison Hodge.

Pakenham, T., 1979. *The Boer War*. Johannesburg: Jonathan Ball.

Pakenham, T., 1992. The *Scramble for Africa*. Johannesburg: Jonathan Ball.

Patterson, D. S., 2008. *The Search for Negotiated Peace: Women's Activism and Citizen Diplomacy in World War I*. New York: Routledge.

Pretorius, F., 1998. *Die Anglo-Boereoorlog, 1899–1902*. Cape Town: Struik.

Pretorius, F., 2017. *Verskroeide Aarde. 2nd edition*. Cape Town: Tafelberg.

Purvis, J., 2002. *Emmeline Pankhurst: A Biography*. London and New York: Routledge.

Rabe, L., 2011. *Rykie: 'n Lewe met woorde*. Cape Town: Tafelberg.

Reddy, E. S., 1995. *Gandhiji's Vision of a Free South Africa*. New Delhi: Sanchar Publishing House.

Reynolds, C., 2007. 'Die ontwikkeling van 'n elektroniese genealogiese databasis van burgerlike sterftes tydens die Anglo-Boereoorlog 1899–1902'. MA dissertation, NorthWest University.

Roberts, B., 1991. *Those Bloody Women: Three Heroines of the Boer War*. London: John Murray.

Rosen, A., 2013. *Rise Up, Women! The Militant Campaign of the Women's Social and Politican Union 1903–1914.* New York: Routledge.

Russell, B., 1993 (reprint). *The Collected Papers of Bertrand Russell, Vol. 12.* London: Routledge.

Schreiner, O., Olive Schreiner Letters. 'Mary Sauer (née Cloete)', available at: https://www.oliveschreiner.org/ vre?view=personae&entry=61.

Seibold, B. S., 2011. *Emily Hobhouse and the Reports on the Concentration Camps during the Boer War, 1899–1902: Two Different Perspectives.* Stuttgart: ibidem-Verlag.

South African History Online. 'Gandhi and the Passive Resistance Campaign, 1907–1914', available at: http://www. sahistory.org.za/ article/gandhi-and-passive-resistance-campaign-1907-1914 (accessed 10 May 2015).

Spies, S.B., 1977. *Methods of Barbarism?* Cape Town: Human & Rousseau.

Stanley, L., and Salter, A. (eds), 2014. *The World's Great Question: Olive Schreiner's South African Letters, 1889–1920.* Cape Town: Van Riebeeck Society.

Stephen, L. (ed.), 1912. *Dictionary of National Biography.* London: Smith, Elder & Co. Available at: http://www. archive.org/stream/dictionaryo fnati22lees/#page/272/ mode/2up.

Strachan, H. (ed.), 1998. *The Oxford Illustrated History of the First World War.* Oxford and New York: Oxford University Press.

Terblanche, A., 1948. *Emily Hobhouse.* Johannesburg: Afrikaanse Pers Boekhandel.

Thompson, L. M., 1961. *The Unification of South Africa, 1902–1910.* Oxford: Oxford University Press.

Truter, E., 1994. 'Rachel Isabella Steyn, 1905–1955'. Doctoral thesis, Unisa.

Truter, E., 1997. *Tibbie: Rachel Isabella Steyn (1865–1955): Haar lewe was haar boodskap.* Cape Town: Human & Rousseau.

Tucker, S. C., 1998. *The Great War, 1914–1918.* London: UCL Press.

Turner, J., 1988. *Britain and the First World War.* London: Unwin Hyman.

Van Heyningen, E., 2013. *The Concentration Camps of the Anglo-Boer War: A Social History.* Sunnyside: Jacana.

Van Reenen, R., 1970. *Heldin uit die vreemde.* Cape Town and Johannesburg: Tafelberg.

Van Reenen, R. (ed.), 1984. *Emily Hobhouse: Boer War Letters*. Cape Town: Human & Rousseau.

Warner, P., 2006. *Kitchener: The Man behind the Legend*. London: Orion Publishing Group.

Warwick, P., and Spies, S.B. (eds), 1980. *The South African War: The Anglo-Boer War, 1899–1902*. London: Longman.

Letters and telegrams

Botha, L., 1913-12-08. Letter: Louis Botha to EH (JHB).

Brodrick, S. J., 1901-06-27. Letter/Report: St John Brodrick to EH (JHB).

Chamberlain, N., 1901-08-30. Letter: Neville Chamberlain to EH (JHB).

Clark, M., 1906 Dec. Letter: Margaret Clark to R. Milroy (VAB: A357 Smuts-Clark collection).

Davidson, R., 1916-08-10. Letter: Randall Davidson to EH (JHB).

Davidson, R., 1916-09-10. Letter: Randall Davidson to EH (JHB).

Davidson, R., 1916-10-10. Letter: Randall Davidson to EH (JHB).

Farrer, J., 1905-04-28. Letter: Julia Farrer to EH (JHB).

Fraser, G., 1913 Dec. Telegram: Gordon Fraser to EH (JHB).

German Ambassador. Letter: 1923-03-22 to EH (JHB).

Gillett, M.C., 1926-11-12. Letter: Margaret Clark Gillett to *The Times* (VAB: A357 Smuts-Clark collection).

Hely-Hutchinson, W., March 1901. Letter: Hely-Hutchinson to EH (VAB: A156/3/11).

Hobhouse, E., 1900-12-30 to 1901-01-01. Letter: EH to Leonard Hobhouse (VAB).

Hobhouse, E., 1901. Letter: EH to Col. H Cooper (VAB: A156/3/11).

Hobhouse, E., 1901. Letter: EH to Leonard Hobhouse.

Hobhouse, E., 1901-01-08. Letter: EH to Mary Hobhouse.

Hobhouse, E., 1901-01-17. Letter: EH to Caroline Murray.

Hobhouse, E., 1901-01-26. Letter: EH to Mary Hobhouse.

Hobhouse, E., 1901-02-18 to 1901-02-22. Letter: EH to Leonard Hobhouse (VAB).

Hobhouse, E., 1901-03-04. Letter: EH to Mary Hobhouse.

Hobhouse, E., 1901-03-08. Letter: EH to Leonard Hobhouse.

Hobhouse, E., 1901-03-31. Letter: EH to Mary Hobhouse.

Hobhouse, E., 1901-04-09. Letter: EH to Mary Hobhouse.

Hobhouse, E., 1901-04-22. Letter: EH to Mary Hobhouse.

Hobhouse, E., 1901-07-11. Letter: EH to Caroline Murray.

Hobhouse, E., 1901-07-18. Letter: EH to St John Brodrick (JHB).

Hobhouse, E., 1903-08-16. Letter: EH to South African News.

Hobhouse, E. 1903-08-23. Letter: EH to Mary Hobhouse (JHB).

Hobhouse, E., 1903-09-06. Letter: EH to Nora Hobhouse (JHB).

Hobhouse, E., 1903-09-12. Letter: EH to Mary Hobhouse ('Autobiography: Pretoria and the Western Transvaal').

Hobhouse, E., 1903-09-23. Letter: EH to Patrick Duncan (JHB).

Hobhouse, E., 1903-09-27. Letter: EH to Mary Hobhouse ('Autobiography: Pretoria and the Western Transvaal').

Hobhouse, E., 1903-09-30. Letter: EH to Mary Hobhouse.

Hobhouse, E., 1903-10-04. Letter: EH to Barbara, Dorothy and Leonard.

Hobhouse, E., 1903-11-17. Letter: EH to Mary Hobhouse.

Hobhouse, E., 1903-11-23. Letter: EH to Mary Hobhouse.

Hobhouse, E., 1903-11-26. Letter: EH to Patrick Duncan (JHB).

Hobhouse, E., 1903 Dec. Circular: Emily to Dutch Reformed churches (Anglo-Boer War Museum no. 04123).

Hobhouse, E., 1904-01-30. Letter: EH to *Manchester Guardian*.

Hobhouse, E., 1904-03-15. Letter: EH 'Chinese Labour', *The Times*, 14 Mar 1904; publication 15 Mar 1904.

Hobhouse, E., 1905-06-15. Letter: EH to Charlotte Toler.

Hobhouse, E., 1905-06-25: Letter: EH to Charlotte Toler.

Hobhouse, E., 1905-07-02. Letter: EH to Charlotte Toler (VAB: A357 Post-war correspondence, Smuts-Clark collection).

Hobhouse, E., 1905-07-09. Letter: EH to Leonard Hobhouse.

Hobhouse, E., 1905-07-23. Letter: EH to Charlotte Toler (VAB: A357 Post-war correspondence, Smuts-Clark collection).

Hobhouse, E., 1905-08-06. Letter: EH to Charlotte Toler.

Hobhouse, E., 1905-09-16. Letter: EH to Charlotte Toler.

Hobhouse, E., 1905-12-25. Letter: EH to Charlotte Toler.

Hobhouse, E., 1906-04-04. Letter: EH to Margaret Clark.

Hobhouse, E., 1906-05-20. Letter: EH to Charlotte Toler.

Hobhouse, E., 1906-05-23. Letter: EH to Margaret Clark (VAB: A357).

Hobhouse, E., 1906. Letter: EH to Leonard Hobhouse, Whitsunday 1906 (VAB: A156).

Hobhouse, E., 1906-06-23. Letter: EH to Lord Elgin.

Hobhouse, E., 1906-08-19. Letter: EH to Charlotte Toler (VAB: A357 Post-war correspondence, Smuts-Clark collection).

Hobhouse, E., 1909-04-06 to 1909-04-10. Letter: EH to Johanna Osborne (VAB: A53 Johanna Osborne collection).

Hobhouse, E., 1909-10-08. Letter: EH to Johanna Osborne.

Hobhouse, E., 1909-10-22. Letter: EH: 'A new Suffrage Society', Cambridge Independent, London.

Hobhouse, E., 1909-11-19. Letter: EH to Johanna Osborne (VAB: A53 Johanna Osborne collection).

Hobhouse, E., 1910-01-14. Letter: EH to Johanna Osborne (VAB: A53 Johanna Osborne collection).

Hobhouse, E., 1910-04-04. Letter: EH to Johanna Osborne.

Hobhouse, E., 1910-04-30. Letter: EH to Johanna Osborne.

Hobhouse, E., 1910-06-19. Letter: EH to Jan Smuts (Ditsong National Museum of Cultural History, Pretoria).

Hobhouse, E., 1910-07-06. Letter: EH to Johanna Osborne.

Hobhouse, E., 1910-11-30. Letter: EH to Johanna Osborne.

Hobhouse, E., 1911-06-10. Letter: EH to Johanna Osborne.

Hobhouse, E., 1913-06-09. Letter: EH to Caroline Murray (Molteno-Murray Family Papers, BC330, University of Cape Town Libraries: Special Collections).

Hobhouse, E., 1913-11-09. Letter: EH to John X Merriman (JHB).

Hobhouse, E., 1913-12-06. Letter: EH to Sanni Metelerkamp (private collection).

Hobhouse, E., 1913-12-08. Letter: EH to Mrs Woods (private collection).

Hobhouse, E., 1913-12-08. Letter: EH to Sanni Metelerkamp (private collection).

Hobhouse, E., 1914-06-21. Letter: EH to Arthur Hobhouse (private collection).

Hobhouse, E., 1914-08-06. Letter: EH to Arthur Hobhouse (private collection).

Hobhouse, E., 1914 Oct. EH: 'To Women throughout Europe' (JHB).

Hobhouse, E., 1915-01-01. EH: 'To the Women of Germany and Austria: Open Christmas Letter', *Jus Suffragii* (The Right of Suffrage).

Hobhouse, E., 1915-04-09. Letter: EH to Johanna Osborne (VAB: A53 Johanna Osborne collection).

Hobhouse, E., 1915-07-05. Letter: EH to Jane Addams ('Jane Addams Papers', Swarthmore College Peace Collection, Reel 8/1124-1125).

Hobhouse, E., 1915-09-04. Letter: EH to Jane Addams ('Jane Addams Papers', Swarthmore College Peace Collection, Reel 8/0713).

Hobhouse, E., 1916-06-20: Letter: EH to Gottlieb von Jagow ('Jagow Letters', Foreign Office Archives, Germany, Vol. R20465).

Hobhouse, E., 1916-06-21: Letter: EH to Gottlieb von Jagow ('Jagow Letters', Foreign Office Archives, Germany, Vol. R20465).

Hobhouse, E., 1916-06-25. Letter: EH to Gottlieb von Jagow ('Jagow Letters', Foreign Office Archives, Germany, Vol. R20465).

Hobhouse, E., 1916-07-01. Letter: EH to Edward Grey (JHB).

Hobhouse, E., 1916-07-05. Letter: EH to Edward Grey (JHB).

Hobhouse, E., 1916-07-12. Letter: EH to Robert Cecil (JHB).

Hobhouse, E., 1916-07-16. Letter: EH to Leonard Hobhouse (JHB).

Hobhouse, E., 1916-08-05. Letter: EH to Walter Hines (JHB).

Hobhouse, E., 1916-08-08: Letter: EH to Archbishop of Canterbury (JHB).

Hobhouse, E., 1918-09-18. Letter: EH to May Murray (Molteno-Murray Family Papers, BC330, University of Cape Town Libraries: Special Collections).

Hobhouse, E., 1918-12-29. Letter: EH to Henry Hobhouse (private collection).

Hobhouse, E., 1919-11-19. Letter: EH to Jane Addams ('Jane Addams Papers, Series 1', Swarthmore College Peace Collection).

Hobhouse, E., 1919. Telegram: EH to Jane Addams ('Jane Addams Papers, Series 1', Swarthmore College Peace Collection – Cable/Nov1919/A37/CHBL47).

Hobhouse, E., 1919-1920. EH to 'Friends – Various Relief Worker Letters – Jan. 1919-Jul. 1920' (Friends House Library YM/MfS/FEWVRC/10/1/5/12, London).

Hobhouse, E., 1925. Letter: EH to Leonard, Mother's Day 1925 (JHB).

Hobhouse, E., 1925-05-27. Letter: EH to Betty Molteno (Molteno-Murray Family Papers, BC330, University of Cape Town Libraries: Special Collections).

Hobhouse, E., 1926-02-07. Letter: EH to Tibbie Steyn (VAB: A156, M. T. Steyn collection).

Hobhouse, E., 1926-04-11. Letter: EH to Tibbie Steyn (VAB: A156, M. T. Steyn collection).

Hobhouse, E., 1926-05-01. Letter: EH to Tibbie Steyn (VAB: A156, MT Steyn-collection).

Hobhouse, E., 1926-05-16. Letter: EH to Tibbie Steyn (VAB: A156, M. T. Steyn collection).

Hobhouse, E., 1926-05-23. Letter: EH to Tibbie Steyn (VAB: A156, M. T. Steyn collection).

Hobhouse, E., 1926-05-30. Letter: EH to Tibbie Steyn (VAB: A156, M. T. Steyn collection).

Hobhouse, E., 1926 May. Letter: EH to Tibbie Steyn, (VAB: A156, M. T. Steyn collection).

Hobhouse, L, 1914-08-05. Letter: Leonard Hobhouse to EH (JHB).

Hobhouse, L., 1914-08-08. Letter: Leonard Hobhouse to EH (JHB).

Hobhouse, L., 1914-08-26. Letter: Leonard Hobhouse to EH (JHB).

Hobhouse, M., 1905-02-02. Letter: Mary Hobhouse to EH (JHB).

Hobhouse, M., 1905-03-10. Letter: Mary Hobhouse to EH (JHB).

Hoover, H., 1916-08-14. Letter: Herbert Hoover to EH (JHB).

Leipzig City Council, 1924-12-24. Letter: Leipzig City Council to EH (JHB; translated from German into Afrikaans by Lizette Rabe.)

MacMillan, C., 1915-12-16. Letter: Chrystal MacMillan to Jane Addams (Jane Addams Papers, Swarthmore College Peace Collection, Reel 9/0597).

Merriman, A., 1901-08-08. Letter: Agnes Merriman to EH (VAB).

Merriman, J.X., 1901-07-26. Letter: John X. Merriman to Leonard Courtney.

Merriman, J.X., 1913-12-09. Letter: John X. Merriman to EH (JHB).

Military telegrams, CSO, 1903. Code Cables: 9/9/1903 Documents: CO 210 6515/03 (VAB).

Monument Committee, 1913-12-17. Telegram: Monument Committee to EH (JHB).

Murray, C., 1902-02-28. Letter: Caroline Murray to EH (VAB).

Rowntree, M., 1906-06-18. Letter: Marion Rowntree to EH (VAB: A357).

Schreiner, O., 1908. 'Olive Schreiner to Emily Hobhouse, 29 May 1908', Hobhouse Trust, Olive Schreiner Letters Project transcription.

Schreiner, O., 1908. 'Olive Schreiner to Emily Hobhouse, 3 Oct. 1908', Hobhouse Trust, Olive Schreiner Letters Project transcription.

Schreiner, O., 1912. 'Olive Schreiner to Emily Hobhouse, 22 July 1912'. National Library of South Africa, Cape Town, Special Collections/ Olive Schreiner Letters Project transcription.

Schreiner, O., 1913. 'Olive Schreiner to Minnie or Mimmie Murray née Parkes, April 1913'. National English Literary Museum, Grahamstown: Olive Schreiner Letters Project transcription.

Schreiner, O., 1903-04-03. 'Olive Schreiner to Emily Hobhouse, 3 April 1903'. National Library of South Africa, Cape Town, Special Collections/Olive Schreiner Letters Project transcription.

Schwimmer, R., 1914-08-18. Letter: Rosika Schwimmer to EH (JHB).

Smuts, J., 1903-10-25. Letter: Jan Smuts to EH (JHB).

Smuts, J., 1913-12-10. Letter: Jan Smuts to EH (JHB).

Spencer, E.C., 1904-05-07. Letter: Charles Spencer to Kate Courtney. London School of Economics: 9/02/133.

Subscribers to the Fund, 1904: Personal thank-you letter to EH (private collection).

Von Jagow, G., 1916-06-20. Letter: Gottlieb von Jagow to EH ('Jagow Letters', Foreign Office Archives, Germany, vol. R20465).

Diaries

Clark, M., 1905. Diary: Margaret Clark: 23 Jan. 1905 – 8 Oct. 1905 (VAB: A1/330/1 – transcription by Prof. Doreen Atkinson).

Courtney, K., 1904. Diary: Kate Courtney, May 1904 (private collection).

Hobhouse, E., 1905. Journal of Emily Hobhouse: 1 Jan. 1905 – 6 Apr. 1905 (JHB).

Hobhouse, E., 1916. Diary: Emily Hobhouse: 1 Jul. – 14 Jul. 1916 (JHB).

Hobhouse, E., 1916. Journal: Emily: 'Volume I, 1916' (JHB).

Hobhouse, E., 1916. Journal: Emily: 'Volume II, Belgium and Germany' (JHB).

Hobhouse, E., 1916. Journal: Emily: 'Volume III, Visit to Germany and Belgium: The story of my visit to Germany during the Great War' (JHB).

Newspapers, pamphlets, reports, journal articles and other material

Advertisement, 1921. E. M. & Sons. Sale of Warren House (St Ives Archives).

Berry, C., 2010-08-19. Report: Alfred Gillett Trust, GB2075 MCG, Papers of Margaret Clark Gillett and Arthur Bevington Gillett, 1774–1983, available at: https:// alfredgilletttrust.files.wordpress.com/2014/11/ mcg.pdf.

Bishop, G., 1895. Newspaper cutting (newspaper unknown) in *Parish Album: A Parish Album of St Ive*, 16 Feb.

Bouwer, A., 1960. 'Elf babas land gelyk', *Sarie Marais*, 11 May.

British Listed Buildings, 1985. Chantry, St Ive: English Heritage Building ID 61375.

Burnley Express, 29 Jun. 1901.

Caldwall, S., 1991. 'Segregation and Plague: King William's Town and the Plague Outbreaks of 1900-1907', *Contree*, p. 10.

Cape Times, 22 Jul. 1901.

Clark, M., Undated summary of MC's time in SA – 7 pages (VAB: A357, Smuts-Clark collection).

Clark, M., and Hobhouse, E., 1907. Report: 'Transvaal and Orange River Colony – Spinning, Weaving as Boer Home Industries – May 1907' (VAB: A357, Smuts-Clark collection).

Census, 1871. 'Enumeration District 7 Civil Parish of Callington, Eccl. District of Cornwall, 1871–Transcript of Piece', RG10/2234 (Liskeard Museum Archives).

Cheltenham Looker-On, 22 Jun. 1901.

Corder, C., and Plaut, M., 2013. 'Gandhi's Decisive South African 1913 Campaign: A personal perspective from the letters of Betty Molteno', *South African Historical Journal*, 66(1), pp. 22–54.

Crangle, J. V., and Baylen, J. O., 1979. 'Emily Hobhouse's Peace Mission, 1916', *Journal of Contemporary History*, 14(4), pp. 731–44.

Davies, M.L., 1909. Letter: Margaret Llewellyn Davies, *The Common Cause*, 21 Oct., p. 9.

De Zuid-Afrikaan, 1903. 'Miss Hobhouse te Kaapstad',

Nov., p. 6, available at: https://digital.lib.sun.ac.za.

Die Burger, 1926. 'Vandag herbegrafnis Mej. Emily Hobhouse', 27 Oct.

Die Burger, 1926. 'Bysetting van asse mej. E. Hobhouse', Oct.

Dunning, R., Hobhouse family history: documents in a private collection.

Du Plessis, A., 1999. 'Kantskole het meisies uit kampe ná die oorlog opge-hef', Volksblad, 18 June 1999.

Enteraden Ltd, 2015. 'Cheyne Court and Rossetti Garden Mansions – History', available at: www.enteraden.co.uk (accessed on 9 Feb. 2015).

Evening Telegraph, 1916. 'How Miss Hobhouse Obtained Passports', 31 Oct.

Funeral notice, 1926. St Mary Abbots, Kensington; 11 Jun. 1926; In memoriam – Emily Hobhouse (private collection).

Funeral programme, 1926. 'Plegtige Teraardebestelling van Emily Hobhouse – Volgorde van Verrigtinge' (Anglo-Boer War Museum, no 4441/3).

Goldman, P.L.A., 1913. Folder/R.S. Goldman, Transvaal Archive section of the National Archive in Pretoria.

Hobhouse, E., 1887. List of paupers, St Ive parish 1887 (Liskeard Museum Archives).

Hobhouse, E., 1901. Pamphlet: 'Appeal of Miss Hobhouse to Mr Brodrick' (Pamphlet no. 86, London School of Economics, 349/6820501488 HOB).

Hobhouse, E., 1901. Recommendations to St John Brodrick, June. (JHB).

Hobhouse, E., 1901. Report: 'The Concentration Camps: Mr Brodrick's concessions and Miss Hobhouse's comments on them.'

Hobhouse, E., 1901. Report: 'A Letter to the Committee of the South African Women and Children's Distress Fund', 2 Dec., The Argus Printing Company.

Hobhouse, E., 1903. Speech: 22 Aug. 1903 (Anglo-Boer War Museum – Document no. 5348/18).

Hobhouse, E. 1913. Speech/pamphlet: 16 December.

Hobhouse, E., 1915. Foreword: 'International Congress of Women, The Hague, 28 April to 1 May; Report', University of Illinois.

Hobhouse, E., 1916. 'Union of Democratic Control 1 October 1916', in Belgium To-Day, pp. 132–4.

Hobhouse, E., 1916. 'Interview with a high official of the German foreign office', The Nation, Oct. 1916 (British Library: MFR/2456 no 381).

Hobhouse, E., 1916. 'Miss Hobhouse's Tour', The Times.

Hobhouse, E., 1916. Notes: 'Lambeth, Aug. 2.16, 11.30 am' (JHB).

Hobhouse, E., 1919. Pamphlet: 'Russian Babies' Fund' – March 1919 (VAB).

Hobhouse, H, 1916 and 1926. Private memoranda (private collection).

Kapp, P, 2002. 'War and Reconstruction: Four Comparative Case Studies', Scientia Militaria, 31(2), pp. 92–116.

Leipzig City Council, 1922. Report no. 13/7/1922 (JHB). (Translated from German into Afrikaans by Lizette Rabe).

Lists: UK Outward Passengers, 1890-1960. Liskeard Museum Archives (Emily Hobhouse File).

Marschall, S., 2004. 'Serving Male Agendas: Two National Women's Monuments in South Africa', Women's Studies, 33(8), pp. 1009–33.

Manchester Guardian, 1901. 'Extracts of Campbell-Bannerman Speech', Bath, 2 Nov.

Manchester Guardian, 1926. 'Miss Hobhouse; The Funeral Service at Kensington', 12 Jun., p. 10.

Manchester Guardian, 1926. 'Emily Hobhouse – General Smuts's Speech at Bloemfontein', 18 Nov.

Military correspondence, 1903 (VAB: CO 210 6515/03).

Minchinton, W., 1958. 'The Virginia Letters of Isaac Hobhouse, Merchant of Bristol', The Virginia Magazine of History and Biography, 66(3).

Molteno, B., 1901. 'Statement re Miss Hobhouse's removal from the Avondale Castle' (VAB: A156/3/11).

Murray, C., 1901. Report: 'Arrest and Deportation' (VAB: A156/3/11, Adv. Gladys Steyn and Mrs M.T. Steyn collection).

Murray, C., 1926. 'Impressive Memorial Service' (summary of EH's funeral – Molteno-Murray Family Papers, BC330, University of Cape Town Libraries: Special Collections).

Nottingham Evening Post, 1916. 'A Mischievous Lady', 7 Nov.

Parliamentary report, 1901. 'The Rates of Mortality in the Concentration Camps in South Africa', British Medical Journal, 1901, 2:1418.

Raath, S., and Warnich, P., 2012. 'From a concentration camp to a post-apartheid South African school: A historical-environmental perspective in developing a new identity', *Y&T* [online] n.7 [cited 2017-09-08], pp. 139–67.

Reynolds, C. Available at: http://celestereynolds.weebly.com.

Royal Cornwall Gazette, 1892. 'Shocking Destitution at St. Ive', issue 4623'; 3 Mar.

Schwyzer, F., and Hobhouse, E., 1919. Report: 'Save the Children Fund; Germany – Report on Conditions affecting Child-Health in Leipzig', Dec. 1919 (VAB: pamphlet no 614.7).

Smith, C, 2010. 'Halssnoer van Emily Hobhouse terug in Vrystaat', Volksblad, 13 Nov.

Smith, I.R., and Stucki, A., 2011. 'The Colonial Development of Concentration Camps (1868–1902)', *The Journal of Imperial and Commonwealth History*, 39(3), pp. 417–437.

Steyn, R.I., 1921. Appeal from Mrs Pres. Steyn (Anglo-Boer War Museum collection no. 58/2).

Steyn, T., 1926. 'Emily Hobhouse', *Die Huisgenoot*, 25 Jun.

Testimonial, 1904. Lady Courtney: 'Testimonial to Miss Emily Hobhouse' (Alfred Gillett Trust, ref: MCG 32/7 – letters to friends and family).

The Friend, 1926. 'Impressive Memorial Service', 28 Oct.

The Times (London), 1900. 'Peace Meeting in Liskeard; Uproarious Proceedings – speakers refused hearing, platform stormed', 2 Jul. (Liskeard Museum Archives).

The Times (London), 5. Jul. 1901.

The Times (London), 7 Jul. 1901.

The Times (London), 26 Jul. 1901.

The Times (London), 1926. 'Death of Miss Emily Hobhouse', 10 Jun., issue 44294.

Trelawny, W., Will of W. S. Trelawny (Liskeard Museum Archives).

Van Heyningen, E., 2010. 'Fools Rush In: Writing a history of the concentration camps of the South African War', *Historia*, 55(2), p. 17.

Walsh, A., 1907. 'Miss Hobhouse's Work in South Africa', *The Advocate of Peace*, 69(3), Mar. 1907, pp. 63 4. World Affairs Institute, available at www.jstor.org.

Wessels, E., and Heunis, V., no date. Report: 'Die Kantskool by Koppies' (Anglo-Boer War Museum collection).

Will, 1926. 'Estate of the Will of Miss Emily Hobhouse (deceased), date 6 July 1926' (JHB).

Wikipedia. 'Carding', available at: https://en.m.wikipedia. org/wiki/Carding.

Yorkshire Post, 1916. 'The case of Miss Hobhouse', 15 Nov.

Acknowledgements

This book would not exist in its current form without the help of a number of people and institutions. It is my pleasure to acknowledge them:

Jennifer Hobhouse Balme, Emily's grandniece, shared with me Emily's documents, letters, diaries, scrapbooks and photos that she had in her possession and welcomed me into her home with great hospitality.

Special thanks to my wife, Carol Hodes, my best sounding board and greatest supporter, who was with me every step of the way in the process of making this book (even when it required a lot of tolerance).

Also: Aldi Schoeman; Alfred Gillett Trust Archive; Alix Carmichael; André and Claudi Jooste; André le Roux; Andries Wessels; Anri Delport; Anglo-Boer War Museum (Johan van Zyl, Vicky Heunis and Etna Labuschagne); Arina Kok; Birgit Seibold; British Library; Ditsong National Museum of Cultural History (Annemarie Carelsen); Doreen Atkinson; German Federal

Archive (Federal Foreign Office); Esmaré Weideman; Friends House Library; George Claassen; Graphics24 (Jaco Grobbelaar); Jonathan Wormald; Koos Bekker; Linde Dietrich; Little, Brown (Duncan Proudfoot, Amanda Keats, Charlotte Cole, John Fairweather, Alison Candlin; Liskeard Museum Archives (Anna Monks); Lizette Rabe; London School of Economics (Women's Library); Malani Venter; Robert Molteno; Robert Dunning; Ruan Huisamen; Sally Brazier; Sue Seager; St Ive Church; Swarthmore College Peace Collection; Tafelberg Publishers (Annake Müller, Eben Pienaar, Eloise Wessels, Erika Oosthuysen, Jean Pieters, Kristin Paremoer, Nicky Stubbs); Tobie Wiese; Free State Archives Repository (Rentia Roodt); University of Cape Town Libraries – Special Collections; University of Cape Town – Department of communication and marketing (Aamirah Sonday, Kylie Hatton and Riana Geldenhuys).

Index

447